A TEACHER'S G
SCIENCE AND F
IN THE CLASSR

A Teacher's Guide to Science and Religion in the Classroom provides practical guidance on how to help children access positive ways of thinking about the relationship between science and religion. Written for teachers of children from diverse-faith and non-faith backgrounds, it explores key concepts, identifies gaps and common misconceptions in children's knowledge, and offers advice on how to help them form a deeper understanding of both science and religion.

Drawing on the latest research as well as the designs of successful workshops for teachers and for children, there are activities in each chapter that have been shown to help children understand why science and religion do not necessarily conflict. The book highlights children's interest in the so-called "Big Questions" that bridge science and religion and responds to the research finding that most children are missing ideas that are key to an explanation of why science and religion can be harmonious.

The book explores key concepts and ideas including:

- Nature of science
- Power and limits of science
- Evolution, genes and human improvement
- Miracles, natural disasters and mystery
- Profiles of scientists, including Galileo and Newton

A Teacher's Guide to Science and Religion is an essential companion for preservice and practising teachers, providing session plans and pedagogic strategies, together with a cohesive framework, that will support teachers in fostering children's curiosity and enthusiasm for learning.

Berry Billingsley is Professor of Science Education at Canterbury Christ Church University and Principal Investigator of LASAR (Learning about Science and Religion). Berry has also worked in media producing science shows for children, and has led teacher education programmes in science teaching and related national and international research.

Manzoorul Abedin is a Research Fellow with LASAR at the Faculty of Education, Canterbury Christ Church University. He specialises in designing and presenting teacher education sessions and in addition, children's workshops on questions bridging science and religion.

Keith Chappell is a biologist and theologian. He teaches ecology and evolutionary biology and is currently an Associate Fellow with LASAR, Canterbury Christ Church University.

A TEACHER'S GUIDE TO SCIENCE AND RELIGION IN THE CLASSROOM

Edited by
Berry Billingsley,
Manzoorul Abedin and
Keith Chappell

Routledge
Taylor & Francis Group

LONDON AND NEW YORK

First published 2018
by Routledge
2 Park Square, Milton Park, Abingdon, Oxon OX14 4RN

and by Routledge
711 Third Avenue, New York, NY 10017

Routledge is an imprint of the Taylor & Francis Group, an informa business

British Library Cataloguing in Publication Data
A catalogue record for this book is available from the British Library

Library of Congress Cataloging in Publication Data
A catalog record for this book has been requested

ISBN: 978-1-138-21181-0 (hbk)
ISBN: 978-1-138-21182-7 (pbk)
ISBN: 978-1-315-45197-8 (ebk)

Typeset in Times New Roman and Helvetica Neue
by Florence Production Ltd, Stoodleigh, Devon, UK

To Mike Poole,
whose work has inspired this book

CONTENTS

CONTENTS ▪ ▪ ▪ ▪

FOREWORDS

Recent years have seen a substantial growth in interest on how science and religion relate to one another. However, there is still surprisingly little advice available to teachers and educators about how this issue might be addressed in the primary or secondary classroom.

This book valuably helps to address this need. It eschews the overused metaphor of conflict between science and religion without pretending that the relationship between them is always harmonious. Instead, what the contributors do is provide a range of ways of thinking about the relationship between science and religion – more importantly, of getting students to *think* about this.

The result is a book that should improve the way that science is taught. We need books like this. Science is a wonderfully powerful and extremely useful way of understanding the material world – but it can overextend itself. We want students to understand the questions that science can address and the questions that it can't – questions, for example about morality, about aesthetics and about meaning.

Michael J. Reiss
UCL Institute of Education, London

I remember feeling very excited at the prospect of using *A Teacher's Guide to Science and Religion in the Classroom* when I read the book proposal last year. Therefore it is a great privilege to be writing a foreword for this book. As a senior lecturer in religious education working in initial teacher training, I am careful to use resources that will enable my trainees to plan and prepare RE lessons that cause pupils to question, reason, explore and explain. In this book, I know I have found a rare and exciting resource that will facilitate such learning both within my lectures and, furthermore, in schools.

It is my opinion that teachers have needed a publication such as this for some time. Within this book, you will find a sound and reasoned set of ideas for approaching the teaching of science and religion in the classroom. The book is underpinned by valuable research and contains helpful, practical examples to illustrate how the theory discussed can be put into practice during lessons. Not only will this book facilitate careful planning for pupils' learning, it is my belief that exploring the themes contained within each chapter will also encourage the development of teachers' confidence to discuss science and religion within the classroom.

Within my religious education seminars, I often have some trainees who admit that they lack confidence in teaching RE. More often than not, they are held back by fear and anxiety over causing offence when discussing both religious and non-religious worldviews. Although these apprehensions are understandable, I wonder at times if we are so afraid of causing offence that we are ceasing to ask the questions that we really want to and, as a result, are losing the courage to ask them in an honest and authentic manner. A sad consequence of this might be diminished opportunities to share ideas and encounter viewpoints that differ from our own. If this is the case with us as teachers, how will we ever be able to progress our pupils in their thinking and explore ideas with them? I would argue that just as my trainees are nervous about engaging with religious and scientific ideas for fear of causing offence, our pupils might feel the same way.

In order to overcome this, we need to be honest with our pupils. I often take my trainees by surprise when I inform them that if they engage with scientific and religious ideas in a lesson, they risk causing offence at some point. Not because we would desire to, but because we do not always know the best way to ask questions or explain our viewpoints. However, this does not mean that we should stop trying. I also feel that it is important to highlight to trainee teachers that we do not have to be perfect as educators. We just have to be willing to engage with ideas, be open in discussions and confident enough to react with humility if ever causing offence. In doing so, teachers can model to their pupils how to engage with ideas in science and religion honestly, without being silenced for fear of awkward conversations. They will happen at some point. It's how you react to it that matters.

It is my viewpoint that we need to equip our children and young people with the skills to listen, question and distinguish truth from fiction. I was encouraged as I read David Hutchings' work on storytelling and Galileo, as this chapter provides clear teaching pedagogy on how teachers may use a "story within a story" to encourage pupils to consider and question their knowledge. Similarly, the thinking and observation skills promoted in this book enable pupils to discover ways in which scientists generate knowledge and how they can then do this for themselves. Perhaps one of the most important lessons we can pass on from this book to our pupils is the pursuit of wisdom. In pursuing wisdom, we should seek to gain as many possible answers as we can before discerning truth. This is a notion found in both secular and religious thinking. As Mark Laynesmith's chapter illustrates, seeking many possible answers is a skill utilised by scientists, while the book of Proverbs in the Bible states that there is wisdom in seeking advice from many counsellors (Proverbs 11:14). In encouraging our pupils to pursue wisdom, we provide them with a precious and valuable mindset, which can serve them in their future lives. The journey can start in our classrooms as we discuss the concepts and themes contained within this book. What a privilege we have as teachers to be in such a position.

May you enjoy using this book to enrich your lessons. I know I will.

Claire Parkin
Senior Lecturer in Primary Religious Education
St Mary's University, Twickenham, London

I have been involved in religious education (RE) in schools for most of my professional life. In Britain, we have the wonderful arrangement whereby RE is a compulsory subject of study for all pupils, irrespective of the type of school they are in. But I did not start as an RE teacher. I began my career as a biology teacher, having graduated from the natural sciences tripos at Cambridge. However, in my first teaching post, I was soon spotted as a churchgoer and recruited into teaching RE by the school's senior managers. I loved it and went back to higher education to study theology with the express purpose of pursuing a career in RE teaching. I then returned to secondary school teaching and spent seven years teaching both biology and RE. But I was in for a shock. Despite the quality of my first degree in science, some of my students questioned my credibility as a science teacher because I also taught RE. As the years have gone by I came to realise this was not a personal issue; the quality of much greater scientific minds than mine has been questioned simply on the grounds that the people involved have been known Christians. This presumed scientific scepticism about religious faith seems to be an influential mindset.

One of the treats of the Cambridge natural sciences tripos was the option to study the philosophy of science. I availed myself of that opportunity and I think it's fair to say it changed my life. Prior to the course, I harboured a fairly naïve view of science, although I had never really thought much about the nature of science and none of my teachers had raised it with me. As a Christian, I was pretty certain that there were inherent clashes between my faith and my science – but I kept that in the background. The philosophy of science opened my eyes, with my introduction to Thomas Kuhn's notion of paradigms and Michael Polanyi's treatise on personal knowledge being encounters that have influenced me ever since. And I started to read Christian authors like Donald Mackay and began to realise there was no need for the expectation that science must challenge Christian faith.

Unfortunately, the conflict thesis is still widespread and doing a lot of damage. The National Institute for Christian Education Research (NICER) at Canterbury Christ Church University recently completed a year-long study of how teachers in church schools interpret their role.[1] During a focus group with 12-year-old pupils at a jointly run Anglican/Catholic school, pupils informed us that they had expected to be told that evolution was wrong and that creationism was right when they joined the school. What we know is the case from the extensive research of LASAR is that school pupils seem to think that there is a clash between science and religion and that they have to make the decision as to which they follow. My guess is that there are significant issues of teenage identity tied up with this perception.

It still staggers me how widespread is the view that evolutionary theory is necessarily atheistic. I am convinced that challenging these misconceptions is an educational priority. So I am a great fan of the work of LASAR and am delighted in particular to write a foreword to this book. The combination of theoretical reflection and practical classroom ideas that it provides will be a great support for teachers.

Trevor Cooling
ProfessorChristian Education at Canterbury Christ Church University
and Chair of the RE Council of England and Wales

1   Trevor Cooling with Beth Green, Andrew Morris and Lynn Revell, *Christian Faith in English Church Schools: Research Conversations with Classroom Teachers* (Peter Lang, 2016).

LIST OF CONTRIBUTORS

Manzoorul Abedin, Research Fellow, Faculty of Education, Canterbury Christ Church University, UK

Berry Billingsley, Professor, Faculty of Education, Canterbury Christ Church University, UK

Jane Borgeaud, Senior Lecturer, University of Winchester, UK

Richard Brock, Postdoctoral Fellow, King's College London, UK

John Bryant, Professor Emeritus, Biosciences, University of Exeter

Keith Chappell, Associate Fellow, Faculty of Education, Canterbury Christ Church University

Martin Coath, Associate Lecturer, School of Geography, Earth and Environmental Sciences, University of Plymouth, UK

Sharon Fraser, Associate Professor of Science Education, University of Tasmania, Australia

Mark Gilbert, Mathematical biologist, University of Oxford, UK

Chris Hatcher, Evolutionary ecologist, University of Loughborough, UK

David Hutchings, Physics teacher and author; Institute of Physics committee member

Mark Laynesmith, Anglican chaplain and team coordinator, University of Reading, UK

Ard Louis, Professor of theoretical physics at the University of Oxford, UK

Simon Peatman, NCAS Climate research scientist, University of Reading, UK

Matt Pritchard, Science Magician and Curator of Wonder

Bethany Sollereder, Associate Faculty Member, theology and religion, University of Oxford, UK

Siew Fong Yap, Head of Science, Kingsway Christian College, Perth, Australia

INTRODUCTION

Berry Billingsley and Manzoorul Abedin

Most people wonder about the so-called "Big Questions" – such as how did the universe get here? – at various points in their lives and for many reasons. Commonly at such times thoughts turn to what science and religion seem to say.

Research over the years has consistently shown that a majority of children perceive that science and religion conflict. The LASAR (Learning about Science and Religion) project was established in 2009 to find out more about children's ideas and also to look at how questions and themes bridging science and religion are managed in schools.

Stereotypes, such as that science and religion are mutually exclusive, that someone with a religious faith is not likely to become a scientist and that scientists are typically atheists, are frequently articulated in some parts of the media, popular TV shows and jokes. The impact of these stereotypes each time they recur in popular culture on children's developing thinking is difficult to estimate but it has been established via large-scale surveys that, by the end of primary school, a significant proportion of children aged 10 already say that science and religion are mutually exclusive. Survey findings (n = 712) with children in this age group found that about one-third (34%) agreed with the statement "Science and religion disagree on so many things that they cannot both be true", while just under one-third (27%) of the cohort disagreed. Fewer than one in five (16%) of children agreed that "Science and religion work together like friends" while almost half (46%) of those surveyed disagreed (Billingsley & Abedin, 2016). But while the media do influence children's thinking, it is the way in which schools respond that decides whether these stereotypes can either persist and spread or fail to get a foothold.

The findings from LASAR's research have highlighted that not only in secondary but also in primary schools, teachers tend to present and discuss questions via compartmentalised curriculum boxes. While immersing students in the questions, methods and norms of thought of one discipline at a time is an essential and important aspect of education, there are many topics and questions that are missed out by this approach. Further, the research concluded, if teachers don't create opportunities for questions that go beyond subject silos, children pick up the message that these kinds of questions are unwanted.

Even so, children's curiosity and enthusiasm for exploring the so-called Big Questions, such as what does it mean to be human and how did the universe get here are consistently high for all ages (see Figure 1.1).

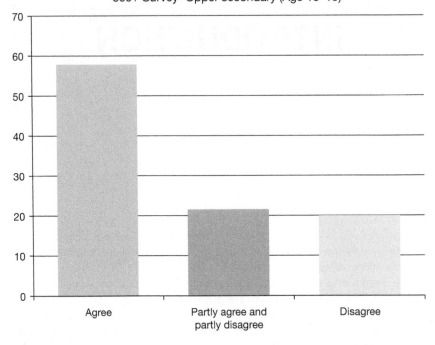

I am interested in thinking about what it means to be human
500+ Survey- Upper secondary (Age 13–15)

Figure 1.1

While enthusiasm to think about the origins of life and the universe remains high across the age groups, studies with secondary school students indicate that in this age group, levels of belief in creation by God fall. A survey of 2613 secondary students by LASAR (Billingsley, 2017) found that just over one-fifth (21%) agreed with the statement "I believe that God created the universe", while 45% disagreed. The proportion of students in each year group who believe that God created the universe decreases for children in older age groups (from about a quarter – 26% in Year 7 down to 17% in Year 11). The percentages of students who perceive science and religion to conflict on the questions of why life and the universe exist rise from younger to older age groups. Comparing students in Year 7 through to Year 11, for the origins of the universe the level of disagreement with the idea that science and religion fit together rises from 45% to 60% and for the statement relating to how life began, the percentages and changes in percentages are very similar. In the light of the conflict that many students perceive to exist, some choose sides depending on where they feel they belong – as one 14-year-old girl explained: "I think God created the universe, but if you don't have a religion, then you might think that it was the Big Bang. Because I have a religion, I think it was God who created it." Another group of children say they are confused and within this group some say they hold onto both, even though they see them as competing. While filling in our survey, one student noted that she had struggled with many of the questions because "There's the science part of me that says 'no, it's the big bang', and then there's the religious part of me that said 'it was God', so it was quite confusing." A significant proportion of children say they take the side of science, saying "it has more evidence" or "it is certain".

Interviews with primary and secondary school students show that there are common challenges for both age groups. One of these challenges is that most children have no one who seems like the right person to ask about these types of questions. Very few, in particular, have someone they can talk to about science and religion at the same time. Comments by children aged 10 who participated in a survey included: "I ask my teacher about science and our reverend about religion." Children perceive the people they know to be committed either to science or to religion, such as: "Our dean believes that God created the beginning of the universe . . . [the other children in my class] would think that maybe the Big Bang created it and not God" (10-year-old boy). For secondary school students, the scarcity of opportunities to learn about how science and religion relate is reinforced by the allocation of science and religious education to different subject specialists. The RE teacher is generally perceived by children not to be a science specialist and as one student explained: "No one really asks the science questions because you'd really more ask your science teacher about that instead of asking your RE teacher." At the same time children perceived that it would be "off topic" and/or culturally sensitive to ask questions that touch on religion in their science lessons. One student explained: "We don't ask science teachers questions any more at the moment, because we don't think that they'd answer them . . . they won't answer that because it's not on their topic" (Billingsley & Chappell, 2016; Billingsley, Nassaji & Abedin, 2016; Billingsley, Taber, Riga & Newdick, 2016).

What all of this means is that children in school struggle to find opportunities to ask questions and talk about big questions that bridge science and religion. This is unfortunate because exploring these questions can help young people to form a deeper understanding of both science and religion and encourage them to become more thoughtful and questioning about what they learn in school. The implications of this conflict for teaching and learning have been reported in the United States (Smith, 2010), the United Kingdom (Fulljames, Gibson & Francis, 1991; Taber, Billingsley, Riga & Newdick, 2011), Australia (Billingsley & Fraser, in press) and other places around the world (Deniz, Donnelly & Yilmaz, 2008; Ha, Haury & Nehm, 2012; Hansson & Redfors, 2007). Children's attitudes to science and to careers in science can be affected by their perceptions of how science relates to their religious beliefs (Esbenshade, 1993). Although the conflict view is widespread, it is not a necessary position. Unless students receive effective teaching, they are unlikely to develop the epistemic insights needed to understand why science and religion are not necessarily competing (Billingsley, Taber, Riga & Newdick, 2016; Reich, 1991). Also, whether or not students have a religious faith, it is important that all students appreciate the diversity of metaphysical stances that can be compatible with science (Hokayem & BouJaoude, 2008). The need for children to have access to positive views of how science and religion relate is therefore becoming a higher priority in schools. This follows a growing appreciation by the public, by church education authorities and by teachers that children need to have effective teaching if they are to appreciate why the conflict view of the relationship between science and faith is not the only position available to them.

Chapters in this book together emphasise the need for children to see the value and significance of questions that do not sit neatly in one subject or another. Primary and secondary students need frameworks and bridges to enable them to move successfully between their subject compartments – and this book provides a number of lesson plans and pedagogic strategies towards that goal. For many decades the practice at almost every level of education has been to teach students about scholarship and knowledge via a compartmentalised system of individual curriculum boxes. The compartments are sustained by subject-specific curriculum documents, examinations, teacher education and – in secondary schools – specialist teacher recruitment and subject specific classrooms (Cloud, 1992; Ratcliffe, 2009). In this way pedagogy can squeeze students' curiosity and channel their thinking away from creative activities such as identifying good questions to ask and devising ways to address them. Taken together, various chapters in this book provide a cohesive framework to help students make sense of words and ideas such as "evidence" that are referred to in many subjects and modules.

ADDRESSING THESE GAPS – WHERE TO START

Children's perception of science and religion as conflicting depends on many things. It depends in part on what they are hearing from the media, in the playground and at home. If children repeatedly encounter the message that science and religion are mutually exclusive, then, with no reason to suppose otherwise, it seems reasonable to say that most will accept this position unquestioningly as true. But this is not the only factor at work. One of the key steps on the journey towards appreciating why science and religion are not *necessarily* incompatible is to consider the idea that science and religion are mostly concerned with different types of question. This matters because it explains why they are not necessarily rivals – even when they appear to be discussing the same topic. The idea that different disciplines can work together is not something that children very often consider. In school, the questions that children meet are categorised into different subjects. So in science children look at science questions, in history they look at history questions etc., but children do not often meet a question that is presented as one that could be addressed by more than one of those disciplines. One way to help build up these ideas with children in primary school is to give them a question that has multiple answers so that they can pick out which one or ones may be scientific. You could say to children: "Yesterday, I was sitting at home and suddenly the doorbell rang. Why do you think the doorbell rang?" and then invite them to think of as many answers as they can. Once children have generated a number of suggestions, tell them that the answer you were looking for is that a little clapper struck it several times, vibrated the bell and made a sound.

This answer is likely to be different to the ones the children thought of but is also likely to be compatible with them. It would be compatible for example with: "My friend was at the door." This activity can be a stimulus for noticing that if a question is to be investigated using science, it means it must be possible to investigate it by making observations of the physical universe. To try another example for themselves, children could generate multiple answers to the question: "Why did the book fall off the table?" More able children might be able to explain what type of answer each one is and whether it is testable scientifically. In other words, does their explanation describe the "the physical processes that made it happen" or "a human story which fills in a bigger picture"? The point is that both types of explanation can be true at the same time – and, indeed, we might find it useful to have both together. This kind of thinking can be described as building up an answer that has many layers of explanation. Each layer is another discipline (scientific, historical). Children could be asked, for example, to research an answer that has several layers of explanation to address the question. "Why did the *Titanic* sink?" In the chapters that follow, there are examples of questions that bridge science and religion and also examples of questions that bridge science and other disciplines.

DOES IT MAKE A DIFFERENCE?

In this book, there are teaching ideas for a series of topics on which science and religion both seem to have something to say. These teaching ideas have been developed and refined over many years through workshops with different age groups. Many of the workshops can be adapted for use either in primary or secondary, but, in this book, they are ordered from upper primary to upper secondary. The impact of sharing these teaching points with children can be dramatic. LASAR works with primary and secondary schools to provide children with an off-timetable day with three workshops. Students complete a survey at the beginning and end of the day. Table 1.1 shows "before" and "after" data for primary children, and the impact of the workshops is clearly visible.

The popularity of sessions run by the LASAR project indicates the value that schools place on giving students opportunities to engage with these questions – however arguably – these opportunities should be embedded into the standard education that all students can access. The key challenge, therefore, that the book identifies and addresses is that most children are missing ideas that are key to an explanation of why science and religion can be harmonious. While the book is designed to help teachers address these gaps, the guides and activities are written for teachers of classes with children from diverse (faith and non-faith) backgrounds. The book does not promote the notion (which would be false) that harmony is the only view of science and religion, but rather is focused on the goal of ensuring children have access to both conflict and non-conflict views. The Religious Education Framework (the national non-statutory curriculum for religious education) asserts the importance of ensuring children build this understanding – and can explain why some people see science and religion as compatible and some do not. In addition, the national statutory science curriculum in England (and internationally) requires children to learn about the power and limits of science – an idea that is central to understanding why science and religion can coexist in harmony. As such the ideas and concepts covered in the book are focused on a particular goal – to give children greater access to positive ways to think

■ Table 1.1

		Agree	Neither agree nor disagree	Disagree
Many scientists believe in God (or a Greater Being)	Pre-event	31	41	23
	Post-event	66	27	5
Science and religion work together like friends	Pre-event	16	33	49
	Post-event	41	35	21
The scientific view is that God does not exist	Pre-event	45	33	18
	Post-event	26	40	30

about science and religion within a context of explaining the reasonableness of both positive and negative positions on how science and religion relate.

The ideas addressed in different chapters include:

■ Can all questions be answered scientifically? Which types of question are more or less amenable to science and why?

■ Miracles and science: What have scientists (with and without a religious faith) said about events that are described in religious texts as miracles?

■ Why are there people including scientists who believe that there is a God or gods when they have no proof?

■ Science seems to say the universe began with a Big Bang while religions talk about creation. Can we have both or do we have to choose?

■ Galileo, Newton and Mary Anning are just some of the scientists from the past who expressed a strong belief in God. What are their stories?

■ Evolution – a workshop that focuses on teaching the key ideas using practical activities.

■ Ways to imagine God – including "god of the gaps", deism and theism.

■ Does science tell us that our personalities are shaped by factors beyond our control – leaving no room in practice to believe that humans can choose whether or not to act morally?

■ Given what we now know from genetics and neuroscience, does this mean that the scientific position is that the soul does not exist?

■ Are humans the exception and are we the only intelligent life in the universe – what do some scientists and theologians say?

■ Chapters to suggest ways that these teaching ideas can be fitted into a school lesson, day off-timetable or special event.

OVERVIEW OF CHAPTERS

Chapters are structured in 18 units. The aims and the contents of the chapters are clearly written with each chapter introduction providing a sneak peek at the key questions, background, learning opportunities and, where relevant, resources and further readings. The resources for the primary and secondary schools and their suitability are clarified in the beginning of each chapter and when appropriate advice given on how the content can be differentiated and broken down according to individual teacher needs. Resources are predominantly based on the structure of schools in the UK, but the chapters are also purposefully written so that teachers can relate the topics to their own school system as appropriate. Chapters in general give information about the relevant age and level for each unit. Moreover, resources that focus on science and religion do not do so following any specific theological tradition with an aim to address different world religions and faiths. The lesson plans and resources presented in the book have been developed by teacher-researchers and reviewed by an academic advisory panel. Chapters have also been tested and rewritten in the light of comments and criticism. These quality-assuring elements have ensured that the resources in this book are to the point, easy to apply and up to date.

The first chapter "All you need is science, or is it? Exploring scientific, theological and other 'ways of knowing'" offers a distinction between information and wisdom and between necessary and sufficient knowledge and shows how the variety of "ways of knowing" offered by different disciplines can relate to one another within the concept of "emergence". Author Mark Laynesmith then moves to the classroom to justify why teachers need to encourage pupils to consider a range of possible answers to any question. A sample lesson plan is then given, including classroom-based exercises that allow theological answers to sit alongside other "ways of knowing" the world.

In "Creating linkages: you don't have to reinvent the curriculum!", Sharon Fraser has used the Australian Curriculum materials to consider how cross-curriculum linkages between science and other subjects can be established and provide students with opportunities to challenge their commonly held beliefs about knowledge. Informed by research conducted by the University of Reading, UK, and the University of Tasmania, Australia, in the Being Human project (Being Human: Discovering and Advancing School Students' Perceptions of the Relationships between Science and Religion), she shows that through an interrogation and finessed understanding of the "habits of mind" of science, students are better positioned to both challenge the privileged position of science in our society and to explore the "habits of mind" of other disciplines, including religious education.

"How science changes over time" collates a number of activities to try in the science lesson to explain that our scientific curiosity is stimulated by making and talking about observations, and the data (evidence) gathered via the senses. These activities are carefully synchronised for students to appreciate an important nature of science (NoS) that scientific knowledge changes and builds over time. Authors Berry Billingsley and Manzoorul Abedin cite research that has consistently suggested that there are surprisingly entrenched misconceptions about the nature of science (NoS) among many people, including teachers and students. The chapter starts with a variety of classroom activities on "gravity" to underscore what prompts scientific ideas and how scientific methods are used and gradually developed to evaluate those ideas through repeated reproduction and verification of observations. Through these activities, the chapter highlights the importance of understanding that there are many notable moments in history when science has made a significant leap and many more moments where smaller bounds of progress have been made.

Matt Pritchard's "Unleashing wonder and mystery in the classroom" facilitates a discussion on limitations of a methodical approach to teaching science. He does this by exploring how magicians approach wonder and mystery and providing a framework for utilising science magic to increase student engagement and learning. The chapter ends by highlighting the interplay between science, faith and mystery. David Hutchings offers a fresh look at Galileo's life to explore the "science vs religion" story and demonstrates how the power of stories can be used as a narrative to overpower the conflict thesis in the classroom. Martin Coath and Berry Billingsley's "How scientific is that? A practical guide to discuss the power and limitations of science in secondary schools" offers a graphical representation of the degree to which questions can be addressed using science, illustrating the core of the "power and limits" discussion. Mark Gilbert then returns to the theme of the effectiveness of storytelling in teaching. The chapter "Isaac Newton" – the topic of the chapter, briefly outlines Isaac Newton's extraordinary life, looking at, on one hand, how Newton was able to significantly advance several areas of scientific enquiry and, on the other hand, how his interest in alchemy and the occult confuses our concept of science as a clear upward progression. Newton, Gilbert argues, saw his worldview as providing justification for Christian faith and discussing many dimensions of Newton is an interesting way to explore the interactions between science and religion.

Chris Hatcher, in "Evolution", recognises that, typically, there are few resources available for teachers to use to teach this subject area while attitudes and concerns held by teachers, students and parents remain largely unknown regarding the teaching of evolution. The chapter has outlined a systematic way of teaching about the process of evolution including the prerequisite content necessary to be able to understand these tricky concepts. Although perceived in the media as a potentially quite contentious issue, Hatcher shows that a lot of faiths are in agreement with the theory of evolution. Yet, teachers hold reservations about teaching the topic and adopt different strategies compared to other science topics as a result. The chapter encourages teachers to teach evolution with confidence, including avoiding misconceptions, and encouraging scientific enquiry.

Keith Chappell's "Miracles" introduces the idea of miracles and creates a discussion on why they are potentially a controversial subject in the area of science and religion. It does so by first presenting the views held by students, their concerns and potential barriers to being open to science and/or religion as a result of the debate. The background section of the chapter contains views of some scholars on the subject from a religious and non-religious background and of scientists who believe in miracles and their explanations for their occurrence. The chapter then ends by providing practical ideas challenging the assumptions about the incompatibility of science and religion in this area.

In "God and natural disasters", Bethany Sollereder explores various Christian theological responses to the question of natural disasters. She then examines and critiques the implications of several different approaches, both well known and new, among academic theologians. All the positions are presented as possibilities and none of them is given as "the Christian answer". Siew Fong Yap's "Science at the movies. Remediating the misconceptions and developing ethical reasoning" seeks to explore and implement an engaging approach towards integrating science, societal values and religion through the use of socio-scientific issues utilising the medium of films and/or movies in the middle school and upper secondary science classrooms. Richard Brock's "Beyond experimentation: teaching a broader model of what scientists do" contends that understanding the nature of science presents a challenge for teachers who wish to define what science is and what it is not for the students in their classroom. This is because teachers and students have preconceptions about what "doing science" means and what kinds of activity are appropriate for the science classroom. This chapter examines some of those assumptions and presents a range of suggested activities to encourage both students and teachers to adopt a broader model of the nature of scientific activity. The ideas suggested in this chapter are intended as possible additions to lessons to give students a broader image of what it means to be a scientist.

John Bryant in "Genes, determinism and human improvement" presents a number of examples to show that even with genes that contribute to the structure, function and minute-by-minute activity of human bodily systems, there are interactions between "nature and nurture" and these interactions become more complicated when one considers features such as personality, behaviour and intelligence. Bryant argues that there is evidence that religious experiences can lead to clear behavioural changes and sometimes changes in personality traits. The big questions of how to extract reliable information about the world and how to separate fact from mere opinions are complex issues.

"How do I obtain reliable knowledge about the world?" by Ard Louis illustrates how experiences of a scientist can shed light on the big questions of life and on the construction of different worldviews – a set of values and assumptions on which people base their lives.

Simon Peatman's "Awe and wonder in science" considers that, for some scientists, the awe and wonder they feel when seeing beauty in nature points towards a "creator God" who has designed all things, and for others, providing a rational, scientific explanation of natural phenomena does away with a need for God, removing these phenomena from the world of spirituality into the realm of the purely physical. The chapter then provides a framework for exploring these two lines of thinking, using as an example an experiment that can be performed as part of a lesson. In "Evolution and religion: Mary Anning – embracing faith and science", Keith Chappell evaluates Mary Anning's role in the development of the sciences of geology, palaeontology and evolutionary theory and her significance for women in science, which now is a part of the primary science curriculum in the United Kingdom. In addition to providing an example of a scientist with faith, the story of Mary Anning presents a picture of science rooted in observation and deduction rather than the notion, held by many children, that science is purely experimental and "done" in the laboratory. In the final chapter in the book, "Thinking beyond the classroom", Jane Borgeaud reviews different classroom materials provided in other chapters of the book in order to argue that the inclusion of such materials within such a curriculum is not specific to religion and science, and normalises the idea that scientists can have a religious faith. She cites research findings with Year 6 pupils on science and religion found that the children frequently indicated that they did not know of scientists with a religious faith. She also suggests that creating a themed day or week specifically centred on science and religion would allow a deeper study of the diversity of views and normalise the idea that it is thought provoking yet safe for students to have the two themes discussed together.

In sum, then, chapters in *A Teacher's Guide to Science and Religion in the Classroom* encourage teaching science as multidisciplinary, bridging its subject boundaries with religion and other disciplines in schools. The way of addressing this is through stimulation of open-minded discussion on how science and religion relate and designing classroom activities and generally making balanced pictures of the different worldviews. The key challenge for teachers is to relate these topics to the students in an intelligible way and adjust the resources in the light of the students' age and their ability to understand them.

REFERENCES

Billingsley, B., K. S. Taber, F. Riga, and H. Newdick. (2013). Secondary school students' epistemic insight into the relationships between science and religion—a preliminary enquiry. *Research in Science Education*, 43(4), 1715–1732.

Billingsley, B. and M. Abedin. (2016). Primary children's perspectives on questions that bridge science and religion: findings from a survey study in England. In BERA (British Education Research Association) annual conference, Leeds.

Billingsley, B., R. Brock, K. S. Taber and F. Riga. (2016). How students view the boundaries between their science and religious education concerning the origins of life and the universe, Review of *Science Education*, n/a-n/a.10.1002/sce.21213.

Billingsley, B. and K. Chappell. (2016). What are young people's perceptions of power and limitations of science in the context of thinking about what it means to be human? In BERG (Biology Education Research Group – Royal Society of Biology) annual conference, London.

Billingsley, B., M. Nassaji and M. Abedin. (2016). Can science tell us everything about being human? Research based intervention to teach secondary students about the nature of scientific questions. In TEAN (Teacher Education Advancement Network), Birmingham.

Billingsley, B. (2017). Scientism, creationism or category error? A cross-age survey of secondary school students' perceptions of the relationships between science and religion. *Science Education Journal*.

Billingsley, B. and S. Fraser. (in press). Ways children reason about science and religion in primary school: Findings from a small-scale study in Australian primary schools. In *Science, Religion and Education*, edited by Berry Billingsley, Keith Chappell and Michael Reiss. New York: Springer.

Cloud, J. D. (1992). Ending our practice of compartmentalization, Review of *School Administrator*, *49*(2): 24–25.

Deniz, H., L. A. Donnelly and I. Yilmaz (2008). Exploring the factors related to acceptance of evolutionary theory among Turkish preservice biology teachers: Toward a more informative conceptual ecology for biological evolution. *Journal of Research in Science Teaching*, *45*(4), 420–443.

Esbenshade, D. H. (1993). Student perceptions about science and religion. *The American Biology Teacher*, *55*(6): 334–338.

Fulljames, P., H. M. Gibson and L. J. Francis (1991). Creationism, scientism, Christianity and science: A study in adolescent attitudes. *British Educational Research Journal*, *17*(2): 171–190.

Ha, M., D. L. Haury and R. H. Nehm (2012). Feeling of certainty: uncovering a missing link between knowledge and acceptance of evolution. *Journal of Research in Science Teaching*, *49*(1): 95–121.

Hansson, L. A. and Redfors (2007). Physics and the possibility of a religious view of the universe: Swedish upper secondary students' views. *Science & Education*, *16*(3–5): 461–478.

Hokayem, H. and S. BouJaoude (2008). College students' perceptions of the theory of evolution. *Journal of Research in Science Teaching*, *45*(4): 395–419.

Ratcliffe, M. (2009). The place of socio-scientific issues in citizenship education. In *Human Rights and Citizenship Education*, edited by A. Ross. London: CiCe.

Reich, H. (1991). The role of complementarity reasoning in religious development. *New Directions for Child and Adolescent Development*, *1991*(52): 77–89.

Smith, M. U. (2010). Current status of research in teaching and learning evolution: II. Pedagogical issues. *Science & Education*, *19*(6–8): 539–571.

Taber, K. S., B. Billingsley, F. Riga and H. Newdick (2011). To what extent do pupils perceive science to be inconsistent with religious faith? An exploratory survey of 13–14-year-old English pupils. *Science Education International*, *22*(2), 99–118.

CHAPTER 2

ALL YOU NEED IS SCIENCE, OR IS IT?

EXPLORING SCIENTIFIC, THEOLOGICAL AND OTHER "WAYS OF KNOWING"

Mark Laynesmith

AIMS OF THE CHAPTER

- This chapter explores how teachers might encourage pupils to consider a range of possible answers to any question, allowing theological answers to sit alongside other "ways of knowing" the world.
- A distinction between necessary and sufficient knowledge is introduced and one between information and wisdom.
- The chapter shows how the variety of "ways of knowing" offered by different disciplines can relate to one another within the concept of "emergence".
- A sample lesson plan is given.

INTRODUCTION

Time is short! One of the things this means is that when we try to make sense of the world we often try to reduce a question to the simplest answer. These "short-cut" answers can be highly useful. However, they can also hide the fact that there are other *kinds* of answer that run in parallel. Moreover, the kind of "short-cut" answer we choose to privilege may reflect certain cultural conventions and assumptions. For example, "Why is my hair the way it is?" may often receive a simple biological answer: "Because of your DNA." But this answer needs to sit alongside other, possibly more pertinent, answers such as: "Because of your culture."

Teachers frequently ask questions, and answer children's questions. They do so for a variety of purposes: to provoke children's thinking, to find out what children's ideas are, to monitor and regulate progress in an activity, and to check on understanding. The focus of this chapter is on how teachers' framing of questions and answers implicitly shapes children's thinking, their enquiry skills, and their views of the cosmos.

"THIN" AND "THICK" DESCRIPTIONS OF REALITY

What is the best way to answer a question? The English Franciscan theologian William of Ockham (c. 1287–1347) is credited with the idea that when providing an answer to a question, we should prefer the one that is based on the simpler, more testable, theory. More complex and difficult to test theories should (at least initially) be ignored. "Ockham's razor", as it has come to be known, is a principle long shared among philosophers. It is a highly useful tool in the field of science enabling researchers to focus on what is *most probable* first, and thus to provide simple, elegant and accurate answers.

Outside the laboratory, Ockham's razor has its drawbacks. In the field of history, for example, simple answers are rarely considered satisfactory. Consider the question: "Why did the Second World War break out in 1939?" A student would be expected to provide a range of factors, assessing their relative significance. A simple, mono-causal answer would be considered insufficient. Among the social sciences and humanities Ockham's razor generally gives way to a different approach to knowledge: "thick description". This phrase was coined by the philosopher Gilbert Ryle (1900–1976) and, via the ethnographer Clifford Geertz (1926–2006), has entered the domain of the humanities. This means that the best answer, *to some kinds of question*, will be one made up of a number of different factors, often held in tension.

DIFFERENT WAYS OF KNOWING: HOW SOCIETY CONSTRUCTS KNOWLEDGE

So, in answering questions about the world, we have a choice between two different kinds of answers: "thin" and "thick". Both have their place and value. How we choose to answer a question may also depend on what the answer is intended for. This touches on an often hidden dimension to knowledge acquisition: *power*.

The relationship between ways of knowing and social power has been a key part of "social constructivism", a notion developed in the second half of the twentieth century by Peter Berger (b. 1929) and Thomas Luckmann (1927–2016). Social constructivism proposes that how someone chooses to understand something will, in part, reflect the cultural norms of the one understanding. While knowledge is certainly not considered arbitrary, social constructivists point out that the ways we interpret the world often change according to culture and context. Let us take an example possibly pertinent to a teacher:

> A child in class is displaying poor attention. This is causing the child to fall behind and is also disruptive to other children. One way of interpreting this reality might be (broadly speaking) *biological*: the structure or chemistry of the child's brain is causing ADHD. The response to this interpretation might be to encourage the parent(s) of the child to speak to a doctor about prescribing Ritalin. This may be a valid response.
>
> By the same token, a *sociological* interpretation might either contravene or augment the biological interpretation by alerting the teacher to the effects of the home environment (e.g. abuse, neglect, poverty etc.). A response based on this "way of knowing" might lead to an intervention by welfare services or the police. This, too, might be a valid response.

A third interpretation might be *pedagogical*: the child is simply spending too much time sitting still and not enough time in physical activity. The response to this interpretation might be a practical adjustment of the curriculum or the school day. Again, this might be a valid response.

Each of these ways of knowing the distracted child *might* be correct. They might even overlap and mutually reinforce one another. Indeed, in constructing a "thick" description of the problem, we might additionally consider the relevance of other knowledge domains: *nutrition* (poor diet), the *architecture* of the learning environment (stuffy rooms), and so on.

Importantly, the resulting decision about how to respond to the distracted child (or any other question) may well depend on how much time has been spent exploring each of these different "ways of knowing". This, in turn, might be dependent on the economic resources of the school, the training of the teacher, the social policies of the government, the constraints of time, and so on. Thus, in an often hidden way, society can be said to "construct knowledge".

WHAT IS A WISE ANSWER? "NECESSARY" AND "SUFFICIENT" KNOWLEDGE

In theory, if we wanted to create a really "thick" answer to a question, it would be *necessary* to include the largest possible number of different ways of knowing. In practice, a more limited range may be *sufficient*. Knowing how to arrive at a sufficiently good-enough answer to a question (say, that of the restless child) will ultimately rely on something more than mere information: it will require *wisdom*.

Wisdom is a key category in many ancient religious and philosophical systems. Its significance in modern pedagogy is most associated with the thought of Nicholas Maxwell (b. 1937). Established by him to encourage universities and schools to seek and promote wisdom, the association Friends of Wisdom defines wisdom as the "capacity to realize what is of value in life, for oneself and others. It includes knowledge, understanding and technological know-how, *and much else besides*" (my emphasis). Wisdom is more than information, it includes a dimension of valuation.

In the context of this chapter, I suggest that children are introduced to wisdom when they are encouraged to explore the *fullest possible* range of explanatory ways of seeing the world, rather than being limited to a single intellectual domain. Or, to use the social scientific parlance discussed earlier, when children are introduced to "thick description".

BEING WISE WITH SCIENTIFIC AND THEOLOGICAL "WAYS OF KNOWING"

In popular discourse, and especially in the media, discussions about issues of public policy often revert to reductionism: Ockham's razor rules. For example, media exploration of new medical advances and their possible social effects will rarely engage with a broad range of "ways of knowing". Instead, typically, one or two scientifically-trained specialists might be asked to give their views on the matter. But not all kinds of question are fully answered if only scientific answers are listened to. A biologist, for example, can answer the question "Can we do X to a human being?" But the further question "Should we?" is not a biological matter. Rather, it involves cultural and ethical issues for which an anthropologist, a lawyer, an ethical philosopher, or even a theologian might have useful skills and insights with which to provide a wise, "thick" answer.

Time constraints, the limitations of the media, cultural fashions, and the lure of technological quick fixes, can all mean that complex issues can sometimes be reduced to over-simplistic answers. What can be lost is the ability to discern a *wise* answer. The same problem can also be manifested within education. Subject compartmentalisation and a lack of integration between the sciences, social sciences and humanities can unwittingly lead to answers that are too narrow (something that topic-based learning aims to rectify).

Moreover, with recent advances in neuroscience, genetics, and computer-based technologies the inattention to what is wise (as opposed to what is simply possible) can have a significant impact on areas of common life such as criminal justice, education, and health-care. An ability to know the world from a variety of perspectives, and from that to extrapolate a *wise* response will be of major benefit to our children.

"EXPLANATORY EMERGENCE": HOW (POSSIBLY) TO INTEGRATE DIFFERENT "WAYS OF KNOWING"

If the argument that "knowing" the world from a variety of perspectives is more likely to give rise to richer understanding and wiser forms of decision-making, how practically might this be done?

Typically, "science" and "religion/theology" are set up as alternative viewpoints from which children and adults are forced to choose, but is this helpful? Various models of how to relate "science" and "religion/theology" have been proposed. Most famous is Stephen Jay Gould's (1941–2002) concept of "non-overlapping magisteria" (NOMA) in which a ceasefire between science and religion is proposed. Each is allowed its own sphere of influence: science comments on the realm of "fact", religion the realm of "value".

Approaching the question through the lens of "emergence" provides an alternative, less polarised way of integrating different "ways of knowing". "Emergence" can refer to several things. Here I use the term to refer to the manner in which complex natural phenomena cannot be explained merely by analysing their constituent parts. For example, at the simplest level of the universe, energy, the discipline we call "physics" is the best and most appropriate way of discussing things. But as energy takes on material forms (atoms, molecules), a "step up" is required into the discipline we call "chemistry" since *the discipline of physics is no longer enough*. Likewise, study of more complex forms of chemicals in, say, plants or animals, requires a "step up" into the domain of "biology" and so on.

Thus, a physicist's answer to the question: "What is a cat?" should be (strictly speaking) merely: "A local collection of energy." This is an accurate, even *necessary* answer, but is hardly a *sufficient* or illuminating one. A wiser, more sufficient answer is given if we "step up" the explanatory ladder and ask a biologist. Broadly speaking, the sciences sit within one another, rather like the ever smaller dolls stack up inside a Russian doll. That they do so arguably reflects the fact that nature itself has this emergent quality.

Ever more complex, emergent, "ways of knowing" do not, however, cease with the sciences. To adequately study the behaviour of a collection of biological beings, for example a group of humans, requires a more complex explanation than even a biologist is able to provide. It requires (at least) the skills of a sociologist or an anthropologist. Similarly, to understand a human *culture* – the significance of a group of humans over time – we need to "step up" into an even higher domain: "history". Although rather more messy than the sciences, the social sciences and humanities reveal something of the Russian doll model, too.

To describe the *most* emergent level of existence, namely "consciousness" and the "ideas" that are entertained by conscious beings, one has to "step up" into the domain of philosophy. A subset of philosophy is theology: those ideas that have to do with transcendent and (theologians would argue) "revealed" truth.

Within this model of "explanatory emergence" each level of study – each "way of seeing" – potentially brings to light new dimensions of reality. A physicist, a biologist, a sociologist, an economist, a historian, and a philosopher will all have interesting, valid and unique views on the question "What is a human?" Clearly, we might discount some answers to some types of question as being relatively uninformative. Nevertheless, the practice of scanning a number of different levels of meaning might well be useful in forming a *wise* view of how we might value something.

IS THE UNIVERSE ITSELF EMERGENT?

As has been suggested "explanatory emergence" (the model of nested "ways of knowing") may well map onto the nested nature of reality itself. This seems to result in a "bottom-up" view of the universe: physical properties give rise to chemical ones, chemical ones give rise to biological ones, and so on "up" into (as far as we know) the highest form of emergence yet: human consciousness.[1]

Supplementing this, there is an argument to be made about "top-down" or "downward" causation. In short, although "I" certainly am a "product" of my energy, my genes and so on, nevertheless "I" can, within limits, shape my constituent parts. Genetics determines whether I have curly or straight hair; this is called *upward causation*. However, consciousness enables me to choose what I do with my hair (straighten it, dye it, and so on); this is *downward causation*. Although there will always be limits, technological and scientific advances are providing ever greater scope for downward causation. Genetic-based medical techniques, for example, offer humans the possibility of artificially *producing their own biology*. This ever-growing possibility returns us once again to the question about what is the wise thing to choose to do.

SIDE-BY-SIDE WISDOM: AVOIDING COMPETING ANSWERS

One beneficial result of separating out the variety of "ways of knowing" in this manner is that we are helped to avoid confusing disciplines. For example, it might help us not to conflate, confuse, or put into competition theological and biological views of humans. In the Christian theological tradition (of this author at least), humans are rightly interpreted as a gratuitous product of the universe (we didn't choose to exist, we are "creatures"); we have a scope for freedom bounded by certain constraints (we exist somewhere within a continuum of "free will" and "determinism"); we bear "transcendent" characteristics and are capable of recognising goodness, truth and beauty (we are "made in God's image");

but we are also flawed and incomplete (we are "sinful"). This theological "way of knowing" is different from a biological view that humans are constituted by cells and organs honed by many years of evolution. *Both* views can be true at the same time. Allowing these different kinds of answer to sit alongside one another is to choose to avoid the error of radical biological reductionism, on the one hand ("you are simply your genes"), and radical theological reductionism, i.e. Creationism, on the other ("God made everything in six days").

Notice, too, that different "ways of knowing" will use different "languages" in which to couch their answers. Scientific answers will primarily depend on mathematical or empirical modes of speaking. By contrast, answers given in the humanities are more likely to be based on persuasive *narratives* and these may combine empiricism with rhetoric, personal reflection, myth, legend, poetry, tradition, metaphor, symbol and so on.

Theology, in particular, is likely to couch its answers in a rich variety of "languages". This may be somewhat baffling for other "ways of knowing". However, there is an important reason for this. Theologians, at least since Thomas Aquinas (1225–1274), have asserted that *God is not an item in this world* (not an "object" for study), but rather *the world's author* (and thus "outside" reality). This means that theology can *only* talk about God by means of metaphor and analogy, saying how God is *like* or *unlike* any particular object. "God is love", a theologian may say, but what (s)he strictly means is "God is *like* certain human experiences of love." Theological answers, although they do not avoid empiricism, will always be tentative ones. Couched in metaphor and symbol, they are answers that recognise that they are given at the limits of possible human knowledge.

AN EXAMPLE LESSON PLAN

Introducing different "ways of knowing" within the framework of emergence

Is science all you need?

This outline was originally developed for a half-hour session for Year 6 and above children in groups of up to 20, but is flexible enough to be expanded for size and age. It is intentionally discursive in structure.

a)   Begin by explaining that the purpose of the lesson is to explore whether science is all we really need to make sense of life.

b)   Start by erecting a straw man to draw students' attention to the concept of "reductionism" with a simplistic statement (written on a board), such as:

I love my children, but that's just because of my genes.

Discuss the biologically reductionist assumption here; the partial truth of genetic explanations and the limits of these (e.g. *Do all biological parents love their children automatically? Why not? What about parents who adopt?*).

The word "reductionist" might be introduced (reducing an argument to what is the simplest answer). The teacher may also wish to distinguish between a *necessary* answer and a *sufficient* one (biology provides only part of an answer, but not the whole).

c) Explain that you are going to explore some other "ways of knowing" the world:

> We've already seen our first "way" of explaining things: biology. Biology's answer is built on things like DNA, cells and living organisms. What other "ways" of explaining the world are there?

Teachers may need to coax, for example by asking what different subjects are studied at GCSE, A level and at university.

For ease, the teacher may wish to have the following disciplines written out on cards: Physics, Chemistry, Biology, Psychology, Economics, History, Philosophy, Theology. Each one can be blu-tacked onto a whiteboard as the students think of them. The subjects should be assembled in an open circle with "Physics" roughly in the eight o'clock position, "Theology" in the four o'clock position. Other subjects could be added by pen at the appropriate location in the circle, or simply noted.

Either as each subject is mentioned, or after the whole spectrum is displayed, students can be asked what the subjects of each *kind* of way of knowing are. These could be pre-printed on cards that students are asked to position appropriately.

For example:

> Which of these ways of knowing deals with energy, light, tiny particles? (answer: physics)

> > Chemistry: molecules, chemicals, chemical processes
> > Biology: DNA, cells, living organisms
> > Psychology: neurons, the brain, thought processes (the teacher may wish to allude to differences between physiological and social psychology)
> > Economics: resources, money, exchange systems
> > History: ancient artefacts, past societies, stories
> > Philosophy: ideas (truth, goodness, beauty), values (right/wrong), morality
> > Theology: ultimate worth, the soul, the link with the spiritual

The intermediate stage of the exercise will result in the something like Figure 2.1.

If using a smartboard, to humanise the lesson photographs of representatives from each discipline could be offered alongside each subject.[2] The teacher should highlight the fact that the spectrum moves from the "sciences" through the "social sciences" towards the "humanities".

Sum up:

> Here are a range of "ways of knowing" the universe. Let's play a game and see how each "way of knowing" helps us see something different about reality.

d) Pin up, in the centre of the circle of subjects, a card with the question written on it:

> Why is my hair the way it is?

Go through each subject in turn exploring the kinds of answer each discipline/expert might give and how each answer works. Start with biology. A possible answer might be:

My genes code for hair colour and curl.

Other types of answer:

Physics (my hair is *X* colour because of reflected *light*)
Chemistry (my hair is made of certain kinds of *molecule* – NB absence of vitamins will cause hair to fall out . . .)
Psychology (my hair can fall out due to *stress* or I can go grey)
Economics (I can *afford* this hairstyle; or I have to work in the fields all day and my hair is sun bleached/I can *afford* a holiday somewhere hot! NB the crossover with the sciences)
History (cultural reasons – *fashion:* why do men mainly have short hair?)
Philosophy (*ideas* of about what is beautiful, "clean" or appropriate)
Theology (my hair might be covered up or cut to indicate my *attitude* to God, e.g. a vow)

Any and all of these answers might be valid. After all the kinds of answer have been exhausted, teachers may wish to ask students which are their *favourite* answers, perhaps by voting, and *why*. Discuss:

Do we have to pick only one "way of knowing" for this question? What would a wise answer be?

e)   Now re-run the experiment. Remove the card with the hair question. Replace with a card with "*Who am I?*" written on it.

Ask "*What would a physicist say to this question?*" (e.g. I am energy)

Other types of answer:

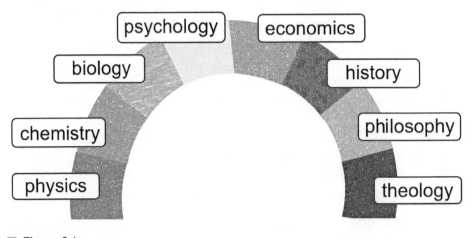

■ **Figure 2.1**

Chemistry (I am a mix of *chemicals*)

Biology (I am a specialised *animal*, a product of evolution etc.)

Psychology (I am a *thinking*, *emotional* animal)

Economics (I am a producer, consumer, shopper, worker, part of a *system of exchange*)

History (I am of X *identity*/nationality, the product of this country, these stories)

Philosophy (I am *mind* or ideas and values)

Theology (in the Christian tradition: I am a *creature* made in the image of God, sinful, being redeemed)

Once again, teachers may wish to ask students which are their *favourite* answers to this question and *why*. They may also be asked whether they preferred to use some "ways of knowing" for the hair question, but different "ways" for the question of what is a human. Why might they prefer to answer these questions in different ways?

This may lead to a general discussion: *Are some kinds of "ways of knowing" better for some kinds of question? Why might this be?* (Possible answers may build on the idea of social constructivism, mentioned earlier: because of the media presence of certain ideas, compelling representatives of a specific "way of knowing", the purpose of knowledge sought.)

The teacher may, finally, wish to include a personal and vocational angle, asking: *Which "ways of knowing" (subjects) are you more drawn to, and why?* (It could be because of role models, the perceived economic value of a discipline, an existing skill etc.)

f)   Last, we may introduce "explanatory emergence".

With the range of disciplines on display, the teacher may wish to introduce the concept of emergence. This part of the lesson may be best delivered initially in a monologue, with discussion after:

■   *Physics* is a good "way to know" small things, but at a certain level we find it helpful to shift up into the "way of knowing" called *chemistry*.

■   To describe an animal simply as a collection of chemicals, however, seems to miss the point: we need to talk about cells and organs, so it is helpful to also be able to "know" a thing using *biology*.

■   When biological organisms become as complex as a brain, we might need to "shift up" into the "way of knowing" called *psychology*, which allows us to speak of thought and emotion.

■   However, to really understand a whole society, we need to "know" more than just about how individual brains work: we need to talk about social systems, including buying and selling, so we use the "way of knowing" called *economics*.

■   Simply talking about money, however, doesn't fully help us understand cultures, for that we need to shift up into the "way of knowing" called *history*.

■   Some ideas are more permanent, bigger, than any single period of history. To understand these ideas, we need use the "way of knowing" called *philosophy*.

■   Finally, some philosophical ideas have to do with more than we can see or prove. They point to the possibility of something that transcends, that is beyond. This "way of knowing" is called *theology*.

The various "ways of knowing" nest within one another like layers of a Russian doll. Point out that school curricula (in theory) make room for all of these "ways of knowing" so as to give us the best all-round, wisest, view of the nature of reality.

g)   Emergence and universal history.

To conclude, the teacher may wish to point out that the spectrum of "ways of knowing" maps out the history of the universe as a story of both *upward* and *downward causation*. This section could be expanded into a lesson in its own right.[3] For example:

> [*Highly simplified*] As far as we know, existence starts with the big bang [*point to physics*], then after millions of years of cooling chemicals start to form [*point to chemistry*]. Out of these complex chemicals emerge very basic plants and (at first) simple animals [*point to biology*]. Among animals, creatures eventually arise with complex nervous systems and ultimately a specialised organ called a "brain" [*point to psychology*]. Some of these animals live in social units and, among them, one group (humans) developed cultures including exchange [*point to economics*], storytelling, art [*point to history*]. "Ideas" arise from these cultures that have validity across time [*point to philosophy*]. Some of these ideas include speculation about what life is for, and why we are here at all and that we might possibly come to "know" the source of this mystery [*point to theology*]. This is a story of upward causation lasting nearly 14 billion years.

A clockwise arrow could be drawn starting with physics and ending with theology. The teacher can then introduce the idea of *downward* causation by curving the arrow around from theology back towards physics, anticlockwise. Explain:

> Yet something very curious has now happened in the history of the universe. We seem to have reached a moment when the universe can reflect on itself. As well as the lower levels of matter making the higher levels, the higher levels can increasingly shape the lower levels. We conscious animals can make choices about, and remould, the lower levels from which we emerge. Our biology makes us, but we also can shape our biology, through our choices (e.g. to have children or not), through the use of medicine and now through genetic engineering. Our values and beliefs can increasingly shape the very things that enabled them to arise.

h)   Conclusion.

The teacher will want to return to the original question: what can scientific "ways of knowing" give us that other "ways" cannot? What is gained from a wider, "thicker" approach to answering questions using multiple "ways of knowing" than just scientific ones? How do we recognise a "wise" answer?

NOTES

1   I sidestep the enormous debate about the distinction between "weak" and "strong" emergence. Weak emergence refers to the claim that if one could know all of the lower level data of a phenomenon one could, in theory (even if rarely in practice), predict its higher level emergent properties (e.g. the shape of a snowflake could be predicted if one knew the properties of all of its constituent molecules). "Strong" emergence suggests that something *qualitatively new* is brought into being at each step "up". David Chalmers (b. 1966) suggests that strong emergence only exists (as far as we know) in the "step up" into consciousness. In human consciousness, something new comes into being that knowledge of physical properties alone could not predict.

2   For instance, Einstein for physics, Marie Curie for chemistry, Stephen Jay Gould for biology, B.F. Skinner for psychology, Ann Pettifor for economics, Mary Beard for history, Socrates for philosophy, and Robert Beckford for theology.

3   There are many resources for exploring this story. See, for example, the Big History Project (www.bighistoryproject.com).

CHAPTER 3

CREATING LINKAGES

YOU DON'T HAVE TO REINVENT THE CURRICULUM!

Sharon Fraser

AIMS OF THE CHAPTER

- Introduce the Melbourne Declaration, the Australian Curriculum and the possibilities for cross-disciplinary learning in Australia.
- Paint the picture of the position of religion in Australian secular and independent schools.
- Consider what young people in Australia have to say about science and religion.
- Unpack what we could do within the Australian Curriculum: Science to help children to move across subject disciplines to develop new expertise.

INTRODUCTION

At the heart of the Australian national curriculum is the Melbourne Declaration, which was signed by all the state and territory Ministers for Education and the Prime Minister of Australia in 2008. This document has been crucial in shaping education throughout the country. From the perspective of the focus of this chapter, the Declaration makes two key points: first, it highlights the impact of global integration and international mobility on Australian society, underlining the importance of appreciating and respecting social, cultural and religious diversity. Second, it identifies that, for *all* Australians, being able to engage with scientific concepts and principles, and approach problem solving (solution finding) in new and creative ways, are essential capabilities. The signatories to the document also agreed to aspire to and achieve the highest possible levels of collaboration between all school sectors, government, Catholic and independent, and at all levels of government (federal, state and territory). Essentially, the Declaration is an aspirational document that identifies two overarching goals for education in Australia:

Goal 1: Australian schooling promotes equity and excellence.
Goal 2: All young Australians become successful learners, confident and creative individuals, and active and informed citizens.

A national curriculum was viewed as one of the key vehicles for achieving these two goals and, eight years later, the Australian Curriculum is approaching finalisation.

As education is a state issue, with each state and territory having its own laws governing the provision of both government and non-government education, the states (and different school sectors) continue to interpret it and incorporate it within their own state-based curricula.

The curriculum learning areas include, fairly unsurprisingly, the single subject areas of English, mathematics, science and health and physical education, and multiple subject areas of humanities and the social sciences, the arts, technologies and languages, and they are presented as a progression of learning from Foundation (kindergarten) to Year 12. Importantly, however, the curriculum aims to develop "general capabilities that underpin flexible and analytical thinking, a capacity to work with others and an ability to move across subject disciplines to develop new expertise" (MCEETYA, 2008, p. 13). To this end, alongside disciplinary knowledge, the curriculum outlines seven general capabilities that comprise "an integrated and interconnected set of knowledge, skills, behaviours and dispositions that students develop and use in their learning across the curriculum" (ACARA, 2013, p. 5) and three cross-curriculum priorities, which are intended to be of benefit to individuals and Australia as a whole.

Of interest to the discussion here are two of the seven general capabilities, specifically "critical and creative thinking" and "ethical understanding". Students who develop capabilities of critical and creative thinking are able to "generate and evaluate knowledge, clarify concepts and ideas, seek possibilities, consider alternatives and solve problems" (ACARA, 2013, p. 78) and display dispositions such as "inquisitiveness, reasonableness, intellectual flexibility, open- and fair-mindedness, a readiness to try new ways of doing things and consider alternatives, and persistence" (p. 79). While to develop an ethical understanding involves students recognising the complexity of many ethical issues and "building a strong personal and socially oriented ethical outlook that helps them to manage context, conflict and uncertainty" (p. 122); they are expected to develop such understandings through the "investigation of a range of questions drawn from varied contexts in the curriculum" (p. 123). While the extent to which Australian teachers explicitly focus on the development of these capabilities as they teach science is not currently known, the potential of using these focus areas to develop resilient and capable school graduates is immense.

THE SCIENCE CURRICULUM

As stated, the Australian Curriculum: Science is one of the eight learning areas mandated from Foundation to Year 10. It is built around six key ideas (see Figure 3.1) that are embedded within each year level description, and are intended to guide teaching and learning and support the coherence and developmental sequence of science understanding within and across year levels.

The science curriculum is sequenced in relation to three interrelated strands: Science Understanding (SU – science content knowledge) unpacked through four sub-strands (biological sciences, chemical sciences, physical sciences and earth and space sciences); Science Inquiry (SI – the scientific process) and Science as a Human Endeavour (SHE – the nature of science within context). Creators of the curriculum felt that school science should mirror the work of scientists, thereby reflecting the nature of science, built around inquiry and undertaken in response to and in order to influence society's needs. While SU and SI are relatively self-explanatory for those of us who teach science, the SHE strand would benefit from unpacking. This strand has been defined as a "movement in science

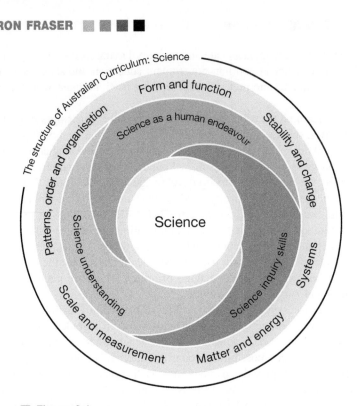

The structure of Australian Curriculum: Science

■ Figure 3.1

education" (Sammel, 2014, p. 850) which enables learners to be critical thinkers and to understand what science is, how it develops and influences and is influenced by society.

The SHE does this through exposing students to two sub-strands: the Nature and Development of Science, and the Use and Influence of Science. The former sub-strand helps students to understand the unique nature of scientific endeavours and how scientific knowledge is the result of the actions of many researchers and is always contestable. The second sub-strand explores how scientific knowledge and its applications (e.g. robotics; medical interventions) affect their lives and how such knowledge can be used to inform their understandings, decisions and actions. Thus SHE gets to the heart of scientific literacy, whereby students are helped to understand "the fundamental conceptual, epistemic and social dimensions associated with the scientific community . . . of how to think, communicate and argue in the beliefs and language of science" (Sammel, 2014, p. 850). As is the case for the other two strands of science (SU and SI), SHE is mapped as a developmental sequence from Foundation to Year 10 (science sequence of content, ACARA, 2015c) such that by the end of Year 10, students should be able to:

[E]valuate the validity and reliability of claims made in secondary sources with reference to currently held scientific views, the quality of the methodology and the evidence cited. They construct evidence-based arguments and select appropriate representations and text types to communicate science ideas for specific purposes. (science sequence of achievement, ACARA, 2015b)

The exploration of science and its relationship with faith, religion or cultural beliefs is not specifically named within the curriculum. Yet considering science learning for the purposes of producing scientifically literate graduates embraces the notion that students are able to interact with science knowledge within the contexts in which they find themselves, which includes both the sociocultural and religious (faith, spiritual) environments. Of issue here, however, is the way in which the science curriculum is implemented in schools and the extent to which teachers are open to such ways of thinking and teaching. Tuovinen (2013) unpacked some of the descriptors of the three strands of the Australian Curriculum: Science, with respect to how particular topics could be considered from a science-faith perspective. For example, as students engage with the idea that science "involves observing, asking questions about, and describing changes in objects and events" (SHE: ACSHE021), Tuovinen suggests that this could be a useful time to introduce them to the idea that there may be some questions that science is unable to answer. Similarly, he calls for teachers to make explicit links between ethical thought or action (general capability) and spirituality and faith positions. Faith-based schools are well placed to create such opportunities, but government-funded schools across Australia may be less so.

RELIGION IN AUSTRALIA AND THE CURRICULUM

In Australia, parents have the option to send their children to state schools (government funded) or private schools (e.g. faith-based schools; independent schools); while all systems receive some government funding, state schools provide free education while the latter charge tuition fees. Australia differs from the UK in that religion is not taught by classroom teachers; neither is it part of the ordinary secular curriculum of government schools. In fact, there is a perceived polemic in Australia between the religious and the anti-religious (Byrne, 2013). The positioning of religion in secular education has received a level of scrutiny in recent years, with the analysis of ideologies, policies, pedagogies and practices undertaken in some depth (Byrne, 2014). While there is legal provision in Australia for non-denominational religious education in schools, it has never been practised in more than an insignificant way. Jurisdictions throughout Australia vary with regard to the religious content of their education system, with secular education (which might include general religious education but not polemical theology) protected by law in many states and territories.

There is no training for religious education of teachers graduating from most Australian teaching degrees and, as has been mentioned already, it is not named as a learning area in the curriculum. In Australian state schools and non-denominational private schools, if religious education *is* offered, it is regulated (no more than 30 minutes a week) and provided by school chaplains or their equivalent, not by classroom teachers. In those states and territories in which the provision of some sort of religious instruction is mandatory, student attendance is not. In order for a child to participate in religious education activities/classes, parents are required to give permission and can expect the school to provide alternative activities (e.g. values/ethics classes) if they do not want their child participating. Faith-based schools provide their own denominational religious education and/or instruction. Hence opportunities for students to participate in discussions about religion vary between schools and states throughout Australia. The extent to which there are opportunities to engage in meaningful and useful conversations about science and religion together is as yet unknown and the focus of ongoing investigation, some of which is reported here.

SHARON FRASER ■ ■ ■ ■

WHAT DO YOUNG AUSTRALIAN STUDENTS THINK ABOUT SCIENCE AND RELIGION?

Research conducted collaboratively by researchers from the University of Reading, in the UK, and the University of Tasmania, in Australia, in the Being Human project (Being Human: Discovering and Advancing School Students' Perceptions of the Relationships between Science and Religion) has revealed ways in which primary (Year 6) and secondary (Years 10 and 11) school students perceive science and religion. To find out how children think about science and religion, the project carried out surveys and interviews with over 500 primary school-aged children in England and Australia. Together these data provide powerful insights into children's understandings. For the purpose of this chapter, three emerging themes will be discussed that emerged from the perspectives of Australian students from Year 6, gained through interviews (n = 20). These themes are:

1   Science is facts and proof and religion is belief.
2   Science and religion are compartmentalised.
3   Ideas are emerging and not previously considered together.

Each of these themes will be explored briefly, elaborating their meaning through the use of quotations from interviews with students, using pseudonyms.

Science is facts and proof and religion is belief

Students believe that science is dynamic, and all about facts that help us live in and impact on the world, in fact, "the whole world is basically science" (Esty6), and we study it so that "we can get a better understanding of what, why we're here, what we're doing here, and how to do more things and become better" (Jeff6). Religion, by way of contrast, is something you just believe in, and "what you believe in is what you believe in . . . that doesn't mean you have to agree" (Arnold6). Science "proves" things, and it will continue to prove more and more things as we keep asking questions and our technologies develop. The importance of evidence in science is well understood and recognised as being important, but children struggle when talking about their religious ideas as just being beliefs. One child identified the Bible as being a sort of evidence, although admitted that it could also have just been made up stories, while another considered the Bible to be a source of tension for science: "evolution . . . they have a lot of evidence that that is true, but it doesn't fit with the Bible" (Silvester6). These perceived differences are often experienced as a dichotomy and are given as reasons to reject one or other account or to admit that it is confusing and they just don't know yet.

Science and religion are compartmentalised

The majority of children recognise science and religion as being different, although they talk about these differences solely in terms of the explanations they provide, rather than the questions they ask or purposes they serve. Some children perceive the people they know to be committed either to science or to religion, considering that a person's background would influence their decisions: "Well, I reckon half of them [their classmates] would . . . believe in science like me. But the other half, they're like really religious families, would believe in religion" (Bailey6). People are categorised as being sciencey: "I guess teachers, they do science. My dad's into science" (Jake6), or religious, depending on their job or how they behave (e.g. in chapel). Children would talk to sciencey people about science but not religion and vice versa, or not talk about with people about science and religion together: "I talk about religion, wait, not together, but I talk about religion and science to my mum and dad" (Bob6). One child recognised a dichotomy between the ideas portrayed in science/scientists and religion/religious people, and felt that he needed someone in the middle between science (e.g. science teacher) and religion (e.g. chaplain) to help him come to understand the truth: "I reckon I will ask some questions the next time I have a chance, to just see . . . if like Reverend Luke believes in . . . religion and science going together well" (Bob6).

Ideas are emerging and not previously considered together

During the interviews, a number of children contradict themselves as they responded to the different questions, indicating how emergent their ideas are about science and religion. The children indicated that they rarely think of science and religion together, and sometimes when they do, it is because they: ". . . just basically want to know which one's actually right" (Bailey6). Most children recognised it as an interesting thing to do and welcomed the opportunity to do so: "I would now because I, now I've thought about them. Yeah. 'Cause I never really thought about them before" (Suzie6). One child mentioned that it is when he struggles with concepts/ideas that are hard to imagine or explain, for example the Big Bang, that he might think of science and religion together. A large proportion displayed a thirst to "find out" about things they don't know and how science and religion "fit together" and their interest has been piqued by participating in the research.

POSSIBILITIES FOR EXPLORING SCIENCE AND SPIRITUALITY, FAITH AND RELIGION IN THE CLASSROOM

As the common expression goes: "Where there is a will, there is a way." If teachers have the will to provide opportunities for their students to engage in the development of their scientific literacy to the extent that Sammel (2014) envisages, there is nothing in the Australian Curriculum: Science to prevent them. Tuovinen's paper (2013) provides us with some useful starting points towards the creation of useful classroom activities that enable our students to engage positively with spiritual or faith-based and scientific thinking, while drawing from curriculum content and pre-existing lesson plans. In Australia, teachers of science (Foundation through to Year 12) have access to an increasing number of online resources, including both lesson and whole unit plans. Resources such as Primary Connections and Science by Doing, and websites such as Scootle and Science Web provide an extensive array of materials that can be used and adapted to suit context and purpose. What follows are several suggestions as to how, with little difficulty, teachers can enable cross-disciplinary learning and faith-based discussions and elicit the consideration of tricky questions.

TAKING A CONTENT (SU) APPROACH

As teachers of science, we might be quite comfortable with the idea that content is an important focus of learning in this discipline. A level of understanding of science content is essential to teaching the subject well, as is diverging from the explicit curriculum (Eisner, 2001) such that opportunities for inter-disciplinary conversations and learning are created. It is possible to do so relatively easily by taking units of work and thinking beyond the named learning outcomes (LOs) taken from the curriculum documents and extending them. This process is illustrated by looking at an Early Childhood (Foundation Year) unit of work: Needs of Living Things, developed by the Australian Science Teachers Association (ASTA) and available from the Science Web website.

The overall goals of the unit can be seen in Figure 3.2. The author of the unit plan believes that it contributes to the achievement standard outlined for Foundation:

Unit Overview	1 Needs of pets	2 Needs of animals	3 Needs of plants	4 Our needs and wants	5 Needs of wild animals

Outline of unit

All living things have basic needs for their survival – food, water, shelter and air. Students may have prior knowledge of caring for a younger sibling, an animal or plants. They will know what it is like to feel hungry, thirsty and tired. They may not identify air as a basic need until guided to do so.

This unit aims to bring students' prior knowledge to a conscious level, making explicit all the basic needs of living things. Through the firsthand experience of a guest presenter, students recognise how people look after a pet to meet its basic needs. Focus questions help identify what senses the animal uses to help meet those needs. Students use the experience to create a model of a pet and identify how they would meet its needs.

Through caring for a class pet/s as well as growing seeds, students observe firsthand how to meet the needs of animals and plants and consider the consequences of their needs not being met. The need for air is addressed by considering situations where air is not available. Students analyse their own needs and are guided to recognise that sometimes wants are confused with needs. They are also guided to see that all basic needs must be met, not just some of them. Finally, students extrapolate what they have learned to an animal that lives in the wild. They consider how bilbies have to provide for their own needs and also learn about the senses that help them to do so.

A class science journal is used as a tool for recording the students' learning journey and provides for meaningful literacy modelling. It is used to review and organise observations and ideas, and can include images and student contributions. Real life, hands-on experiences and sharing observations with others are a key part of creating meaningful, shared understandings. Individually students create a model, draw observations and identify wants and needs in a game and a grocery catalogue. The unit also provides for students to engage with a learning object (ICT as a cross-curriculum priority).

Whilst employing the students' own senses as a tool for scientific observation, this unit could be extended through additional lessons analysing the way animals (including humans) use their senses to help them survive. The lessons and background information provide useful web links for extension possibilities.

■ Figure 3.2

By the end of the Foundation Year, students describe the properties and behaviour of familiar objects. They suggest how the environment affects them and other living things . . . Students share observations of familiar objects and events.

As the unit is written, it enables learners to engage in SU (ACSSU002; Biological Science), SHE (ACSHE013 – Nature of Science) and SI (ACSIS014; ACSIS011; ACSIS233; and ACSIS012).

Key to modifying this unit of work to enable it to foster discussions that facilitate learners to interrogate and/or link science and their beliefs/religion together, at an appropriate developmental level, is to extend their exploration of needs of living things beyond the physical to encompass the emotional, spiritual needs of humans (Polanyi, 1974, cited in Tuovinen, 2013). Considering Maslow's hierarchy of needs (1970) as a framework (see Figure 3.3) is useful for exploring the children's needs beyond the physiological, to incorporate notions of happiness.

An enhanced conceptualisation and usage of the term "environment" is also an avenue for exploration. Biology Online (2008) defines environment as:

1 The external conditions, resources, stimuli etc. with which an organism interacts.
2 The external surroundings including all the biotic and abiotic factors that surround and affect the survival and development of an organism or population.
3 The totality of the surrounding conditions and elements in an individual.

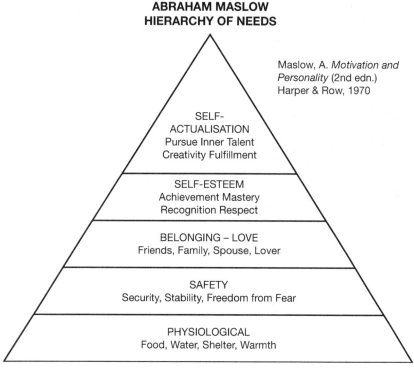

ABRAHAM MASLOW
HIERARCHY OF NEEDS

Maslow, A. *Motivation and Personality* (2nd edn.) Harper & Row, 1970

SELF-ACTUALISATION
Pursue Inner Talent
Creativity Fulfillment

SELF-ESTEEM
Achievement Mastery
Recognition Respect

BELONGING – LOVE
Friends, Family, Spouse, Lover

SAFETY
Security, Stability, Freedom from Fear

PHYSIOLOGICAL
Food, Water, Shelter, Warmth

■ Figure 3.3

Merriam-Webster (2016) provides the following first two statements as a "full definition" of environment:

The circumstances, objects, or conditions by which one is surrounded.

The complex of physical, chemical, and biotic factors (as climate, soil, and living things) that act upon an organism or an ecological community and ultimately determine its form and survival: the aggregate of social and cultural conditions that influence the life of an individual or community.

While children in the Foundation Year do not need to be able to comprehend the subtle differences in these two definitions, it is essential that we as teachers do so that we can guide the activity accordingly.

With these two modifications in mind, teachers of Foundation students are able to modify the fourth lesson: "Our needs and wants" to move beyond the relatively simplistic dichotomy of needs versus wants, towards a rich conversation about what it means to be both animal and human. Such a conversation does not require any dilution of the SU goal (i.e. Living Things have Basic Needs, including Food and Water; ACSSU002), rather it enables these young learners to understand this and build further to consider what more there is to being human and requiring of these basic needs.

TAKING AN INQUIRY (SI) APPROACH

Scientific inquiry has been defined in the *National Science Education Standards* as:

[T]he diverse ways in which scientists study the natural world and propose explanations based on the evidence derived from their work. Inquiry also refers to the activities of students in which they develop knowledge and understanding of scientific ideas, as well as an understanding of how scientists study the natural world. (National Research Council 1996, p. 23)

As with most curricula from around the world, scientific inquiry is writ large in the Australian Curriculum. By the end of Year 10, students are meant to be able to:

develop questions and hypotheses and independently design and improve appropriate methods of investigation, including field work and laboratory experimentation. They explain how they have considered reliability, safety, fairness and ethical actions in their methods and identify where digital technologies can be used to enhance the quality of data. When analysing data, selecting evidence and developing and justifying conclusions, they identify alternative explanations for findings and explain any sources of uncertainty. Students evaluate the validity and reliability of claims made in secondary sources with reference to currently held scientific views, the quality of the methodology and the evidence cited. They construct evidence-based arguments and select appropriate representations and text types to communicate science ideas for specific purposes. (ACARA, 2015a)

In order to achieve this level of capability, children should engage in a hands-on/ minds-on (Gough, 1990) approach to SI. Students should be actively involved in learning, with lessons appealing to their curiosity, challenging their thinking and involving their bodies, through experimentation and the physical manipulation of materials. They should be encouraged to propose their own questions, potentially view them from different perspectives, set up and carry out investigations, evaluate the information they uncover and support their conclusions using reasoned arguments and evidence.

Science as a discipline does not, however, "own inquiry"; in fact, inquiry "is not a 'method' of doing science, history, or any other subject . . . it is an approach to the chosen themes and topics in which the posing of real questions is positively encouraged, whenever they occur by whoever they are asked" (Wells, 2000, p. 61). Religious education also engages in inquiry learning, which is:

> the active processes in which students are engaged as they pursue increased under-standing of religion and religious matters . . . These active processes may include communicating questions, intuitions, conjectures, reasons, explanations, judgments and ideas in a variety of forms. They will also include the development of skills and dispositions to think and act in ways that are, as Groome put it, *humanising for life in all its fullness*. (Elliott, 2004, p. 3)

The similarities between these definitions are tangible, drawing us to the conclusion that an effective education provides opportunities for students to engage with different, but interrelated views of the world (see Figure 3.4), through inquiry. Each discipline has its own unique "habits of mind" (e.g. science requires validation of data; English literature engages with subjective interpretations), none of which is right or wrong, only different (Exline, 2004).

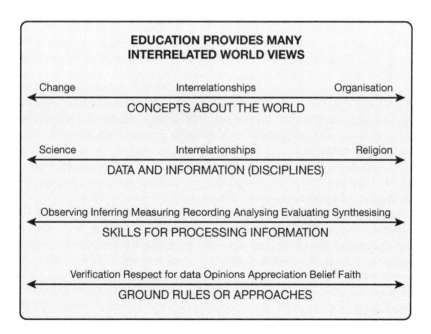

■ Figure 3.4

Science as a discipline exists because of inquiry and hence, when teaching science, we must enable our students to develop their SI through explicitly teaching through inquiry, and developing learning activities that help them critique its habits of mind, with respect to strengths and limitations. Together with the students, critique the "scientific method" (only one?) and identify when this/these process(es) are appropriate for answering which types of question. In doing so, we have before us a perfect opportunity for explicating the similarities and differences between the manner in which inquiry is enacted within science and across the disciplines. It is important to create inquiry brainstorming sessions that result in questions that can, and cannot, be answered through science, and using this as an opportunity to explicitly discuss the limits of science in answering some questions in isolation from other world views. As the Australian Curriculum: Science is underpinned by inquiry, there are numerous opportunities for us to encourage students to engage in, and critique inquiry and to consider which questions can and cannot be investigated scientifically (Murphy, 2001 and Polkinghorne & Beale, 2009, cited in Tuovinen, 2013) and why this is the case.

TAKING A SHE PERSPECTIVE

As has been discussed previously, the SHE perspective provides teachers with the space to critique the nature and development of science and the use and influence of science. To the perceptive and open-minded science teacher, it is clear that as the curriculum unfolds for older learners, more and more opportunities for conversations about the nature and development of science present themselves. In Year 7, for example, one of the content areas, Earth and Space Science, provides us with the opportunity to delve into early understandings of the universe (i.e. predictable phenomena on Earth, including seasons and eclipses, are caused by the relative positions of the sun, Earth and the moon; ACSSU115), including the now defunct, geocentric model of the universe. An example of a unit from the Queensland Curriculum and Assessment Authority (QCAA), provided in Table 3.1, shows how a focus on space science can address a substantial number of different components of the curriculum, including two key aspects of SHE and both general capabilities and cross-curriculum priorities.

One of the assessment tasks (in the 'Explain' phase of the unit's plan) helps students to come to understand the sun, Earth and planets through an investigation of an early astronomer. The unit plan does not provide any further detail about the focus of the activity, but it is easy to see how such a task could be expanded to further delve into the nature of science over the centuries.

Students can explore how important researchers from different civilisations, religions and world views (see Table 3.2) have been to our present day understandings of the heliocentric model of the universe.

We can alert them to the often neglected or ignored contributions of Arab and Islamic astronomers (between 700 and 1200 AD), who built on the science of both the Greek and Indian scholars during the dark ages (Sayili, 1981). This blending and extending of ideas that have developed over the centuries ultimately led to new science, which then influenced Western science during the Renaissance. Students will be fascinated to research the various motivations for studying the sky, one of which for the Arabs was for the purpose of time-keeping, as the Islamic religion requires believers to pray five times a day at specific positions of the sun. Astronomical time-keeping was the most accurate way to determine when to pray, and was also used to pinpoint religious festivals.

■ Table 3.1

Identity curriculum			
Content descriptions to be taught			**General capabilities and cross-curriculum priorities**
Science Understanding	Science as a Human Endeavour	Science Inquiry Skills	
Earth and space sciences • Predictable phenomena on Earth, including seasons and eclipses, are caused by the relative positions of the sun, Earth and the moon (ACSSU115) **Physical sciences** • Earth's gravity pulls objects towards the centre of the Earth (ACSSU118)	**Nature and development of science** • Scientific knowledge changes as new evidence becomes available, and some scientific discoveries have significantly changed people's understanding of the world (ACSHE119) **Use and influence of science** • People use understanding and skills from across the disciplines of science in their occupations (ACSHE224)	**Processing and analysing data and information** • Construct and use a range of representations, including graphs, keys and models to represent and analyse patterns or relationships, including using digital technologies as appropriate (ACSIS129) • Summarise data, from students' own investigations and secondary sources, and use scientific understanding to identify relationships and draw conclusions (ACSIS130) **Evaluating** • Reflect on the method used to investigate a question or solve a problem, including evaluating the quality of the data collected, and identify improvements to the method (ACSIS131) **Communicating** • Communicating ideas, findings and solutions to problems using scientific language and representations using digital technologies as appropriate (ACSIS133)	◆**Literacy** • Use appropriate scientific language specific to the topic ▦ **Numeracy** • Create tables and charts to display information and find patterns • Calculate degrees of tilt and temperature variation ▣ **ICT capability** • Use a range of digital technologies to assist with investigating the concepts • Use simulations and animations to investigate ✿**Critical and creative thinking** • Use thinking skills to complete group activities and open-ended tasks ♯♯**Personal and social capability** • Work together to participate in learning experiences **Aboriginal and Torres Strait Islander histories and cultures** • Research moon myths and culture, including Aboriginal and Torres Strait Islander Dreaming stories

▨ **Table 3.2** Some of the researchers essential to the progression of our understanding of
the universe

Scientist	Century	Contribution
Ptolemy	~100 AD	Developed a geocentric model for understanding the structure of the solar system
		Influenced the gears and motors used in modern planetariums
		Ptolemaic model was not seriously challenged for over 1,300 years
al-Khwarizmi	~820	Invented algebra
		Performed numerous calculations of the positions of the sun, moon and planets
		Constructed a table of the latitudes and longitudes of 2,402 cities and landmarks (basis of early world map)
al-Farghani	~860	Wrote extensively on the motion of celestial bodies
al-Khujandi	~990	Adopted and perfected the Greek-invented astrolabe by building a large sextant inside an observatory near Tehran
		Contributed extensively to our knowledge about the Earth's tilt
Omar Khayyam	~1070	Performed a reformation of the calendar
		Calculated the length of the year with an accuracy to the 6th decimal place
Copernicus	~1473	Developed a heliocentric model for understanding the structure of the solar system
Brahe	~1573	Measured the position of planets (without telescope) using oversized instruments and naked eye observatory
		Calculated the measurement of error in his instruments
Kepler	~1609	Looked for patterns in nature – Kepler's laws of planetary motion
		Used Brahe's data and identified ellipses of planets
		Hypothesised that there was a force joining the planets to the sun
Galileo	~1633	First astronomer to use a telescope
		Observations helped convince people of the heliocentric model
		Revolted against authoritarian attempts to stifle freedom of thought
Newton	~1679	Brought into one theory both our observations of how things move on Earth and how the planets move in the heavens – Newton's laws of motion and gravity.

Hence almost 1500 years of thinking, observing, measuring, creating (instruments) and hypothesising across the world have contributed to our current understanding of the universe. This construction continues today, with new questions being posed as we gain knowledge through the invention of new, more precise instrumentation and our travel to the moon and beyond. Through investigations and conversations of this nature, young learners come to realise that science is an imperfect discipline, one that is dependent on advances in mathematics, technology and engineering at the very least. It is a contestable discipline and should not be thought of as the purveyor of an ultimate truth. Through investigating this long history of scientific endeavours, several points can be highlighted:

- History tells us that these researchers believed in God.
- New scientific knowledge stands on the shoulders of giants.
- It is the nature of science to be contestable: nothing is ever *proved*.
- Just as science changes its ideas, so too can religion; Galileo, for example, once had a fiery relationship with the Catholic church over his proposed heliocentric universe.
- The relationship between science and religion has been complex over the ages, due to changing circumstances/needs, the particular historical situation and the beliefs and ideas of the scientific and religious figures involved (Brooke, 1991).

Instead of setting a relatively simple and science-focussed assignment, aimed at increasing our understanding of who contributed to how it is that we know what we know, perhaps extend the focus of the task to include a debate of one of the following topics:

1 The Big Bang is the one true explanation of the beginning of the universe.
2 Religion has helped the progression of (space) science.
3 We can learn nothing from the creation myths of other cultures.
4 There are no questions about the universe that science cannot answer.

Debating requires students to research, reason, argue, communicate and justify their ideas and opinions, all higher order skills that when used in a science context contribute to the development of scientific literacy skills. The power of the debate topics listed above is that they encourage students to synthesise their understandings gained from the study of multiple disciplines, thereby challenging the siloed nature of the explicit curriculum.

CONCLUSION

In this chapter, we have used the Australian Curriculum: Science to consider how unpacking and extending the SU, SI and SHE strands and developing cross-curriculum linkages provide students with the opportunity to challenge their commonly held beliefs about knowledge. By acknowledging that the explicit curriculum is a guide, not a strait jacket, teachers are able to achieve more than the stated (and siloed) LOs and enable learners to develop the "capacity to work with others and an ability to move across subject disciplines to develop new expertise" (MCEETYA, 2008, p. 13). Science teachers (or teachers teaching science) have a responsibility to provide students with opportunities to think about what science is – and what it is *not*. As we know, science is definitely not proof of anything; rather, it is a way of acquiring knowledge based on evidence, which is acquired through the use of a systematic methodology, including observation and experimentation.

Through an interrogation of, and thence finessed understanding of the "habits of mind" of science, students are better positioned to both challenge the privileged position of science in our society and to explore the "habits of mind" of other disciplines, including religious education. By deconstructing disciplines to their purpose and process in this way, we are then able to help students explore their synergies as well as their differences and prevent their compartmentalisation through carefully designed learning activities. Such activities do not need to be *in addition* to normal teaching; rather, they can build on pre-existing resources, thereby maintaining their alignment with the curriculum and the intentions of the Melbourne Declaration. Constructing learning activities in this way also provides us with the opportunity to address the understandings that have been unearthed in the Being Human research, specifically that students lack an understanding of the "habits of mind" of both science and religion, thereby experiencing them as dichotomous in nature. It is up to us as educators to break down the siloes of knowledge, and provide students with opportunities to consider ideas from different, cross-disciplinary perspectives to gain a richer appreciation of themselves and the natural world.

REFERENCES

Australian Science Teachers Association (ASTA) (n.d.). *Needs of living things*. Retrieved from http://scienceweb.asta.edu.au/years-f-2/unit1/overview/yrf2-unit1-overview.html.

Australian Curriculum, Assessment and Reporting Authority (ACARA) (2013). *General capabilities in the Australian Curriculum*. Retrieved from: http://www.australiancurriculum.edu.au/GeneralCapabilities/General%20capabilities.pdf.

Australian Curriculum, Assessment and Reporting Authority (2015a). *The Australian Curriculum*. Retrieved from: http://www.australiancurriculum.edu.au.

Australian Curriculum, Assessment and Reporting Authority (2015b). *Science sequence of achievement*. Retrieved from: http://www.acara.edu.au/verve/_ resources/Science_Sequence_of_achievement.pdf.

Australian Curriculum, Assessment and Reporting Authority (2015c). *Science sequence of content*. Retrieved from: http://www.acara.edu.au/verve/_resources/ Science_Sequence_of_content.pdf.

Biology Online (2008). Retrieved from http://www.biology-online.org/.

Brooke, J. H. (1991). *Science and religion: some historical perspectives*. Cambridge: Cambridge University Press.

Byrne, C. J. (2013). Free, Compulsory and (Not) Secular: The Failed Idea in Australian Education. *Journal of Religious History, 37*(1), 20–39.

Byrne, C. J. (2014). *Religion in secular education: what in heaven's name are we teaching our children?* International Studies in Religion and Society. Brill: Leiden.

Eisner, E. (2001). *The educational imagination: on the design and evaluation of school programs* (3rd Ed.). New Jersey: Merrill Prentice Hall.

Elliott, M. (2004). Inquiry learning in the religion classroom. In F. Ralston (Ed.). *Curriculum Matters, 3*(1), 3–5.

Exline, J. (2004). *From concept to classroom: inquiry-based learning*. Retrieved from http://www.thirteen.org/edonline/concept2class/inquiry/.

Gough, P. B. (Ed.). (1990). Hands-on/Minds-on: Making Science Accessible. *Phi Delta Kappan, 71*(9).

Maslow, A. (1970). *Motivation and personality*. New York: Harper & Row.

Merriam-Webster (2016). Retrieved from: http://www.merriam-webster.com/.

Ministerial Council on Education, Employment, Training and Youth Affairs (MCEETYA) (2008). *Melbourne declaration on educational goals for young Australians*. Retrieved from http://www.curriculum.edu.au/verve/_resources/ National_Declaration_on_the_ Educational_Goals_for_Young_Australians.pdf.

National Research Council. (1996). *The national science education standards*. Washington, DC: National Academy Press.

Polanyi, M. (1974). *Personal knowledge: towards a post-critical philosophy*. Chicago: University of Chicago Press.

Queensland Curriculum and Assessment Authority (QCAA) (2016). *Sensational seasons and heavenly bodies*. Retrieved from: https://www.qcaa.qld.edu.au/ downloads/p_10/ac_ science_yr7_unit_overview.docx.

Sammel, A. J. (2014). Science as a Human Endeavour: Outlining Scientific Literacy and Rethinking Why We Teach Science. *Creative Education*, *5*, 849–857.

Sayili, A. (1981). *The observatory in Islam*. New York: Arno Press.

Tuovinen, J. (2013). Opportunities Offered by the National Science Curriculum for Exploring the Relationship Between Science and Faith. *Christian Perspectives on Science and Technology*, *9*, 1–12.

Wells, G. (2000). Dialogic inquiry in education: building on the legacy of Vygotsky. In C. D. Lee and P. Smagorinsky (Eds.). *Vygotskian perspectives on literacy research*. New York: Cambridge University Press (pp. 51–85).

CHAPTER 4

HOW SCIENCE CHANGES OVER TIME

Berry Billingsley and
Manzoorul Abedin

AIMS OF THE CHAPTER

- The key aim for this chapter is for students to appreciate that scientific knowledge changes and builds over time.
- For students, to be able to explain that our scientific curiosity is stimulated by making and talking about observations.
- For students, to be able to explain that science is a way of thinking that focuses on what we can say based on data (evidence) gathered via the senses.

INTRODUCTION

"Why does an object fall to the ground when you let it go?" Answer: "Gravity!"

Familiarity with the notion that objects fall because of gravity seems to begin at an early age. At the same time, the word on its own doesn't seem to convey very much explanation, so what does "falling because of gravity" mean – or in other words, how does gravity work and how do we know? Gravity can be seen at work here on the Earth – when you drop a cup or dive into a swimming pool. Every object with mass pulls every other object with mass and the more massive the objects, the greater the force between them. If you hold an object like a tennis ball above the ground, it is pulled downwards because of the pull on the Earth. When the tennis ball is released, it falls. Gravity can also be seen at work if we look into space – and it has been described as the "universal glue" because it maintains the earth and other planets in their orbits around the sun. Newton made this astonishing connection – and the story goes that he was sitting under an apple tree at the time. An apple fell on him or just to his side and he realised that the force that bends a planet's path into an orbit is the same force as the one that pulls an apple from its twig. And the rest, as they say, is history!

Gravity, however, is not the only force in operation when an apple or any other object falls to the ground. On Earth, air resistance also affects the way an object falls and air resistance, in turn, depends in large part on the surface area of the falling object. Many people, including many students, suppose that "light objects fall more slowly than heavy objects" and that if you drop a light object and heavy object at the same time from the same height – the heavier object will hit the ground first. That may turn out to be the case

– but the *key* factor and reason isn't the mass (or heaviness) of the object: it's to do with the surface area and relative contribution of air resistance. So, for example, if you drop a feather and a hammer – the hammer hits the ground first while the feather floats down. The feather has a considerable surface area compared with the far more streamlined hammer. As Galileo predicted – and as the Apollo astronauts demonstrated – without air – a hammer and the feather hit the ground together. The reference to Galileo as the scientist who made this prediction and the experiment that the Apollo astronauts conducted on the moon to test his ideas are both included in the session plan that follows. In their experiment, the Apollo astronauts drop a feather and hammer to show how they fall together when there is no air to slow either object down.

The experiment is a great way to illustrate the idea that, sometimes in science, scientists make a prediction that can only be tested with special equipment or much later in history. Arguably, the experiment that was conducted on the moon would have been even more useful from an educational perspective if the astronauts had dropped two sheets of paper – one scrunched and one flat. It would mean that the two objects being compared would have the same *mass*. Then when both are dropped on the moon, we would be seeing that two objects with different surface area fall at different rates on Earth where there is air but at the same rate on the moon – so that we would only be changing their surface area. Further, students could drop their two sheets of paper in the classroom and then see a similar scenario on the moon.

The primary aim of this chapter is to demonstrate how teachers can facilitate their students to understand that scientific knowledge changes and builds over time. The topic "gravity" has been used as an overarching example. It is important for teachers not just to give a technical explanation of "gravity", for instance, but also to nurture the natural curiosity of children by giving them the time to observe and learn. The chapter discusses "stain removal" activity linking it to "gravity" activities to explain how scientific curiosity of students is stimulated by making and talking about observations. Research has shown that children are enthusiastic about the value of science and are able to conceptualise and design a range of scientific methods, but they also consistently struggle to fit science into a wider epistemological picture. The chapter, by means of a variety of activities, aims to highlight that science is a way of thinking that focuses on what we can say based on data (evidence) gathered via the senses. It is also noted in the chapter that repeated reproduction, verification of observations and experimental results contribute to scientific knowledge.

CHILDREN'S THINKING IN SCIENCE CLASSROOM – RESEARCH EVIDENCE

A recurrent theme in science education over the years has been that children perceive science as a set of facts that are proved by experiments (Leach, Hind & Ryder, 2003; Osborne & Dillon, 2008). This characterisation of science arises in large part because a considerable amount of school science time is spent carrying out "recipe" experiments (also called closed enquiry investigations) that produce an outcome that is known prior to the investigation (Dudu & Vhurumuku, 2012; Sullivan-Watts, Nowicki, Shim, & Young, 2013). From a primary education perspective, Pine, Messer and St. John (2001), who investigated how young children form ideas, stressed that children's scientific reasonings are of considerable importance and cannot be ignored in the learning process that might reflect teachers' own difficulties with certain topics (p. 91). Teachers worry about "not knowing enough" and giving facts to children that do not link into their own experience and thinking can deter them from asking questions, since they will find it difficult to understand the answers (Russel & Watt, 1990). Russel and Watt (1990) argued that the teacher's role in science teaching is to help children develop their understanding starting from ideas that they already have through investigations of topics, discussions, explorations of children's ideas and experiences.

The statutory National Science Curriculum in England has stressed the importance of teaching about the nature of science. The introduction to the curriculum specifies three overall aims, one of which is to "develop understanding of the nature, processes and methods of science through different types of science enquiries that help them to answer scientific questions about the world around them" (DfE, 2013). One identified aspect of epistemic insight is to know how to ask a scientific question and, for example, students in primary school "should be given a range of scientific experiences to enable them to raise their own questions about the world around them" (p. 14) and to "select the most appropriate ways to answer science questions using different types of scientific enquiry" (p. 24). Another identified aspect is to "begin to recognise that scientific ideas change and develop over time". These insights are extended in upper secondary school where students should develop an appreciation of the "power and limitations of science" (DfE, 2014). "Epistemic insight", as Billingsley et al. (2013) argue, is, in this context, an appreciation that and why science and religion are not necessarily incompatible and a capacity to recognise and discuss different metaphysical stances on the power, relevance and limitations of science in a multidisciplinary arena. This definition is motivated by a concern that entrenched compartmentalisation in schools is limiting students' opportunities to learn about the relationships between science and religion (Billingsley, Taber, Riga & Newdick, 2010), the nature of science in multidisciplinary arenas (Billingsley, Brock, Taber & Riga, 2016) and the relevance of science to virtually every aspect of modern life (McComas, Clough & Almazroa, 2002). To move students towards greater epistemic insight, students need more opportunities to consider, enquire into and compare the natures of science with other disciplines.

ACTIVITY 1. INTRODUCING GRAVITY

The first activity and stimulus for this section for students is as follows. Stand, holding two sheets of paper, one scrunched and one flat. You could then ask students the following questions:

- ▨ If I hold up a scrunched ball of paper and I let go, what does it do? (Students will usually say it will fall to the ground.)
- ▨ Ok – so it moves down – why does it move in a downwards direction? (Students will usually say because of gravity.)
- ▨ Does that always happen – if I drop the ball of paper again – will it do the same thing (yes) and does it happen for other objects too – what if I hold out a cup of tea and let it go? (Yes!) I won't test that one!
- ▨ Ok – so we now know that when we let an object go from a height, it falls to the ground – and we've tested that out a couple of times. But that's not the only force for us to think about. Suppose we take two pieces of paper and scrunch one into a

ball and leave the other one flat. Now we will drop them from the same height and at the same time. Before I do – make a prediction – will one hit the ground before the other – if so, which will hit the ground first? (Students usually say the scrunched paper.)

■ And what about the flat sheet – show me with your hand the path that it takes as it falls. (Students usually sway a hand from side to side moving down.)

■ Why? (Because air becomes trapped under the flat sheet and slows down its fall – an effect known as air resistance.)

■ Excellent – so now we have another hypothesis – that a scrunched up sheet hits the ground before a flat sheet – and that a flat sheet wafts from side to side as it falls. How can you test that out?

Once students have answered they could try for themselves. Encourage them to repeat the experiment. By asking students to repeat the experiment and observe the result, the teacher can draw attention to the notion of "repeatability" and "verifiability" of a scientific finding – which, in this case, is an observation that supports the idea that the scrunched up paper lands first. We can also say something about generalisability by, for example, starting out with several pairs of sheets of paper – where each pair is different. We could then notice that "sheets of paper fall more quickly once they are scrunched up".

The teacher can then talk through the scientific thought processes and actions that have just taken place.

We began with a hypothesis that objects fall to the ground if we let them go. We didn't stop there, however, as we also recalled observing that many objects do not fall straight to the ground. We have seen sheets of paper waft from side to side as they descend. This became the focus of a scientific investigation.

The students can now work with you to construct a scientific paragraph about what they have been doing. This might look something like this:

> We drew on our previous experiences of observing objects fall to come up with a hypothesis – that objects fall to the ground when we let them go from a height. We developed our hypothesis further. We said that objects fall towards the ground and also that the way things fall depends on their shape. We had an explanation for this – which is that the object traps air as it falls – and so the bigger the surface of the object the more its fall is affected.
>
> We then carried out some trials to test the hypothesis that flat sheets of paper fall more slowly than scrunched up paper. Our hypothesis seemed to hold true – for all of our trials we found that the scrunched paper falls more quickly than flat paper.

To develop students' thinking about this concept, the teacher can reference the idea of a parachute to facilitate a discussion on why a flat sheet falls more slowly. Gravity pulls a parachute down, but as it falls air gets trapped under the canopy, making the parachute fall slowly.

ACTIVITY 2. THEORY AND HYPOTHESIS

A hypothesis is an idea based on a simple relationship – we see that paper falls more slowly when it is flattened out and now we can use that as a hypothesis to think about

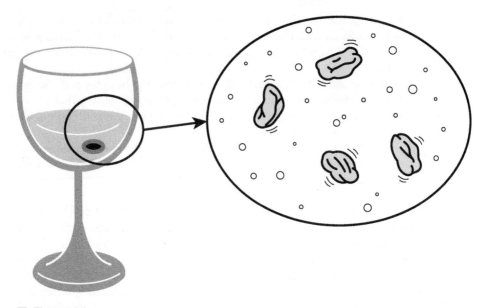

■ Figure 4.1

how other pieces of paper behave. A theory goes further and is a kind of scientific explanation – so our theory about why the paper falls more slowly is that air resistance is slowing it down. Here is another chance for students to come up with a theory.

Take a handful of raisins and put them into diet lemonade. Watch what they do – they rise up to the surface, flip over and then fall down . . . only to rise again. We call it "raisin ballet". Can students construct a scientific theory to explain what happens when the raisins reach the top of the lemonade?

Use the worksheet and the video of raisins in action to help (Figure 4.1). The explanation is that the bubbles of air form on the raisins and carry the raisins to the surface. Air bubbles on the upper surface of the raisin pop into the air and the raisin flips over. Then the air bubbles on the other side of the raisin are released – and the raisin falls. Some students may want to know where the air comes from – it is carbon dioxide – a gas that is in air and it is dissolved in the lemonade. The bumpy surface of the raisin prompts the gas to appear as bubbles.

ACTIVITY 3. FURTHER HYPOTHESIS TESTING

The power of science is that once we have a hypothesis that seems to hold true for all the examples we currently have – we can also use it to make predictions about situations that may be hard to organise at least for now.

In particular, the celebrated scientist who first realised that air affects how things fall in a systematic way was Galileo. The story goes that he dropped a lead ball and a wooden ball from the Tower of Pisa – so show that if the shape is the same they fall in similar ways (with just a little difference).

The teacher encourages students to think about what would happen if two things are dropped where there is no air (e.g. in space or on the Moon or in a vacuum). Galileo predicted that they would reach the ground at the same time. Galileo's idea about the impact of air resistance on how things fall was not tested for several centuries. This incident forms part of the history of science:

- The American space agency NASA's website (also on YouTube) has Galileo's experiment being performed, by an astronaut on the Moon, using a feather and a hammer.
- Which landed on the ground first? (They land at the same time.)

ACTIVITY 4. WHEN DID THE IDEA OF DOING EXPERIMENTS BEGIN?

We all grow up knowing about air and parachutes and the value of doing experiments. But this wasn't always the case. The ancient Greek philosopher Aristotle was born in about 384 BC – i.e. about 2400 years ago. Aristotle's theory about why a stone falls was that it is heading for home. Indeed, Aristotle's theory was more generally that once something is released, it goes home. Birds fly home, people go home, smoke goes "home" to the sky. Galileo not only came up with a better theory (that gravity pulls things down and air resistance affects how they fall), he also encouraged experiments and deliberate observing – rather than only relying on what we anyway see. He is called the father of modern science for this reason.

For most students, this section could end here. Some students may appreciate an extended discussion that identifies the way in which Newton and then Einstein took Galileo's ideas further and came up with their own even more astonishing embellishments to Galileo's theory of gravity.

Newton's theory of gravity

The puzzle occupying Newton's great mind was why planets like the Earth stay in their orbits around the Sun. Moving in a circular path (or more accurately an ellipse) must mean that a force was at work. Otherwise the planets would fly off in a straight line. Imagine whirling a tennis ball on a string around your head, the ball only moves in a circular route while you pull on the string. Let go and the ball flies off in a straight line (and hopefully hits a wall and not a child). Newton was sitting under an apple tree wondering what this force could be – when an apple fell either right onto him or to the side. The idea came to him – that the force at work that keeps planets from leaving their orbits is the same force that pulls an apple down to the ground – gravity. It needs a bit of thought to see why this one force can be the explanation in both cases – but then Newton was good at thinking!

Einstein's theory

To see how Einstein took these ideas further means thinking about "weightlessness" and "free fall":

"Weightlessness" is something that astronauts experience when they are inside an orbiting spaceship. The spacecraft and the astronauts are both moving together under the influence of gravity creating the experience known as "free fall". Students may have briefly experienced free fall for themselves – in a lift as it accelerates downwards. For a moment, the floor is falling away and you no longer feel it "holding you up". You might feel "weightless" and a sense of floating. This idea about gravity was worked out by Einstein – one of history's most creative and imaginative of scientists!

CONCLUSION

Newton said of science and of his experience of being a scientist – that he stood "on the shoulders of giants". By this, he meant that for every good idea he came up with he knew he had to thank scientists before him for working out ideas that were embedded in his own reasoning. There are many notable moments in history when science has made a significant leap and many more moments where smaller bounds of progress, detours and changes of direction have been made. When we put science into a historical context for students it can seem like a story of puzzles that each last for a while until there seems to be a solution and another puzzle comes to light. There are some activities that are designed to enable students to see for themselves something surprising in nature that scientists have discovered. In practice, this means students are told to set up a scenario in which they repeat the experiment or carry out an activity that is intended to work in a particular way. It is import-ant on these occasions to clue students into why they are doing this kind of activity. The experiment has been deliberately designed to produce and showcase a particular known relationship. In that sense, students are working with equipment and instructions that are designed to show them something we already know. The test is not so much to find out what happens but rather to see whether the students can carefully follow the instructions to see the expected result. This is very different to the scenario where students are given a question and are working out their own plan for how to investigate. Both are important experiences to have in their science lessons. In the latter case, students are more likely to experience the excitement and cut and thrust of trying to come up with a good experimental design and there is the scope for different answers depending on how the experiments are set up; in the former case, they are becoming more familiar via some kind of first-hand experience with an idea or relationship or moment in science's history that we still consider relevant and important.

Answers to Figure 4.1 EI detective sheet: dancing raisins

REFERENCES

Aikenhead, G. (1996). Science Education: Border Crossing into the Subculture of Science. *Studies in Science Education, 27*(1), 1–52.

Billingsley, B. & Abedin, M. (2016). Primary children's perspectives on questions that bridge science and religion: findings from a survey study in England. Presented at BERA Conference 2016, Leeds.

Billingsley, B., Brock, R., Taber, K. S., & Riga, F. (2016). How Students View the Boundaries Between Their Science and Religious Education Concerning the Origins of Life and the Universe. *Science Education*, n/a-/a.0.1002/sce.21213.

Billingsley, B., Taber, K. S., Riga, F. & Newdick, H. (2010). Teachers' perspectives on colla-borative teaching about the "big questions" in secondary schools: the silent treatment. Paper presented at the annual conference of the British Educational Research Association.

Billingsley, B., Taber, K. S., Riga, F. & Newdick, H. (2013). Secondary School Students' Epistemic Insight into the Relationships between Science and Religion—A Preliminary Enquiry. *Research in Science Education*, *43*(4), 1715–1732.

DfE. (2013). *National curriculum in England: science programmes of study (for key stage 3)*. London: Department for Education. Retrieved from https://www.gov.uk/government/collections/national-curriculum.

DfE. (2014). *Science key stage 4*. London: Department of Education. Retrieved from https://www.gov.uk/government/uploads/system/uploads/attachment_data/file/318384/Science_KS4_PoS_draft_programmes_of_study.pdf.

Dudu, W. T. & Vhurumuku, E. (2012). Teachers' Practices of Inquiry when Teaching Investigations: A Case Study. *Journal of Science Teacher Education*, *23*(6), 579–600.

Leach, J., Hind, A. & Ryder, J. (2003). Designing and Evaluating Short Teaching Interventions about the Epistemology of Science in High School Classrooms. *Science Education*, *87*(6), 831–848.

McComas, W. F., Clough, M. P. & Almazroa, H. (2002). The Role and Character of the Nature of Science in Science Education. In K. Tobin, D. Baker, B. Bell, R. Duit, M. Espinet, B. Fraser, et al. (Eds.). *The Nature of Science in Science Education* (Vol. 5, pp. 3–39). Leiden: Springer Netherlands.

Osborne, J. & Dillon, J. (2008). *Science Education in Europe: Critical Reflections*. London: Nuffield Foundation.

Pine, K., Messer, D. & St. John, K. (2001). Children's Misconceptions in Primary Science: A Survey of Teachers' Views. *Research in Science & Technological Education*, *19*(1), 79–96.

Russel, T. & Watt, D. (1990). *Evaporation and condensation (Primary SPACE project research report)*. Liverpool: Liverpool University Press.

Sullivan-Watts, B. K., Nowicki, B. L., Shim, M. K. & Young, B. J. (2013). Sustaining Reform-based Science Teaching of Preservice and Inservice Elementary School Teachers. *Journal of Science Teacher Education*, *24*(5), 879–905.

CHAPTER 5

UNLEASHING WONDER AND MYSTERY IN THE CLASSROOM

Matt Pritchard

AIMS OF THE CHAPTER

- An introduction to the multiple reactions a mystery can evoke.
- A discussion of some limitations of a methodical approach to teaching science.
- An exploration of how magicians approach wonder and mystery.
- A simple framework for how science magic can be utilised to increase student engagement and learning.
- Some thoughts about the interplay between science, faith and mystery.

Before reading on, try this:

> Go into a dark room, light a candle and place it next to a wall.
> Now shine a bright light onto the candle.
> Why does the flame not cast a shadow?

THE HUMAN JIGSAW

Mysteries or puzzles can evoke multiple reactions in people. As a magician who presents mysteries to my audiences, I've experienced four main responses. The population is split based on their preference for open/closed solutions and whether they love/hate mystery. (See Figure 5.1.)

The *Indifferent* group has no interest in mystery or finding a solution. A person presenting them with a conundrum will be greeted with this reaction: *"Go away!"*

The *Infuriated* group hates unknowns but also likes closure. *"Tell me how it's done and then go away!"*

There are a number of factors behind these two attitudes. I think people hate puzzles because predominantly they don't like feeling stupid. This can be because they don't like the loss of control of not knowing or because in the past they've been humiliated by someone more knowledgeable. For students, this can be an instant switch off and once triggered it's very hard to reverse. Later in the chapter, I'll be exploring how a safe educational environment can be cultivated where it's OK to be wrong or not know.

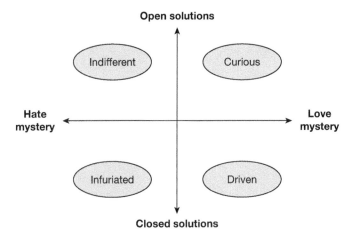

Open solutions

Indifferent Curious

Hate mystery **Love mystery**

Infuriated Driven

Closed solutions

■ **Figure 5.1**

A further reason behind these two groups' attitudes is that they see mysteries and puzzles as a waste of time or childish. Mystery, wonder and play are childlike but is that such a bad thing?

The third group on the grid is the *Driven* population. They love puzzles and won't stop until they know the answer. For them the destination of THE solution is the goal and the journey is to be as short as possible. Once the *"Aha!"* moment has been reached, life continues as normal. They might unlock the door but they won't step inside to explore. With our education system putting so much emphasis on exams and assessments, the danger is that students become short sighted and will only focus on the next task ahead. Later I'll discuss the importance of creating a *"what if?"* environment in which it's OK to go off on tangents and jump ahead.

The final group are *Curious* people. They love puzzles and enjoy exploring new ideas even if they never reach a satisfying answer. For them, the journey is more important than the destination. They unlock doors, walk through them and start inventing new doors to open. Students with this attitude go far. Humans are born curious but, sadly for many, through various experiences, curiosity is lost or ripped away from them. It deeply saddens me that what I believe is one of the most precious and distinctive gifts we humans possess is not better cared for or appreciated.

A WANT FOR WONDER

Science is one of the many ways in which human curiosity surfaces. The universe is one big mystery and scientists attempt to solve it. A common model for how science works is that we observe something and think about how it works by forming a hypothesis, which then leads to a testable prediction. If the prediction proves correct, the hypothesis stands and, if it doesn't, the hypothesis is modified before retesting. Iterate until the theory is a good model for reality – a map of the world to help us navigate. All very methodical, clinical and, dare I say it, boring (see Figure 5.2).

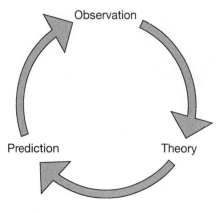

Observation

Prediction   Theory

▨ **Figure 5.2**

Science does not always work this way. Science is messy. Scientists are messy. History is littered with new discoveries that have come from surprises, accidents and mistakes. Untested theories accepted for centuries. Theories and predictions popping up before the experiments are there to back them up. New discoveries coming from theoreticians playing with neat mathematical concepts (maths has a tendency to creep into the real world). Discoveries from asking the powerful question *"I wonder what if?"* And then going out to search for this predictive *what if*.

We do science students a disservice by only teaching the methodical approach starting with observation. Innovation comes from being observant, being playful and asking questions. Not necessarily in that order. Innovation comes from making mistakes, going off piste and being bold. Innovation isn't always smooth and progressive. It's both tediously slow and breathtakingly fast. Marathons and sprints. Endurance and adventure.

We do science students a disservice by teaching a certain, safe and static science. At the core of the scientific method is an adventure fuelled by curiosity and a willingness to adapt, evolve and improve. To be innovative you need to be comfortable with mystery and risk. On the front line, there is no certainty. And, if you're on the front line, you're sticking your neck out. Publish a new paradigm-shifting idea and your name is on the paper for the world to see. If you're correct, then you're a genius. If not, you're a crank. The difference between a Nobel Prize and unemployment is experimental data.

We do science students a disservice by teaching them THE answer rather than the questions and the questioning attitude. A powerful question is worth more than a thousand answers. The journey is more rewarding than the destination. Science isn't a puzzle that can be neatly solved. There are multiple configurations and angles it can be viewed from. This isn't nauseating post-modernism but at science's core – the multiple realities spring-ing from both quantum mechanics and relativity killed off the predictable clockwork universe. There can be multiple solutions or descriptions that are all correct. By giving an answer too quickly, we stifle creative thinking and offer students fast food snacks rather than a wholesome feast.

We do science students a disservice by promoting a hierarchy of school subjects and, ultimately, a belief of scientism. Yes, the scientific method is powerful and has led to some amazing discoveries but it only scratches the skin of life. History, art, theology, philosophy, music etc. have a place in the body of knowledge. We often erect subject walls, especially with a school timetable where hour slots are assigned to each of the subjects. Students find the crossovers between subjects difficult and miss out on the huge potential of mutual exploration. Some of the most exciting areas of current research are happening at the interface; biophysics or behavioural economics, for example.

We do science students a disservice by teaching an emotionless humanless science. Yes, we need intellectual rigour but that doesn't have to be at the expense of the joy and awe (and sometimes repulsion) of new discovery. Science is a story of people discovering things. Story is powerful for both engagement and memory. Stories help build resilience. By eliminating the human element, we also eliminate these benefits. On the flip side, there is a danger of promoting some scientists into savant demigods whom no student can ever aspire to be like. Mad scientist stereotypes with crazy hair and wacky accents are to the subject's detriment.

Teachers are under a ridiculous amount of pressure from exam targets, marking, red tape, student discipline and parents. I do not want to add more to their workload. However, I believe that science students' education can be enhanced by promoting a mindset that embraces:

- mystery
- wonder
- surprise
- play
- risk
- questions
- possibilities.

You'll note that I've not mentioned the word "fun". I have a dislike of those who claim that science *is* fun or worse those who claim to *make* science fun. As if it's boring, difficult and needs a spoonful of sugary silliness to make it more palatable. Exploding a few balloons, making slime and dancing around as a lab coated loon can be temporarily entertaining. They can be great hooks for engagement, however, they're not a long-term solution to inspiring pupils.

Science can be fun but it's not fundamentally fun. I believe the "fun" is a byproduct of having the mindset above. This mindset is both sustainable and transferable to other subjects and, ultimately, sets the student up for a lifetime of learning. It's about setting up intrinsic motivations in the students rather than the extrinsic "carrot and stick" approaches. It's about creating independent learners.

A SCIENCE MAGICIAN?

> The world will never starve for want of wonders; but only for want of wonder. (G.K. Chesterton, *Tremendous Trifles*)

In both my personal and professional life, I've had two main interests: science and magic. The overlaps and tensions between the two are fascinating.

I studied physics at Durham University and then went on to do a PhD in atomic physics. Alongside the academic route, I was working as a magician at parties, weddings and fringe theatre shows. Magic has been a passion since I was 10 years old. I love the creative problem solving that goes into devising a magic trick. I love the reaction a well presented magic trick creates in an audience. The surprise, shock and reality testing befuddlement. Both magic and nature can create a sense of awe in an observer:

Awe – An overwhelming response to something new, big, beautiful or surprising. It can be uncomfortable. It also is something we experience from the outside as an observer rather than a participant. There is a distance. A disconnect. Whether that's looking through a telescope or walking inside a cathedral.

Awe is just the starting point, however. We do not want to create mere observers. The next and harder step is unleashing wonder:

Wonder – Engagement, participation, play. Wonder is like Dr Who's TARDIS. You step inside and the space magically becomes so much bigger. The horizon has shifted and there's new territory to explore. The observer becomes an explorer. Serious play. How deep does this rabbit hole go?

To be gripped by playful wonder is a most joyous experience. For me it is one of those areas where I experience what the psychologist Mihály Csíkszentmihályi calls "flow" (or what others call "being in the zone"). Being so immersed in activity that time both stands still and speeds up. You become a confident risk taker leaping from idea to idea; seeing links and connections that were once invisible. You see a bigger picture.

Magicians live with a dual reality. During a performance, they aim to create for their audiences a sense of wonder as they witness the impossible. Behind the scenes various secret methods are employed to create this illusion of supernatural powers. What the audience and magician experience during a show are quite different. To use simple labels, I shall call these views "effect" and "method".

Take for example the vanishing of a coin. The magician borrows a coin and places it into her closed hand. Moments later the coin has vanished. That's the effect on the audience. The magician has a different view. She picks up a coin and while transferring into her other hand, secretly retains it in her first hand and conceals it from view. The coin is never placed into the closed fist. A simple vanish but also one that can be trivial for the spectator to figure out if performed without extra elements.

A key concept in magic is "misdirection". This is an all encompassing term for directing the audience away from the method onto the effect. The label isn't the best choice of word but it's one that is universally used. Many people think they've only been fooled because the magician made them look away at the wrong time. Misdirection is about manipulating a spectator's attention and perception, thinking and memory. Minimising the method and maximising the effect (Figure 5.3).

■ Figure 5.3

It's more than just words, eye movement, body language and timing. In a well crafted magic show, there's a constant stream of new information to grasp. No time is left to process old information because if a spectator starts to think about the trick, he might start to unravel it. The audience is carried along on a wave and at the end of the ride, they've not had time to think and deconstruct. Memories of details have been blurred. In fact, a magician will often take deliberate steps to blur or rewrite a spectator's memory by falsely recapping or embellishing previous events. A golden rule for beginners in magic is to only perform a trick once because an audience that know what to expect are primed to be sceptical. On first viewing, inconsistencies can be easily overlooked.

In a lot of ways, a scientist is the opposite of a magician. An observer spots something curious – an unexpected event; a coincidence; a pattern. She then works towards understanding how that phenomenon came about. Rather than a rushed blur of activity and sensory overload, the scientist deliberately deconstructs the phenomenon and eliminates any superfluous elements. She will use empirical testing and mathematics. She will repeat the experiment to eliminate coincidences and errors (Figure 5.4).

When a spectator discovers how a magic trick works, the power of both the effect and the magician vanishes. Magicians' secrets are therefore closely guarded to retain the power imbalance. Magicians can be very selfish with their knowledge. They want to give their audiences a taste of wonder but won't teach them how to cook. Science is about revealing rather than concealing. Taking a mystery, opening it up to examination and sharing the discovery. For scientists, often the physical workings of nature are more magical, more beautiful, more mind stretching than the initial curious observation. There are mysteries within mysteries. An intellectual adventure. A deeper magic.

To an outsider, they will often view science as destructive. Taking apart, cutting up, categorising. Like a frog dissection where you've turned something remarkable into a pile of useless flesh and bones. However, science is also an exceedingly creative subject to pursue. Not just because of the diverse range of problem solving that goes on but because once you grasp the "how?" you can then ask the predictive "Now what if?" Changing variables, combining and extending can lead to new discoveries. Magicians and scientists may differ on explaining workings but both groups value wonder and where that takes them.

I call myself a science-magician as I aim to inhabit this dual reality. To approach it from both directions and to wrestle with the tensions:

■ Creating magic based on scientific principles
■ Revealing the magic of science and the natural world

One doesn't dominate the other. They reinforce and weave a wondrous web:

It doesn't stop being magic just because you know how it works. (Terry Pratchett, *The Wee Free Men*, Corgi Books, 2004)

■ Figure 5.4

Before reading on try this:

6210001000

How many zero digits does this number contain?

How many ones?

How many two?

. . .

How many nines?

Did you notice anything? Why does it work? Is this the only number with this feature? Does this have applications elsewhere?

SCIENCE MAGIC IN THE CLASSROOM

"Wow! How? Now . . .?"

The challenge in a classroom setting is to be able to unleash this playful wonder and cultivate a magical mindset. I find utilising science tricks following the three-step process outlined below is a fruitful approach. For younger students, the rhyming phrase "Wow! How? Now?" is an especially effective memory hook and encapsulates the scientific method introduced at the start of the chapter:

"Wow! That's amazing."

"How does it work?"

"Now I wonder what if . . .?"

Let me give you an example of how this works in practice with one of my favourite science tricks – the anti-gravity tin. I'll break the steps down and give some practical guidance along the way. These science tricks can be used as a discussion starter, as part of a longer investigation or a regular exercise throughout the school calendar.

"Wow! That's amazing"

At the front of the class I create a short ramp (~40cm long and lifted up by 5cm at one end). A biscuit tin is placed on its side at the top of the ramp. As expected it rolls downhill. The tin is now placed at the bottom of the ramp and defying gravity it rolls up to the top. This never fails to produce gasps. We're so used to things falling that to see something do the opposite causes confusion. Gravity is the most familiar force to humans. *"What goes up must come down"* but when it doesn't we're perplexed. It feels like the universe has broken, which can be quite unsettling (Figure 5.5).

This first step piques interest by using a magic trick, stunt or puzzle that catches the audience off guard either by surprise or by a counterintuitive result. The more visual the better – especially for younger or less able students – as the situation is easily grasped even if it's

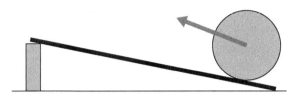

■ Figure 5.5

not fully understood. Magic and mystery are powerful engagement tools that cut through even the most apathetic teenager. The mystery cries out to be solved. Unknowns are uncomfortable. Especially in an age where answers are just a Google away. The students want to know what just happened. This step shouldn't be rushed. Something wondrous has sprung into life but it can easily be crushed. Let the mystery breathe. Let the students be amazed.

"How does it work?"

At this point, the student's questions, answers and accusations of trickery start erupting. It would be easy to provide a nice comfortable solution to the problem. That would be missing a golden opportunity. The mystery would be solved and life would continue with just a minor hiccup of intrigue. Instead, I turn the question back on the students: how do *they* think it's done? With the biscuit tin example, I invariably get the answer of magnets thrown back at me. There is something seemingly supernatural about a magnet's invisible power and action at a distance. They're the obvious candidate for the method behind the magic.

I challenge the students to keep giving me alternative solutions to the tin rolling uphill. Answers range from invisible string through to hidden hamsters. Initially, the ideas dry up after the first few suggestions but if you cultivate a safe environment open to possibility and allow time, more ideas will surface. The key here is not to reject ideas as stupid as that is a sure fire way to crush the creativity in the room and to make the person feel stupid. Their confidence will take a hit and you've undone any progress.

The given answers highlight common science conceptions and, perhaps more importantly, misconceptions. In the biscuit tin example, one of the solutions I've previously been given is that either gravity has been sucked out of the tin or that anti-gravity has been placed inside. A teacher can then follow up these ideas with follow-up work to explore new avenues or to guide the students back. They can also deepen the mystery. For example, if the students are convinced magnets are in use, the metal tin can be swapped with a plastic tin and the trick repeated. A simple science trick can draw in and link multiple areas of scientific knowledge.

Depending on the situation, the students' answers can be harvested in a number of different ways:

■ Ask the students to raise their hands if they've got an answer. This simple technique is the quickest but favours the confident and doesn't allow everyone to have a voice. Most of the attention in the class can be lost if students don't feel involved or are not clever enough to provide an answer.

■ "Think pair share." Each student partners up and has a brief discussion in their pairs as to how the trick works. Everyone gets to voice his ideas even if not in public.

Pairing up can aid the initial thought process and removes the fear of public humiliation. A teacher can then ask for some groups to feed back. Pupils are more willing to share when it's not their idea as they can't personally be wrong.

■ If time allows, getting students to sketch down their answers on paper is very effective. Doodling helps visualise the problem. A teacher can ask for group feedback or all the sketches can be stuck to a wall for the whole class to view. At the end of the session, the teacher has a physical record of class thinking and can spot common misconceptions that can be followed up in later lessons.

Ok, so before we continue, let me explain how the biscuit tin rolls up hill. I did consider keeping the mystery but wanted to share the workings so you can replicate it.

A little construction is needed for this trick. The first thing you need is a counterweight. I made mine simply by making a stack of coins and taping around the circumference. More precisely I made two stacks of ten 2p coins. Twenty coins in total. I then taped these two counterweights to one inside edge of the tin. I'd suggest if the tin has a seam, you place the weights next to that to help identify its position when looking on the outside. You can if you want, conceal the hidden weights by replacing the tin lid but I just leave it off and make sure I always hold the tin opening away from the audience.

Next make a ramp. Mine is made from a wooden board ~40cm long and lifted up at one side by ~5cm. You may need to experiment to find the best incline for your tin. Add a non-slip rubber mat to the surface of the ramp. This is to ensure the tin always rolls and doesn't slide off.

Place the "anti-gravity tin" on a ramp with the counterweight on the uphill side. Let go of the tin and it should roll up hill giving the illusion of defying gravity. That is until the counterweight rolls around until it reaches the bottom of the tin.

The added weight changes the centre of mass (COM) of the tin, which would normally be at the centre of the cylindrical tin. The COM is now situated close to the extra weight on the edge of the tin. Gravity acts on the COM and pulls it downwards.

In order for the COM to move downwards, the tin has to roll uphill. Physics and not magic.

An alternative to using the non-slip mat is to stick the rubber sheet to the outside perimeter of the tin. It makes the tin self-contained and can work on any surface.

"Now I wonder what if . . .?"

Once the students have exhausted their ideas for how the trick is done, I will often reveal how it was done. Not to make the incorrect students feels stupid. And not that I want to crush the mystery but because of a combination of these reasons:

■ The educational benefit of knowing how a scientific principle can be exploited to create unexpected results. As I've said earlier, sometimes the science can be just as magical as the magic trick.

■ I want the students to go away and experiment themselves by performing the trick to others. Most of the tricks I use are simple to construct and very low cost in terms of materials. Almost all of the tricks are made from household items. It's about making the science accessible. It's about showing that science is all around us. It's about opening our eyes to the wonder in the everyday.

I would like the students to extend the trick by asking one of the most important questions in science: "Now I wonder what if . . .?" By changing a variable, eliminating a feature or combining ideas, what will happen? This is a key part of innovation. A small change can have a dramatic effect. There are now multiple avenues to explore. A small mystery at the start of a lesson can create enough ideas to explore for the rest of the session. The students are engaged and empowered.

By fostering a mindset of relishing mysteries, students can become positive risk takers. The unknowns don't unsettle them. They embrace them because within an unknown there is a deep well of possibilities to explore.

DUAL REALITY – SCIENCE AND FAITH

> Mystery is not the absence of meaning, but the presence of more meaning than we can comprehend. (Dennis Covington, *Salvation on Sand Mountain*)

Both science and religion try to find answers in mysteries. We gain comfort in the answers they give and yet are discomforted by the discrepancies. At times it feels like trying to complete a puzzle made up of two separate and incomplete sets of jigsaw pieces. The pieces don't fit; there are overlap and gaping holes. It's a mess.

Earlier I explained how magicians inhabit the dual reality of effect and method. How reality can be different depending on your perspective. Have a look at Figure 5.6. What symbol is in the central box? The answer depends on whether you were looking at the left or right diagram. You either interpreted the central box as B or 13 depending on the pattern you recognised. Another reader might have viewed a different diagram and got a conflicting answer to you. Neither of you is right or wrong.

Much has been made of the apparent conflict between science and religion. I find the B-13 ambiguity very helpful, especially when talking to students, in explaining how sometimes dual realities can exist without conflict. Another example. At the start, I mentioned quantum mechanics, which, at its core, has the dual reality of particles and

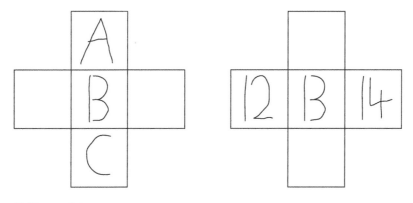

■ **Figure 5.6**

waves. In some circumstances, a wave model is more instructive than thinking of particles and vice versa.

The tools we use to probe the world differ and therefore can yield different answers. With science and religion, we're probing the world for mechanism and meaning. Different questions. Different answers. It's important for students to recognise the differences from having multiple perspectives and not to create a subject hierarchy in which one answer is unduly weighted.

Each subject creates a map of reality. Making connections between ideas and concepts. A navigator can follow that map to understand how the world fits together and use it to move around. Mapmakers make choices though. Not everything is included. Some information is superfluous. Some details are simplified or rearranged to aid navigation. Items are grouped, labelled and condensed. Take the London Underground map for example. It takes a sprawling network of tunnels and makes it accessible to subterranean travellers. Above ground, the information is fairly useless because distances and directions don't match. The Underground map is not *reality*. In a similar way, science (or any subject for that matter) is a *map* of reality but it is not reality itself. This is where scientism comes unstuck. Science, powerful as it is, will not explain everything.

At the start, I sketched the science method of observation, theory, prediction. How a theory is built on a bank of experimental evidence, correct predictions and explanatory power. Religious faith is viewed as the antithesis of the science method. We have the phrase "leap of faith" where we often picture someone trying to make a jump from one cliff edge to the other. (Thanks, Indiana Jones.) It feels like a blind stupid jump into the unknown and the foolish athlete will either succeed or fail spectacularly. You could sum it up as:

Leap of faith = Mystery + Risk

The larger the unknown and the larger the risk you take, the more faith you have. I don't find this caricature of faith a particularly helpful picture, as it's lacking an important element.

Science explores mysteries. Every hypothesis is thrown into an unknown. Every time a scientist conducts an experiment, she has faith that an answer exists and can be found. From Galileo onwards, science is about action as well as thinking. Every time a science paper is published, a risk is taken that the author's ideas might later be shown to be wrong. A central tenet of science is that it evolves – ideas are shaped through the natural selection of evidence. The weak ones die off and the survivors are currently the fittest. Science is an exercise of faith. There is mystery. There is risk. And, crucially, there's also testing. The strength comes from the testing element.

I find the following a better expression of active faith:

Active faith = (Mystery + Risk) × Testing

If there has been no testing or past experience, it doesn't matter how much you want to believe, your faith will be pretty weak. Over time faith will grow and be strengthened as experience and evidence build up. Faith is not static, neither is it a switch that is either on or off. Faith is more like a thermostat that can be varied.

THE WONDER OF THE UNIVERSE

> The eternal mystery of the world is its comprehensibility. (Albert Einstein, *Physics and Reality*, 1936)

To finish this chapter, I want to give an example from a Christian perspective of how science and religion can work together. So let's start with the first job that God gives Adam in the Garden of Eden. In Chapter 2 of Genesis (2: 19–20) there is an animal parade and Adam is given the task of naming the animals. Whatever name is given to the animal, that name is used. Can you imagine the scene? It's a display of the wonder of creation but also an invitation to humans to be part of exploring, categorising and understanding the world. It's an invitation to "do" science. Over the centuries millions of people, from multiple cultures, have taken up this invitation to both wonder at creation and wonder about a creator. Just one example: the astronomer Johannes Kepler said of his work unravelling the universe: *"I was merely thinking God's thoughts after him."* For Kepler, the root of his science and his motivation to do science came from his religious faith.

Later in the Bible it says*: "It is the glory of God to conceal a matter; to search out a matter is the glory of kings"* (Proverbs 25: 2, New International Version). Eugene Peterson in his paraphrase of this verse has an interesting variation: *"God delights in concealing things; scientists delight in discovering things"* (Proverbs 25: 2, The Message). The mystery is why make it a mystery? Why conceal?

At the start of this chapter, I talked about how a mystery can split the population into four groups. The "Curious" delight in discovery. Does God gain pleasure from seeing us discover? Like a birthday gift giver watching the recipient's eyes as they unwrap the surprise. Has the universe been made in order for us to have wonder? And if so, science and religion are surely approaching the same thing but along different paths.

CHAPTER 6

STORYTELLING AND GALILEO

David Hutchings

AIMS OF THE CHAPTER

- This chapter looks at the role and power of stories in teaching.
- The "science vs religion" story – including Galileo – is investigated.
- The competing Galileo accounts lead to a surprising conclusion: that the science vs religion "conflict thesis" is actually a 19th-century invention which convinced many then and is still doing so today.
- This new story of conspiracy can be used as a narrative to overpower the conflict thesis in the classroom.

The penny first dropped a few years ago. I was at a residential adventure camp for 11- to 18-year-olds, several days in and, all of a sudden, things simply fell into place.

How so, you ask? Well, I invite you to picture the scene . . .

Early morning wakeups in remote log cabins; life lived out of an increasingly smelly holdall; physical activities from dawn to dusk; an assorted mix of 100 young people hurled abruptly together; the joys of mass catering on a tight budget; pitched battles with bloodthirsty midges – all in all, an experience that is somehow replenishing and depleting in equal measure. And, by the time the traditional evening meeting rolls round, everyone has pretty much had it.

Despite this, the entire troupe – youth, leaders, and caterers – assemble in the on-site sports hall for some teaching and guidance each and every night. The speaker is right up against it. Tired bodies, tired minds, sideways glances at holiday crushes, fits of giggles, homesickness and daydreams of the next outdoor adventure combine to make getting any kind of message across next to impossible. Here I was, in the audience, as a supposedly responsible adult, finding concentration for even a moment hard work. Unsurprisingly, the brave soul up front, five or 20 minutes in (I couldn't have told you), had long lost the room. And then, right there in the hall, it happened: "Let me tell you a story", he said.

In what appeared to me to be an entirely reflex action, brain hardly aware of the process, I gathered my slouching self up and sat forward. I began listening. My stupor was gone; I was ready to learn. I wanted to know what this story was going to be. *I couldn't help it.*

And, to my great amazement, I realised that I was not alone. Sitting at the back right, I could scan the rows of seats in front and to my left. Everyone – from the peskiest scamp to the world-weariest cook – was on board. Eyes were fixed on the stage. The whole lot of them. It was almost miraculous. This was my "Eureka!" moment. From then on, it all made sense.

"What made sense?!", I hear you say. Well, this: the moments in my lessons (I am a physics teacher) when the students seemed to be at their most involved were not when we were doing some jaw-dropping practical; not when we were covering the mind-blowing space topics; not when we were doing that last-minute revision session; but when I was telling them *stories*.

STORIES AND THE HUMAN CONDITION

Why? What is it about storytelling that seems to grab our attention in a way that nothing else, no matter how stimulating, quite does? The highly esteemed theologian, N.T. Wright, has a theory: he claims that at our most important and basic level we *think* in stories.

It is tempting, at first, to view a story as being merely illustrative of some deeper point. They are the easy-to-swallow point of entry, but need to be discarded as soon as anything of real weight is to be considered; a means to an end. In fact, some might go so far as to claim that storytelling is for children and/or those unready or incapable of more foundational thought. Wright, following significant recent predecessors in many disciplines, challenges this view. Indeed, he seeks to turn it on its head:

> Human life, then, can be seen as grounded in and constituted by the implicit or explicit stories which humans tell themselves and one another . . . Stories are often wrongly regarded as a poor person's substitute for the "real thing", which is to be found either in some abstract truth or in statements about "bare facts".[1]

Bearing in mind that Wright's stock-in-trade is theology, he goes a remarkable step further, saying that these human stories are, in his words, "located" "at a more fundamental level than explicitly formulated beliefs, including theological beliefs".[2]

Let that sink in for a moment. Here is a world-class academic who has been a bishop in the Church of England and who professes a personal Christian faith, writing in what many consider his *magnum opus* that stories are even more primal and integral to human beings than what they believe about life, the universe, and everything. He is not ploughing a lone furrow here: Wright's huge tome references in turn at least a dozen other scholars who have written at length on this same point, some of whom have used the insights of the famous folktale analyst Vladimir Propp (1895–1970) to argue that our storytelling is not childish at all, but is, instead, the best way of dealing with the most profound of all kinds of truth.

If Wright and all these others are correct – and it is an "if", admittedly – then harnessing the power of story might just be the best thing we can do in the classroom. If we are most truly at home with stories, if we follow their rhythms and shapes by our very nature, if we use them to make everything else fit, then they are the ultimate teaching tool. My own experience thus far had suggested precisely this, but I hadn't necessarily realised it until that night in the insect-ridden, sweaty, restless hall.

Combining the observations of a) success at the chalk face and b) the sports-hall-road-to-Damascus experience, I decided to take the plunge: could there be a story for *every* topic I taught? If so, would they be interesting enough? Would there actually be *time* to indulge (me and) the students in this way? Would it improve engagement? Would it improve understanding? Would it improve grades?

WHEN STORIES WORK

It seems, however, that I was not alone in asking these questions. In fact, the conviction that there is some untapped educational value tied up in the concept of "story" has led to the launching of an entire organisation: one that is dedicated to the use of storytelling in primary schools, across all the year groups.

In 2013 and 2014, a group of inventive practitioners embarked on a pilot scheme in a school that took its students from an area of high social deprivation in London – Tower Hamlets. Calling their fledgling enterprise "Storytelling Schools", they undertook the systematic teaching of stories – and, in turn, of storytelling itself – to the students, with intriguing results. The University of Winchester followed the programme and wrote a highly detailed formal report on their findings. These included very positive outcomes for nearly all students and for EAL and FSM groupings, in particular.[3]

Alongside all this educational success, the teaching methods were also considered to be highly enjoyable by both students and staff. A repeated theme was a growth in *confidence*, something that we know all too well is often lacking in those students who never quite flourish in the way we strongly suspect they could.

Much of this, I suspect, makes sense. We *know* that stories help us learn. After all, it is how we tend to begin teaching our own children while they are still very young. I suspect most parents have even been taken aback at some point as to just how much detail really goes into even a toddler's mind when there is a clear and strong narrative involved. Getting muddled between "two" and "three" might well happen when a child is first learning to count or to recognise the symbols; I doubt, however, that there has ever been an issue with forgetting how many "little pigs" there are in the fairy tale. So why, I found myself wondering, does it appear that this storytelling practice gets ditched at some point, by some subjects, in secondary education? When does the changeover to explaining – or, worse, simply declaring – bald facts actually happen?

Why do textbooks suddenly seem to go all bullet-pointy, with stories (if they are there at all) relegated to the occasional "did you know?" box, and thus immediately dismissed by teacher and child alike as not-needed-for-the-exam-so-didn't-read?

I don't know the answers to these questions. Perhaps they are already well researched and in the literature, but it is not often that teachers have the luxury of perusing more academic works (yes, I know, I'm writing in one right now). If they are not, however, I would encourage those who might be able to do so, to do so.

What is certainly true is that storytelling has a rich pedigree as a teaching tool historically. Some expressions – "she's just crying wolf"; "a Good Samaritan helped out"; "they were always star-crossed lovers" – immediately draw on the power of our story memory bank. Each of these comments floats on the surface of a story whose depths speak of the inner-core principles of human nature. Each was used by an ingenious storyteller (Aesop, Jesus, Shakespeare, for those keeping score), seeking to make statements that resonate at a profound level with our human experience.

Take, for instance, the insight of Mortimer Adler, in his remarkable *How to Read a Book* – he says that the best tales "satisfy the deep unconscious needs of almost everybody" and that they are:

[U]ndoubtedly the great stories, the ones that live on and on for generations and centuries. As long as man is man, they will go on satisfying him, giving him something that he needs to have.[4]

Even nowadays, outside formal education, the concept of an overarching narrative is often used to communicate key ideas. Soap opera writers deliberately pen themes designed to help the public learn about various illnesses, social prejudices or even financial choices. In fact, in several cases, soaps have been invented entirely from scratch purely to convey essential facts to the populace. These include a Colorado TV show about the importance of health insurance, AIDS advice written into African plotlines, and even Latin American programming about domestic violence.[5]

In a similar vein, using a story to advertise a product or service turns out to have a very positive effect for the advertiser. A 2013 study[6] looked at the attitude of potential customers before and after viewing online adverts described as having a clear "narrative" nature, and concluded that the outcome was an undeniably "favourable consumer attitude". This was at least partly caused by a higher degree of individual *involvement* – precisely what I had noticed on camp and in the classroom.

Putting this together then, we can deduce the following:

- Stories can grab the attention of even disinterested audiences in a unique way.
- There is a weighty scholarly case that stories are our most foundational form of understanding.
- A storytelling philosophy has been trialled in primary schools with great success.
- Throughout history, many of the greatest teachers have utilised storytelling, to such an extent that those stories remain with us centuries or millennia later.
- Outside education, stories are routinely used to teach the public about crucial issues or to win higher levels of involvement within advertising.

On the basis of all of this, I made a deliberate decision to incorporate stories into as many of my lessons as possible. While it is always wise not to blow one's own trumpet too much (especially in print), I *have* found over and over again that this approach *works*. Not only does it help students to remember the key ideas, it enables them to set them in a context and link them together.

Crucially, they also begin to understand that science is a *human activity* and not some hermetically sealed process that mechanically churns out one new faceless truth after another. Science is no longer aloof or other-worldly; it becomes – because of its weaknesses, its suffering, its hope, its *personalities* – something approachable. In the words of the mighty James Clerk Maxwell (1831–1879):

In Science, it is when we take some interest in the great discoverers and their lives that it becomes endurable, and only when we begin to trace the development of ideas that it becomes fascinating.[7]

SCIENCE, RELIGION, STORIES AND GALILEO GALILEI

Yet what has all of this discussion to do with the main subject of this volume – science and religion? Well, as was stated in the Introduction (and in several chapters, and in many other books, and in the literature) the notion of a rivalry between the two, despite being so utterly demolished by the "experts", simply *will not go away*. And the reason for this, I believe, is that it has taken on the form of that most persistent and fundamental of entities: yes, science vs religion has become a *story*.

So deeply ingrained is this story that I repeatedly encounter amazement in the lab whenever my classes find out that I believe in God. They are staggered. For them, science and God are enemies. I may as well be pronouncing to them that David and Goliath were really best friends or that the hare and the tortoise actually ran a relay.

So here is my thesis: when it comes to science and faith, there is a story that needs to be uprooted and no amount of well-reasoned, carefully argued theology, philosophy, history or educational psychology can dig deeply enough to get at it. The only thing that has enough pedagogical power to conquer a story – to destroy it from its very core – is, I would suggest, *another story*. And nowhere, in all of the debate, is the science vs God plotline more in evidence than in the life and times of the man who (supposedly) best champions hard evidence over silly superstition: Galileo Galilei. Let me offer an illustration of this from my own experience in the very recent past.

Over the last two years, I have been working on a book about the interplay, throughout history, of science and Christianity. Co-written with Professor Tom McLeish FRS, *Let There Be Science* (Lion, 2017) seeks a novel approach – it is, primarily, a book of stories. Our aim is to highlight, at a popular level, what is already generally accepted as the truth in academia: that science and religion have not been historical enemies.

When I visited my alma mater's Physics Department, then, I was keen to let my former tutors know about this work. On the whole, the university has been very accepting and encouraging, as I found it was during my studies. We (Tom and I) have since spoken there, by personal invitation, on the topic. The head of department, although not a Christian, wrote a ringing endorsement of the book. Not all of my experiences, however, were quite so positive.

Stepping into the office of one professor with whom I had worked closely a decade or so previously, I mentioned *Let There Be Science* and its subject matter. Within seconds, he was beginning to fume. Face reddening, he asked me if we had written much about the systematic persecution of scientists by the Catholic Church. "There is a bit of myth-busting", I replied – perhaps too cheekily, I'll admit.

This tipped him over the edge. He glowered at me and proceeded to shout about Galileo. He had been to Italy, he said, and seen the torture equipment prepared for the visionary scientist. In the end, I had to cut my losses – the conversation was going nowhere fast. I left making the offer of a free copy, which was declined: "I wouldn't read it!"

It always seems to be Galileo. If the tortoise represents the victory of patient perseverance over rash raw talent and if David represents the victory of faithful bravery over faithless brawn, then Galileo represents the (eventual) victory of naturalistic Science (with a capital "S") over religious claptrap. And, as long as this story sticks around, the war will be lost – no matter how many battles can be won in the meantime.

It is time, I believe, for this story to be retold. It already has been, of course, in many books and articles written by careful historians, scientists and commentators. What I mean is this: it needs to be retold – indeed, I would even say it *must* be retold, as a matter of some urgency – in the classroom.

In fact, I can think of no other field in education in which a continuing misconception of this magnitude would be allowed to have such a huge impact on the futures of young people. Why should budding scientists feel that they have to reject or abandon belief in God? Why should teenagers with a faith be made to feel so wary of or intimidated by science? The current situation is unacceptable. Enough is enough. It is time to change the story – students need to know the *truth*.

THE MYTH

First, let's recount the mythological tale of Galileo, which usually contains some of the following ideas, but without any real supporting evidence:

> Once upon a time, the Catholic Church insisted that the Earth was the centre of the universe because that is what the Bible says. Then a brave atheist scientist called Galileo used science to prove that the Sun is actually at the centre of the solar system. This was unacceptable to the Church because it called the Bible into question.
>
> As a result, Galileo was put on trial, scientifically defended his position and was [depending on the version being put forward] then burned at the stake/tortured/ sent to jail. His death/suffering was not in vain, however, because eventually science won and the Church lost – we now know the truth, despite the best efforts of religion to keep us all in the Dark Ages.

Well, it is immediately easy to see the problem: it is a great story, and one that is incredibly easy to follow. There is a clear good guy, an obvious villain, sacrificial courage in the face of great threat, and the final decisive triumph of good over evil. It "fits", so to speak – the arc is exactly like so many of our classic tales. No wonder the Galileo affair has stuck around so successfully; it is almost perfectly resonant with us, at some base level, as human beings. Indeed, Bertholt Brecht (1898–1956) saw it as a strong enough tale to carry an entire play – *Life of Galileo* (1943) – which follows the same plotline. To make matters worse, the fable flames have been publicly stoked by luminaries such as Voltaire, Einstein, Bertrand Russell and Karl Popper.[8]

Yet those genuinely in the know – historians of science and the like – are well aware that much of this story is poppycock of the highest order. There is no shortage of texts, long and short, popular and academic, which point out just how inaccurate, biased and ideological the Galileo myth really is.[9] And yet it remains. My contention, as I have already laid out, is that this is because the bare facts are *not enough* – they simply cannot compete at story level; they are out of their depth. The facts, if they are to make any difference at all, must be repackaged. We need a new *story*.

THE TRUTH

The first step is, of course, to gather those facts into one place. I shall do so, briefly, now. Obviously, the interested reader is advised to do more research (see the references) of their own to flesh out any part that they should wish to. In this volume, however, word count and form limit how much can be said. We shall have to be satisfied with this:

░ Aristotle (underlying philosophy) and Ptolemy (practical outworking) had established a working model of the heavens that was Earth centred and made use of the complicated geometric arrangement of lots of circles. This view held for comfortably more than a millennium and was a reasonable, but not exact, fit with observations.

░ Nicolaus Copernicus (1473–1543), a Polish astronomer and lay canon, developed a mathematical model which placed the Sun at the centre of the solar system. This was published without any complaint from the Catholic Church whatsoever, since it had no official position on the issue. In fact, interested Christians of the time were split on exactly what was going on – but it was not acrimonious.

░ The Copernican model was also a reasonable fit with planetary movement, yet was clearly nonsense when considered from the Earth's point of view: an Earth racing through space and spinning on its own axis would (according to the accepted science of the day) lose its atmosphere and fling everyone into the interstellar void. A second weakness was that his model predicted parallax effects among the stars, which was contrary to observations.

░ Galileo (1564–1642), thanks to his new-and-improved telescope design had, by 1612, sighted Jupiter's moons, Sun spots, and the phases of Venus, among other things. He almost instantly became world famous. He also became convinced that Copernicus' model was not simply a mathematical novelty, but was physically true; despite the continuing lack of scientific evidence, such as parallax.

░ A committed Christian for his whole life (he wrote a strong defence of Biblical Christianity in the light of good science in 1615),[10] Galileo was nonetheless a rather belligerent character. Unable to support some of his theories (including heliocentrism) with mathematical or cosmological proofs, he often resorted to mocking opponents rhetorically, causing controversy and significant upset at times. This included making fun of his great German contemporary, Johannes Kepler (1571–1630), for his correct idea that the moon caused the Earth's tides. Galileo's model claimed that the tides were due to the movement of the Earth – which was wrong and would have led to just one tide a day.

░ Things came to a head in 1616, when the loud-mouthed and troublesome Galileo was formally warned by the Inquisition not to write about or teach heliocentrism any more – to which he agreed. This was partially because there was sensitivity around the Protestant accusations that the Catholic Church did not take scripture seriously enough, but mainly because there was, still, a distinct lack of conclusive evidence for the position. Cardinal Robert Bellarmine (1542–1621), Head of the Inquisition, had investigated the matter thoroughly and stated that:

> If there were a true demonstration, then it would be necessary to be very careful in explaining Scriptures that seemed contrary, but I do not think that there is any such demonstration, since none has been shown to me.[11]

░ Galileo remained a favourite of many churchmen, including cardinals, and was often invited to lavish occasions as the main guest, awarded assorted titles, and given honorary roles. Perhaps his biggest supporter was his patron, Cardinal Maffeo Barberini (1568–1644), a man who had a decent understanding of astronomy and who admired Galileo so much that he even wrote celebratory poems about him.

In 1623, Galileo probably thought he had hit the jackpot: Barberini became Pope Urban VIII. Thinking himself unleashed, Galileo penned *Dialogue on the Two Chief World Systems* (1632), which championed the Sun-centred view.

Urban, however, turned out to be more cautious than Galileo had expected. He felt that the certainty being declared in the *Dialogue* was unjustified and insisted that Galileo include a more careful voice, one that declared that the matter was not truly decided or even understood (which, in fact, it really was not).

Galileo, stubborn and brash as ever, did so – by inserting a character named *Simplicio*, effectively "the Fool". Speaking for the Pope, *Simplicio* was portrayed as an imbecile; Galileo's text even called him a "mental pygmy" and a "dumb idiot".[12]

Unsurprisingly, Urban was furious and those who disliked Galileo (and there were plenty) saw their opportunity. He stood trial in 1633 and was offered a plea bargain – he would face a minor conviction if he would admit that he had gone back on his 1616 agreement. Galileo accepted this, but then argued again in his trial, claiming that the *Dialogue* did not promote heliocentrism at all. Since it clearly did, he stirred up more resentment: his charge was upped to the semi-serious "vehement suspicion of heresy", he was found guilty and his book was banned.[13]

Urban was keen to be seen as the immovable and impressive victor in this head-to-head, so he ensured that documentation flew around Europe reporting the result of the trial. The report included wording that strongly implied that Galileo had been both tortured and imprisoned: something that, unsurprisingly, became widely believed.

It was not until 250 years later[14] that the truth came out: Galileo had faced neither prison nor torture. Instead, he was placed under what could be loosely termed as "house arrest" – he stayed in the lavish accommodation of the Archbishop of Siena for a while, and then returned to his own villa, where he died in 1642 at the grand old age of 77.

During this "arrest", Galileo was free to continue working, and it was during this time that he wrote his masterpiece *Dialogues Concerning Two New Sciences* (1638), addressing motion. He was, perhaps, the best treated convict/heretic that there has ever been in history.

Conclusive, physical scientific proof for heliocentrism did not actually arrive until the 19th century, more than 200 years later. Prior to this, anyone favouring the Sun-centred model had only partial reason for doing so – perhaps a gut instinct for it, or a preference for its elegance. It simply was not the obvious truth that revisionists like to claim it was.[15]

WHAT TO DO?

Two things, I would argue, become clear from these facts. First, the commonly assumed Church-versus-science narrative around Galileo is wholly inaccurate. Second, a "simple retelling" of the Galileo story is not really possible – it is a rather complex one, involving politics, power plays, egos, religious sensitivities, scientific subtleties and more.

Attempting to recount the truth in appropriate detail, therefore, would make the whole enterprise too long and complicated for the classroom. For a story to take root, it needs to be simple and dramatic: the full Galileo affair is certainly the latter, but hardly the former. Who, for example, is the "good" guy? Galileo? Well, not really. The Catholic Church?

I don't think so. The Pope? Nope. The edges are all far too blurred. Maybe an older, more interested, and able group could just about have the patience and focus needed to work through all these details, but it seems that for the vast majority of people, the strength and simplicity of the original myth will easily overpower the carefully amended version. Have we hit a stalemate then? I would suggest not.

The stickability of the short-simple-and-wrong Galileo fable is hugely impressive, but it actually draws its power from its *location*. Ultimately, it is really a story *within* a story – it plays out on a larger stage, so to speak. The secret of the Galileo affair's strength is its snug placement inside a dominant overarching narrative: that science and religion are enemies. Is there a way that we can keep the story of Galileo both simple and dramatic while simultaneously changing it to better reflect the truth? Yes: give it a different *home*.

REHOUSING THE STORY

We are not exactly on novel ground here. In several of his works, Shakespeare utilised the concept of a "play within a play". Christopher Nolan's brilliant Oscar-winning *Inception* (2010) took this a step further, using a "dream within a dream". Our solution to the Galileo problem can be a similar one: we shall continue to tell it as a "story within a story", but find it a new dwelling. This will only work if the replacement "bigger" story is clear, dramatic, and resonant with the human condition – like those identified by Adler. Fortunately, such a story exists. And it goes like this:

> In the 1870s, two men fooled the world. Their names were John Draper and Andrew White. Each wrote a book which contained a mixture of misunderstandings, exaggerations, misinterpretations, and even outright lies. Their ideas were so convincing, however, that pretty much the entire western world was eventually tricked. Bizarrely, when experts actually studied both of these books and discovered that they were horribly wrong, no one really took any notice. Even now, 150 years later, most people – including University Professors, politicians, and most of the media – still believe what they said. And, as it happens, you probably believe it too.

The above paragraph refers to John William Draper (1811–1882), Professor of Chemistry at the University of New York and Andrew Dickson White (1832–1918), Founding President of Cornell University. Their books are *History of the Conflict Between Religion and Science* (1874) and *A History of the Warfare of Science with Theology in Christendom* (1896) respectively.

Between them, the pair effectively invented the notion that science and (in particular Catholic) Christianity have always been at war. To do so, they made claims that were at best partially and usually completely untrue, such as the idea that the Church believed in and taught a flat Earth; that the Church prevented autopsies; that the Church killed off classical science, and so on. All of these assertions have been utterly discredited.[16]

The advantage of this alternative encompassing story is that it is simple and it is intriguing. This makes it memorable. Everyone loves a conspiracy theory and it plays on that. How on earth did two men trick most of the world for 150 years?! How can an idea stick around so successfully when all the people with genuine expertise have proved it wrong? And, as I am sure you will have noticed, the story above ends on a bit of a cliffhanger; students virtually fall out of their seats to ask the most obvious of questions: *"What did the two books say?!"*

Here, then, is the potentially winning formula. The almost-impossible-to-dislodge "science vs religion" story finally has a worthy rival: the "two guys tricked everyone" story. And, just as the false Galileo account was so much at home in the first, the slimmed-down-and-corrected version fits perfectly within the second. Look at how it can sound now:

> For example, there is a myth around Galileo. The widely believed version has Galileo as an atheist scientist who proved that the Earth went around the Sun and was then tortured by the Catholic Church because the Bible says the Sun goes around the Earth. Lots of people, even Einstein, fell for this. Many, many people, still believe it. But the story is wrong.

To show that it is wrong, the full detail is not needed. Instead, it becomes sufficient to focus in on just a few key points:

> In reality, though, Galileo wasn't an atheist; he was a committed Christian. He didn't prove that the Earth went round the Sun; his argument was incomplete and some key parts were wrong. The Bible doesn't say the Sun goes around the Earth; it is silent on the science, and the Church itself was split on the issue. Galileo wasn't tortured, or killed, or put in a cell; he died at 77 in his own home, having continued to work as a scientist his whole life.

Some might be beginning to feel uneasy that the Catholic Church is getting off a bit too lightly here. So, to balance things out, and avoid future recriminations, I would suggest a few brief additions if time and audience permit:

> Galileo's real problem was his seeming inability to keep his mouth shut. Some historians would even describe him as a bit of a bully – he insulted Kepler, who was right about tides when Galileo was mistaken – he insulted the Pope himself (who was, amazingly, far less committed a Christian than Galileo was).[17] When the Pope (with scientific justification) urged him not to overstate his case, Galileo reacted by adding a character to his book who represented the Pope, calling him a "fool" and a "dumb idiot" in print. It was not a wise tactic, but Galileo went ahead anyway. In the end, he was put under "house arrest" and his book was banned. Yes, the leadership of the Church made a mistake here, but the heart of the issue was not a debate about who had the better science: it was the familiar story of two larger than life characters, with huge egos, yelling at each other.

When it is placed inside the larger "science-vs-religion-is-actually-an-invention" story, the amended Galileo account works brilliantly. The opposites involved – not atheist, actually Christian; not proved, actually flawed; not dogmatism, actually closer to an even split; not jail or torture, actually leisurely house arrest – dramatically reinforce the extent to which Draper and White furnished their thesis and tricked the world. In my experience, students are captivated by the whole concept. And, since the teacher is simply involved in storytelling, this approach can be taken in almost any curriculum area: science, RS, history, drama and more.

CONCLUSION

Perhaps it would be best to finish with a summary of what we have discussed. We spent quite some time showing the profundity of stories and then the effectiveness of storytelling in teaching. We then linked this to the fact that – despite academic consensus – science and religion are still widely seen as being in opposition: the refusal of this notion to go away was put down to it being a great *story*.

The same was said of the false-but-all-too-common Galileo account, which is a story within a story. In reality, the truth is far more complex, so a simple retelling is not usually practical in the classroom. However, by finding a new overarching narrative – that of Draper and White and their revisionist manifestos – we can indeed make use of a cut-down, revised version of Galileo's life.

In taking this approach, we no longer find ourselves relying on "bare facts", which N.T. Wright (and others) claim will only ever produce rather anaemic effects. Instead, we are building on the mighty power of *story* – for it is the only force available that can overcome itself.

NOTES

1   N.T. Wright, "The New Testament and the People of God", SPCK (1992), p. 38.
2   Ibid.
3   Jonathan Rooke, "The Impact of Storytelling Schools on Children's Writing in Tower Hamlets Primary Schools Evaluation of Roll-out Phase 1: 2013–14" University of Winchester, 2015 [url: http://www.storytellingschools.com/wp-content/uploads/2015/10/4315-STS-Evaluation-Report-Jonathan-Rooke-4.pdf].
4   M. Adler, C. Van Doren, *How to Read a Book*, Simon & Schuster (2014), p. 216.
5   Cesar Chelala, "Soap Operas as Teaching Tools: Using television to spread public health messages", *The Globalist*, 11 June 2016 [url: https://www.theglobalist.com/soap-operas-health-aids-teaching-tools/].
6   Russell K.H. Ching, Pingsheng Tong, Ja-Shen Chen, Hung-Yen Chen (2013) "Narrative Online Advertising: identification and its effects on attitude toward a product", *Internet Research*, Vol. 23 Issue: 4, pp. 414–438.
7   John Read, *From Alchemy to Chemistry*, New York: Dover (1995), p. xiii.
8   Maurice Finocchiaro, *The Trial of Galileo: Essential Documents*, Hackett (2014), p. 2.
9   Two good popular examples are Dinesh D'Souza, *What's so Great about Christianity*, Jaico (2008), pp. 101–111 and David Bentley Hart, *Atheist Delusions*, New Haven: Yale University Press (2009), pp. 56–74.
10   Galileo Galilei, "Letter to the Grand Duchess Christina of Tuscany" 1615 [full text English translation available at http://www4.ncsu.edu/~kimler/hi322/Galileo-Letter.pdf].
11   Stillman Drake, *Discoveries and Opinions of Galileo*, Garden City, NY: Doubleday (1957), p. 165.
12   Allan Chapman, *Slaying the Dragons*, Lion Hudson (2013), p. 105.
13   Finocchiaro, Maurice A, "That Galileo was imprisoned and tortured for advocating Copernicanism", in *Galileo Goes to Jail*, ed. Ronald Numbers, Harvard University Press (2009), p. 71.
14   Ibid. p. 73.
15   Owen Gingerich, *God's Planet*, Harvard University Press (2014), pp. 48–51.
16   See, for example, *Galileo Goes to Jail and Other Myths about Science and Religion*, ed. Ronald Numbers, Cambridge, MA: Harvard University Press (2009).
17   David Bentley Hart, *Atheist Delusions*, New Haven: Yale University Press (2009), p. 66.

HOW SCIENTIFIC
IS THAT?

A PRACTICAL GUIDE TO DISCUSS THE POWER AND LIMITATIONS OF SCIENCE IN SECONDARY SCHOOLS

Martin Coath and Berry Billingsley

INTRODUCTION

Scientism is the belief that *"all problems – including distinctly human problems – are merely technological problems"* (Williams and Robinson, 2014). Someone with a scientistic attitude to life would likely be accused by critics of exhibiting an *"over-reliance on, and overconfidence in, science as the source of knowledge regarding all aspects of human life"* (ibid.). Scientism is not a commitment that scientists frequently make, however – or in other words, scientism is not a necessary presupposition of science. An alternative view, which is held by many scientsits and other scholars too is that there are many "dimensions" to most problems.

Whether or not someone holds to scientism, it is still the case that when complex issues are discussed, we often refer to and call on scientific studies, even if the issues are not explicitly scientific. For example, while decisions about funding nursery school places are ultimately political, social and economic, at some stage in the debate it is reasonable to ask if the benefits of starting school earlier can be measured "scientifically".

The exercises outlined in this paper are designed to aid teachers and workshop facilitators in introducing this important, but complex, insight into discussions of a wide range of issues. They were designed as part of the LASAR research project (lasarcentre.com/project-rationale/) and to support a series of public and school workshops given by the author entitled "The Power and Limits of Science". The approach has been used successfully since 2016 in a variety of forms and settings with secondary students and adult groups.

THE SESSION

Scientific difficulty

The session starts with introducing the conceptual variable of "scientific difficulty". This is an example of something that is not measurable but people can have a surprisingly good "feel" for what it means. Take the following three problems in physics:[1]

1 How well can we model the motion of a weight bouncing on a spring?
2 Can we predict the motion and final destination of all the balls on a snooker table after a break?
3 How accurate are predictions of the rainfall in Plymouth over the next ten weeks?

Even if participants have had minimal exposure to mathematical physics most have no problem in agreeing on a plausible order of difficulty or complexity for these three questions. The weight-and-spring (an example of simple harmonic motion) can be described in a single equation.[2] The snooker balls are a much more challenging problem, but computers can give accurate predictions for these types of problem in some cases; in part, because the balls come to rest quite quickly after the break. Finally, ten-week weather forecasting with precision is currently beyond our available techniques and computational power.

How would these three problems look on a scatter plot? The answer is we cannot properly place them in two dimensions because we have established only one property that we can represent as a distance, i.e. the difficulty. Working on the assumption that these three are *"purely scientific problems"* (PSPs), we will agree to place all PSPs at the very bottom of the diagram. The result is illustrated in Figure 7.1.

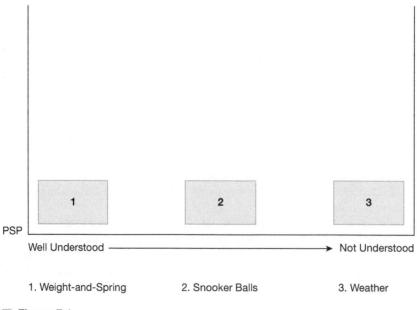

Figure 7.1

In Figure 7. 1, the three purely scientific problems (PSPs) referred to in the text are:

1   Motion of a weight on a spring.
2   Paths and final positions of balls on a snooker table after a break.
3   Accuracy of rainfall predictions over ten weeks.

These are placed on the lowest edge of the diagram reserved for PSPs and spaced along the horizontal axis which is labelled "Well understood" on the left and "Not understood" on the right. Note that we have referred to problems by number, which aids re-use of Post-It notes and saves a great deal of valuable time in groups because the descriptions do not need to be written out.

Other types of difficulty

The incompleteness of this example naturally leads to a discussion about what sort of problems would be placed to occupy the rest of the unused space on the diagram. Space at the top left of the diagram is reserved for well-understood problems that have no scientific component. The top right of the diagram would be the place for discussions that are very hard to resolve and for which science is also of no help.

At this point, the facilitator might ask the group to suggest questions, or problems, or controversies that might populate the top line of the diagram. What sort of things is science *not* useful for? Are there any truly "non-scientific problems" (NSPs)? Suggestions that have come up in previous sessions have included:

1   How should I tie my shoelaces?
2   What is the best way to make a perfect soufflé?
3   How do we decide on the top ten painters of all time?

It is also important to make clear that the process of comparing problems and assigning them a relative difficulty is only useful for the purposes of discussion; there is little hope of achieving universal agreement and no pretence of objectivity. However, it is useful to treat complexity or difficulty informally as a conceptual variable if only for the purpose of sparking disagreement and debate. In the author's experience, it is very successful judged in these terms.

It is up to the workshop leader to bring any discussion concerning the NSPs to a conclusion and to place the three chosen examples (whatever they are) on the diagram giving us something like Figure 7.2.

By placing our three putative non-scientific problems (NSPs) on the same diagram as in Figure 7.1, the tasks are numbered four to six consecutively with the PSPs: 4. Tying Shoelaces, 5. Making a soufflé, 6. Deciding on the top ten painters. These go on the top of the diagram establishing that the vertical axis now represents increasing/decreasing scientific amenability. Placing the tasks as shown in Figure 7.2 reflects our working hypothesis: that tying shoelaces is an everyday, well-understood skill for most people or one that is easily acquired; making a soufflé is less well understood; and that deciding an order of greatness among the world's painters is almost impossible. All these three tasks are achieved without recourse to empirical investigation or mathematical analysis.

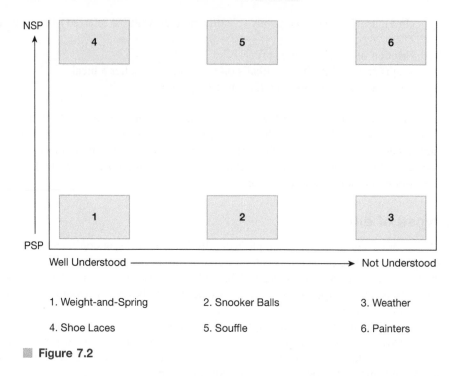

1. Weight-and-Spring   2. Snooker Balls   3. Weather

4. Shoe Laces   5. Souffle   6. Painters

Figure 7.2

Are there any totally non-scientific discussions?

It is usually the case that during the course of placing NSPs on Figure 7.2, there will be objections that science *can* be useful for deciding on the optimal method for tying shoelaces or cooking, despite the fact most people do not use the results of scientific enquiry to help with either. It is important to reiterate that people can legitimately disagree on both the order of difficulty and the degree to which science is useful.

The final point before the practical part of the session is to deal with the *"cooking is partly a science"* objection and establish that the vertical position, the scientific amenability, of the cooking task is a matter of personal opinion, or if the session includes groupwork, it is a matter for discussion and compromise among the group. One possible outcome of these discussions is shown in Figure 7.3.

One possible result of negotiating disagreement on the nature of our NSPs is that the group (or the facilitator) will concede that both shoelace tying and cooking are discussions where science can be useful. This can be represented by a vertical movement of the Post-Its on the PSP –> NSP vertical axis.

Individual or groupwork

The preliminary discussion detailed above in sessions run by the author for Years 12 and 13 and adult groups has lasted up to 25 minutes. The next stage is for individuals or groups to consider a set of sample questions and to contribute some of their own. Using these questions, they will construct a scatter plot that represents either their own opinion or a

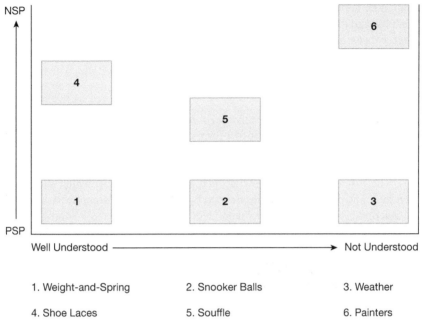

NSP

PSP

Well Understood ⟶ Not Understood

1. Weight-and-Spring   2. Snooker Balls   3. Weather

4. Shoe Laces   5. Souffle   6. Painters

Figure 7.3

group consensus. Each group is given a large sheet of paper, flipchart paper is ideal, and a supply of Post-It notes with which to work.

Many potential issues are controversial and emotional, allowing people to work in groups gives them a chance to compare a range of opinions. Here, there are just four suggestions:

1   How do you cure hiccoughs? There is always lots of advice available from people when you have hiccoughs! Is any of it truly scientific? Does it matter how scientific the advice is if it works for you?

2   Should we eat vegetable oil spreads or butter? Evidence for the health benefits of non-dairy spreads is contradictory. But even if the health benefits were clearly demonstrated, would that inevitably swing the argument? What other reasons are there for choosing what we eat?

3   Should self-driving cars be allowed on the road? This is a very topical argument! Does it depends on the degree of autonomy that is allowed to the car? Whose responsibility is it if there is an accident caused by the machine?

4   Are chimpanzees "nearly human"? This depends entirely on what you mean by "nearly" and for some this is an emotional issue, for others a philosophical one, and for some it is a purely scientific discussion. In any case do we understand the question?

It cannot be stressed too often that the point is not to resolve, or even explore, any of these issues. The facilitator needs to provide strong leadership to avoid the session being derailed by debating the issues, when the point is to decide where they are on a scale of difficulty, and to what degree science can help us with any of them. It is possible for groups to agree that a question is hard to resolve and that science might usefully contribute to the argument, even if they disagree vehemently on the issue itself.

Variations

Two variations on the workshop have been tried with some success. Both represent a move from a continuous representation to a form of categorisation. This approach can simplify the discussion allowing the session leader to ask "which category does this question belong in" rather than placing the Post-Its in a continous space.

The first of these variations is illustrated in Figure 7.4, which simply divides the sheet into nine possible categories defined by three levels of complexity and three degrees of "Scientific", "Partly scientific" and "Not scientific". This is a simple modification of the situation found in Figure 7.3.

In Figure 7.4, the sample questions discussed in the text are moved from a continuous representation (seen in Figure 7.3) to one of nine categories. These start in the bottom left with "Scientific/Well understood" and finish in the top right with "Not scientific/Not understood".

The second variation reduced the number of categories to three and provides a worksheet (see Figure 7.5) with sample questions. This approach is very useful for younger students who can quickly get to the group discussion and the categorisation of the questions, without extended exposition.

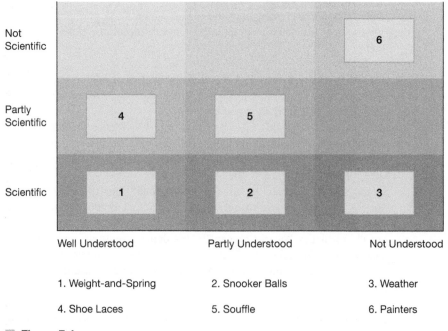

Figure 7.4

Some questions are more amenable to science than others. Please read the following questions and decide in which bubble you would like to put them.

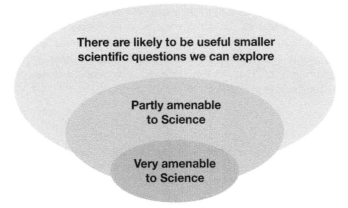

There are likely to be useful smaller scientific questions we can explore

Partly amenable to Science

Very amenable to Science

1. Why did the Titanic sink?
2. What is the most interesting book ever written?
3. Why did the great fire of London spread so quickly?
4. Why do things fall to the ground when you let them go?
5. Would a robot ever be given the status of an electronic person?
6. Why did the Romans come to Britain?
7. Will we ever bring back dinosaurs?
8. If Henry VIII's first wife had given birth to a baby boy, would he have remarried?
9. Why did many women authors write under male pseudonyms?
10. How can we measure the spread of coastal erosion?
11. Is trial by jury the fairest way to judge someone?
12. Is it possible to make a square bubble?
13. Can one survive a lightning strike in a moving car?

■ **Figure 7.5**

We can see in Figure 7.5 that this second variation reduces the number of categories from nine to three and is provided as a worksheet. This allows participants either individually or in groups to work through examples that are provided by the teacher to generate discussion around strategically chosen teaching points.

Discussion

This chapter is designed to be practical and has been written, as far as possible, using the "everyday meanings" of words without undue emphasis on precision or technical vocabulary. This matches the intended outcomes of the exercise, i.e. participants should develop their awareness that complex and difficult issues admit more than simply scientific considerations. There is unlikely to be much room in a single session to enter into extensive discussion about what science is really like or about, so we rely on the participants' existing model of the *nature of science* (NOS).

To support the development of epistemic insight (an appreciation of how scholarship and knowledge work), the session encourages language interactions but also incorporates a graphical, representational, exercise. Graphs and diagrams are not only widely believed to be effective at communicating ideas in science, studies also indicate that when symbolic forms are incorporated into an interactive constructive learning environment *"the emphasis moves from interpreting pre-existing forms to constructing one's own representations"* (Tippett, 2016). This part of the activity can also be conducted in peer groups where participants have been shown to be actively influenced by other members of the group and, crucially, where contributions of individuals are taken further by the whole group as the discussion progresses. This has been referred to as *"collective meaning making in the classroom"* (Rudsberg et al., 2016).

NOTES

1   There are excellent, freely available, video resources that can be used to illustrate these three processes and which are invaluable for promoting discussion.

2   Albeit a second order differential equation.

REFERENCES

Rudsberg, K., Östman, L. and Östman, E. A. (2016). Students' meaning making in classroom discussions: the importance of peer interaction. *Cultural Studies of Science Education*: 1–30.

Sandoval, W. (2014). Science education's need for a theory of epistemological development. *Science Education*, 98(3): 383–387.

Tippett, C. D. (2016). What recent research on diagrams suggests about learning with rather than learning from visual representations in science. *International Journal of Science Education*, 38(5): 725–746.

Williams, R. N. and Robinson, D. N. (2014). *Scientism: the new orthodoxy*. Bloomsbury Publishing.

CHAPTER 8

ISAAC NEWTON

Mark Gilbert

AIMS OF THE CHAPTER

- To underscore the effectiveness of storytelling in teaching science.
- To illustrate Newton's life as an interesting way to explore the interactions between science and religion.

As a scientist who believed in God, Isaac Newton is a counter-example to the popular myth that effective and successful scientists cannot be religious. This is not necessarily a majority view, but did account for around a quarter of pupils aged 13–14 interviewed by a recent study (Taber et al., 2011). As well as being demonstrably false, this myth is also dangerous. First, it allows the lives of professional scientists to be exploited by apologists for atheism, which warps individuals' understanding of both science and religious faith. Second, it may act to discourage pupils with a religious faith or background from pursuing further study in STEM (science, technology, engineering and mathematics subjects). This may, in turn, have broader negative impacts, such as decreasing access to certain types of higher education and employment, reducing social mobility and adding limitations on the public understanding of science.

As well as being a great scientist who was religious, Newton also serves as a counter-example to two other myths: that religious belief cannot be conducive to scientific research and that belief in God is contrary to the spirit of science. For Newton, belief in an omnipotent God was not just another aspect of life, compartmentalised from his scientific work, but was integral to it. Many scholars have suggested that Newton's description of the world in terms of scientific laws reflected a belief in a divine legislator, a "universal ruler" (*general scholium*). In later centuries, these laws would come to be seen as having their own existence, independent of any lawgiver, but for Newton, they depended on God, who "is able to create particles of several sizes and figures, and in several proportions to space . . . and thereby to vary the laws of nature". Not only was Newton's universe governed by God's laws, but it was also a coherent whole, with the same laws operating everywhere. This stood in contrast to the medieval view where different types of behaviour would be expected in the heavens (e.g. celestial motion) than on Earth. Such an approach may have encouraged Newton's bringing together of ideas from different fields in *Newtonian synthesis*. A keen biblical scholar, Newton also applied this methodical approach to the study of biblical prophecy and thus to his religious outlook. This dependency of personal faith on scientific method runs contrary to the myth that science adds nothing to our understanding of faith.

Finally, Newton undermines the myth of a *Newtonian* world-view free from spiritual or divine influence and intervention. Popular revision website, SparkNotes claims that "the essence of Newton's revolution was that he had conceived not only a plausible, but demonstrable model for the workings of the universe, solely relying on mechanics and completely separate of any spiritual influence". This is not really true. Certainly, Newton's laws of mechanics and his laws of gravitation were later shown to account for the stability of planetary orbits, but Newton didn't think so. His planets were inherently unstable and prevented from drifting into outer space or towards the sun by constant tinkering by the Almighty. He is thus an embarrassment to the view that science had become fully separated from religion during the scientific revolution.

NEWTONIAN MYTHS

The everyday work of scientists doesn't necessarily make for a good story. Painstaking repetition of measurements, complex statistics and maintaining experimental equipment are not traditionally associated with bestsellers. Contrariwise, the stories that have built up around some of the greatest scientists are so recognisable that they take on a mythical status and life of their own.

Isaac Newton's contribution to our understanding of the universe confirms his place as one of the world's greatest scientists. He rubs shoulders with giants like Archimedes, Darwin and Einstein. In popular myth, he is forever the long-haired Englishman who saw further than others, whose genius was hit by gravity's apple, and who pulled back the medieval curtain of superstition, showing us to our places in a rational clockwork universe.

Newton has the double distinction of being both the protagonist of popular scientific folklore and also a real investigator. He explored fertile lines of enquiry in celestial mechanics and gravitation as well as dead ends like alchemy. His world-view was informed at least in part by his religious faith, which certainly had an influence on his scientific discoveries. His unorthodox non-Trinitarian Christian beliefs very nearly cost him his job due to his unwillingness to compromise them by becoming ordained as an Anglican priest and affirming a belief in the Trinity (one God in three persons: Father, Son and Holy Ghost).

Like many recognisable historical characters, Newton, his work and ideas have been used to support and justify a range of ideas and causes. Newton has been cast as both a single solitary hero and as the embodiment of the virtues of patience, modesty and industry (Fara, 1999). Since his death, his presence and identity have been employed in arguments well beyond science. These have often touched on the "big questions" and on issues normally associated with religion, such as the existence of God and, particularly, freewill.

These posthumous impacts, together with his significant contributions to several aspects of humanity's study of the universe, and his unorthodox Christian faith, make Isaac Newton's life an ideal subject for those learning about the relationships between science and religion. This chapter explores Newton as both a scientist and as a man of faith. It will consider the outline of his life, Newton's contributions to natural philosophy and how these contributions relate to his religious beliefs.

WHO WAS ISAAC NEWTON?

Isaac Newton was born in Woolsthorpe, Lincolnshire on Christmas Day 1642 (old/ Julian calendar) to an upwardly mobile south Lincolnshire family. Newton's precarious beginnings, months into the English Civil War, befit a hero of popular scientific myth. His father already dead when he was born, Newton was born prematurely, and thought unlikely to survive. Three years later, his mother remarried, this time to the Rev. Barnabas Smith, the sixty-five-year-old rector of North Witham, leaving her son in the care of his grandparents. Smith and his stepson do not seem to have had a good relationship, and years later, when a nineteen-year-old Newton compiled a list of his sins, he included "Threatening my father and mother Smith to burne them and the house over them". Smith died in 1653, leaving Isaac's mother with their three children and with significant wealth.

Aged twelve, Newton was sent to be educated at the County Grammar School in Grantham, where he lodged with local apothecary, William Clarke and his family. The school's curriculum consisted mainly of Latin, Greek, the Old and New Testaments of the Bible, but little, if any mathematics. Newton did not initially excel at school, being placed near the bottom of the lowest class, but rose to become first in the school (Westfall, 1983). Newton's practical skills also developed at this time. He is known to have demonstrated strong mechanical ability and ingenuity, building replica windmills, carts and sundials. His interest in chemistry may have developed from his association with the Clarke family. Religious controversy and conflict were also familiar to the Clarke family. During the Civil War, Clarke was a puritan who had been indicted for high treason when Grantham fell to the royalists in 1643, but was released when it was recaptured by the parliamentarians a month later.

Despite his aptitude and appetite for his studies, aged seventeen, Newton was expected to return home and learn to manage the family estate. This did not go well. Newtonian sheep destroyed neighbouring fields while their master built waterwheels in brooks and read books. After nine months, his mother was persuaded to allow her son to return to school and later to further his studies at Cambridge University. Newton entered Trinity College, Cambridge, in June 1661. Britain was only one year into the restoration of King Charles II after the collapse of the Puritan Commonwealth. This was a period of religious turmoil, with an attempted military coup in January 1661 by the "Fifth Monarchists" who believed that the events of the Civil War and Cromwell's Protectorate were a fulfilment of biblical prophecies in the Book of Daniel relating to the end times.

Religious practice formed an important part of Newton's identity throughout his life. Newton took the moral aspect of his faith seriously and in his late teens, compiled a list of sins he had committed in his youth. On entering Cambridge, he was willing to declare his acceptance of the thirty-nine articles of the Church of England and to take a vow of celibacy. Despite his relatively wealthy background, Newton entered Trinity as a subsizar, a servant expected to do menial work for wealthier students and fellows to pay for his studies. This may have been because his mother refused to fund him. Either way, this status as an effective social outcast would have done nothing to improve his state of social isolation that developed while at the County Grammar School in Grantham. As a student, Newton experienced a curriculum focusing on rhetoric, Aristotelian logic, ethics and philosophy, which despite the tumultuous social and political changes over the preceding thirty years, had been largely unchanged in four centuries (Westfall, 1983). As part of this curriculum, Newton was introduced to the physics developed by Aristotle that had dominated Western thought from the early middle ages. Aristotle's physics held that there were four types of element (water, fire, earth and air) and four types of cause (material, formal, efficient and final). While it is easy for us to ridicule the Aristotelian world-view as primitive and medieval, in learning Aristotelian physics, Newton was exposed to a systematic and structured description of the world. For this world-view to later be replaced by cosmologies based on Newton's work, it was certainly necessary that Newton and his contemporaries be immersed in this earlier formal world-view.

At the same time, Newton also read widely and encountered the intellectual currents of his day. Through his notebooks, we know that he studied the astronomy of Galileo and Kepler and the philosophy of Descartes and Gassendi and Hobbes and Boyle. This clearly sparked his interest in studying natural science and the period Newton spent back in Lincolnshire during the great plague was his most successful. Following the plague, Newton returned to Cambridge and was made a fellow of Trinity College. This provided him with an income with which to pursue research, with Newton rising to become Lucasian Professor of Mathematics (a position more recently held by Stephen Hawking) in 1669 and Fellow of the Royal Society (FRS) in 1672. However, the Trinity fellowship came with the condition that its holder would be ordained as a priest within seven years. Newton took this requirement seriously, reading widely in theology and church history as this requirement approached. However, Newton's reading convinced him that the Church of England was in error concerning the nature of God. He refused to take holy orders and was prepared to vacate his fellowship. However, his success in academia worked in his favour: as Lucasian Professor, Newton was required not to be active in the church so that he could concentrate on his research. Newton argued that this should exempt him from ordination, and was granted special permission to continue in post without religious orders by King Charles II.

Some of Newton's strong convictions about the nature of God were made public in the *general scholium* to the second edition (1713) of his *Principia*. The Supreme God is defined as "eternal, infinite, absolutely perfect". As "Lord over all", He exercises dominion over His Creation and His servants and is a "living, intelligent and powerful" Being. For Newton, God is "all eye, all ear, all brain, all arm, all power to perceive, to understand, and to act". This is an omnipotent, omniscient and omnipresent deity who takes an active interest in His creation, not one who created the universe and then lost interest in it. The less conventional aspects of Newton's faith (e.g. non-Trinitarianism) were not publicised during his lifetime and were only determined later from his writings.

Newton's life took an interesting turn when he was in his late forties. As an opponent of King James II's appointments of Roman Catholics to important positions at universities, he entered national politics and was elected as MP for the University of Cambridge in the short-lived 1689 Convention Parliament that immediately followed the Glorious Revolution in which James II was deposed and replaced by William III (of Orange) and Mary II. In 1696, he moved to London to become Warden, and subsequently, Master of the Royal Mint. While his appointment was mainly due to his support for William and Mary during the Glorious Revolution, he took the role extremely seriously and was very effective at reducing counterfeiting.

WHAT EXACTLY DID HE DO FOR SCIENCE?

Newton made significant contributions across different branches of natural philosophy including optics, mechanics and astronomy. Integral to all of these was mathematics.

Newton's mathematical accomplishments include the classification of cubic curves, the use of power series and developing algorithms (methods) for finding approximate solutions to different types of equation. The greatest of these developments was his systematic study of the relationships between arbitrarily small quantities (infinitesimals), which developed into the area of mathematics known today as calculus. The study of the relationships between infinitesimals is of profound importance to the study of mathematics as well as to the other scientific fields in which Newton was active.

Foremost among these fields was the study of motion, mechanics. Using his mathematical insights in infinitesimal calculus, Newton formulated three laws that applied to all bodies in motion regardless of their shape or size or whether they were immediate physical objects that could be touched or heavenly bodies such as stars and planets. The laws had a predictive element: given enough knowledge about the state of a set of moving objects and no external interference, it would be possible to determine their positions and velocities at any point in the future with an incredible degree of accuracy, with the laws only beginning to break down for objects moving close to the speed of light. Newton's three laws are elegantly simple but also highly counterintuitive. The first law is that a moving object with no external force applied to it will continue to move at the same speed and direction as long as there is no external force. This law explains why an unfortunate astronaut, pushed into deep space with a fixed initial velocity and far from any stars or any other physical objects, would continue indefinitely to move at the same speed and in the same direction. As well as clarifying the more nightmarish aspects of interstellar travel, this law is also relevant in more "down-to-Earth" situations as it encapsulates and effectively defines the concept of inertia. Inertia is the idea that all objects, not just marooned astronauts, remain stationary or continue to move in a straight line unless a force (e.g. an impact with another object, gravity, friction etc.) is applied to them. Given that most objects are constantly being affected by some kind of external force, this is a profound observation and is testament to the power of Newton's mathematical approach.

The second law says that objects are affected by forces in a specific way that depends on the object's mass. An object with a force applied to it will accelerate in the direction of the force with the size of the force equal to the rate of acceleration multiplied by the object's mass. This will be familiar to GCSE science students in the pithy equation "F equals m a". However, neither this nor the first law is as memorable as the mantra-like description of the third law. Every action has an equal and opposite reaction. In physics, this means that every force applied to an object will have an equal force acting against it. We exert the force of our weight on the floor below us and the floor provides a force that pushes back against our weight and (hopefully) stops us from entering the flat downstairs!

The calculus didn't just allow Newton to develop new ideas about the world as with his mechanics, but also enabled him to verify existing theories. Half a century before Newton entered Cambridge, the German mathematician Johannes Kepler (1571–1630) formulated another three laws, the laws of planetary motion. Like Newton, Kepler could not compromise his religious faith (Lutheranism) by converting to Roman Catholicism and his refusal to convert saw him banished from the city of Graz in August 1600, only one month after he had used the observations of Tycho Brahe (1546–1601) to correctly predict a solar eclipse. Kepler's three laws were an important early step along the path that would lead to an understanding of the celestial motions of stars and planets in terms of Newton's mechanics, but to understand this progression, we need to consider the even earlier developments that preceded Kepler.

From ancient times until a hundred years prior to Newton's birth, Europeans generally assumed that the Earth was a sphere. The popularly held idea that educated medieval Europeans believed that the Earth was flat has very little support and is a myth originating in the nineteenth century to support the claim that an idea of a flat Earth based on religious faith was in conflict with a rational scientific spherical Earth.

Despite believing that the Earth was spherical, our medieval forebears would have put themselves at the centre of the solar system with the Sun, planets and stars orbiting the Earth. In discussing day and night, we still use the convenient metaphor of the Sun's rising and setting at the start and end of the day. For our ancestors, these motions were not just metaphorical, and the Sun, planets and stars really did move around a still and spherical Earth. One oddity of this picture was that the planets didn't quite move in regular orbits around the Earth, but moved irregularly, sometimes travelling backwards or in retrograde motion. This was due to two then unknown facts about the solar system. That celestial bodies follow elliptical orbits rather than circular ones, and that the Earth and the other planets orbit the sun (in elliptical orbits) rather than the Sun and other planets orbiting the Earth.

In 1543, a completely new picture of the solar system was revealed, with Polish mathematician Nicolaus Copernicus publishing his *De revolutionibus orbium coelestium* (On the Revolutions of the Celestial Spheres) which suggested that the Earth and other planets followed circular orbits around the Sun. As Copernicus' description assumed that the planets followed circular orbits, epicycles were still needed to explain the apparently odd behaviour resulting from their elliptical paths. The epicycles remained until Kepler, using Brahe's astronomical data, proposed that the planets followed elliptical orbits and moved more quickly when closer to the Sun.

Kepler's laws described the motions of the planets but did not give reference to physical causes. In fact, prior to Newton, cosmology and physics were often viewed as different types of science to astronomy and mathematics, with cosmology and physics more imperfect and considered unable to contribute to the latter. Newton and his contemporaries saw that the force of gravity that keeps us on the ground could explain the centripetal (inward) force that kept the planets in their orbits around the Sun, with Newton using mathematics to show that gravity could account for the observed orbits. Thus, with the publication of Newton's results in his *Principia*, the two distinct areas of enquiry, mechanics and astronomy suddenly became one and the same. This is the sort of "a-ha!" moment that marks a real change in our understanding of the world and is certainly worth communicating to students who are interested in science's wider context (e.g. social, religious etc.). For this reason, we suggest ways of exploring this further with classes and other groups in the exercise.

Another area of science that benefited from Newton's attention was optics. In the early seventeenth century, the prevailing wisdom was that all light was inherently white and that colours were the result of this unvarying light illuminating coloured objects. In 1672, Newton published an observation that contradicted this theory. He had noticed that a prism refracts light at a range of different angles, resulting in beams of white light being refracted into a spectrum of colours. Newton explained this by suggesting that it was the light rather than the objects that had colour, with different coloured light interacting with the prism in different ways. This discovery is a textbook case of the scientific method. Behaviour was observed that didn't fit the existing scientific theory (that colour was a property of objects), so a new theory was proposed (that light had colour). Newton's other contributions to optics include the reflecting telescope, which used curved mirrors rather than lenses, and several ideas that would later inform the development of the laser.

As well as his vast contributions to natural philosophy across fields that have become central to modern science, Newton's interests ranged from the study of scripture and theology to alchemy and the occult. Newton's serious interest in theology began as he was facing the prospect of being required to be ordained as a priest by 1675 in order to keep his fellowship at Trinity. As with his scientific work, the scale and ambition of his religious inquiry was huge. Reading all of the early church fathers, Newton came to conclusions that would prevent him from being able to accept orders in the Church of England. Newton came to believe that Jesus, while being God's son, was not one of the three persons in one God (the Trinity) and that God was not three distinct persons in one substance. This idea (Arianism) had been rejected as a heresy by the Church at the Council of Nicaea in 325, putting Newton well outside the beliefs of mainstream Christianity.

Not taking established interpretations or understanding for granted, Newton sought to find the meaning behind prophecy (the prophets in the Old Testament and the Book of Revelation in the New Testament). To do this he would try meticulously to find the original text, trying to determine the original text of Revelation using twenty-five different Greek manuscripts and citations in the early church fathers. Once the original text had been uncovered, it needed to be interpreted. Newton tried to systematise this step in a similar way to the methodical approaches he had taken in natural science and outlined fifteen rules of interpretation. He was confident that just as every natural phenomenon had one single correct explanation, so every verse of scripture had a single correct explanation.

NEWTON AND HIS MYTHS

Newton's life was one marked by juxtapositions and apparent contradictions. Despite the turmoil and conflict of late seventeenth-century Britain, Newton's most successful year in generating scientific ideas was spent in the rural quiet of Lincolnshire escaping the bubonic plague. Intellectual conflict and personal struggle were not unknown to Newton and he had bitter disputes with both Robert Hooke and Gottfried Leibniz as well as deep inner turmoil over his own beliefs, particularly in his belief in a non-Trinitarian God. However, as a scientist who was committed to thorough personal study of scripture and theology, Newton is a counterexample and embarrassment to the popular narrative of conflict between science and religion.

In this chapter, we have briefly outlined Isaac Newton's extraordinary life. Despite an unremarkable upbringing in provincial Lincolnshire, Newton was able to significantly advance several areas of scientific enquiry. He was able to "lift nature's façade" (Westfall, 1983) and generated ideas that provided work for his colleagues the next few hundred years. By way of contrast, we have also seen how several aspects of Newton's identity may jar with contemporary conceptions of scientists. His interests in alchemy and the occult have caused him to be described as the "Last of the Magicians". That a great scientific mind such as Newton's could engage with these fields confuses our concept of science as a clear upward progression rather than as a winding road with many detours and dead ends. Newton's active religious faith, not only believing in a creator God who sustained the world but also devoting substantial time to interrogating scripture and studying theology, jars with the picture of scientists as atheists who have rejected religion as superstition.

That Newton was religious doesn't provide verification for faith in a creator. Newton saw his world-view as providing justification for Christian faith, while Pierre Laplace, who developed many of Newton's ideas further, saw no need for a God. In conclusion, discussing the many dimensions of Isaac Newton is an excellent way of exploring some of the interactions between science and religion. While there are no firm answers to how science and religion relate in general, with Newton we can explore and humanise some very interesting aspects of this relationship.

EXERCISE

This exercise will encourage pupils to think about the way in which science can provide a unified explanation to different phenomena in the physical world and to think about Newton's insight in unifying astronomy and mechanics. Like Newton, they will see what it's like to connect different concepts.

Print (and laminate) the following sets of cards for each group of pupils:

Group 1: Carnivore's Teeth
Bright Flowers
Drug Resistant Bacteria
Earthquakes
Compasses
Similar species in South America and Africa
Tides
Ballistics
Planetary Orbits
Reflex Reactions
Lightning Storms
Sunlight
Nuclear Weapons
Athletes Foot
Potato Blight
HIV
Static
X rays

Group 2: Evolution
Tectonics
Gravity
Electricity
Nuclear Theory
Germ Theory

Part 1

Give each group of pupils only the cards in Group 1. Ask them to arrange them on the table into groups and suggest those phenomena that might be connected. Pupils may make some connections (e.g. that athletes foot, potato blight and HIV are all diseases, that carnivore's sharp teeth and bright flowers are adaptions from evolution and that tides and planetary orbits are both affected by gravity), but are unlikely to see all the ways in which scientific theory connects the different phenomena.

Part 2

With the pupils keeping their original (Group 1) cards, give them the Group 2 cards, and ask them if this alters the way in which they would lay them out. This may help them see some of the connections they have missed.

REFERENCES

Fara, P., 1999. Catch a falling apple: Isaac Newton and myths of genius. *Endeavour*, *23*(4), pp. 167–170.

Taber, K., Billingsley, B., Riga, F. and Newdick, H., 2011. To what extent do pupils perceive science to be inconsistent with religious faith? An exploratory survey of 13–14 year-old English pupils. *Science Education International*, *22*(2), pp. 99–118.

Westfall, R.S., 1983. *Never at rest: a biography of Isaac Newton*. Cambridge University Press.

EVOLUTION

Chris Hatcher

AIMS OF THE CHAPTER

- What is evolution?
- Why is it in the curriculum?
- What do teachers think about teaching evolution and the relationship between evolution and religion (from survey data)?
- Misconceptions or misunderstanding in learning evolution.
- Strategies for teaching evolution in primary school and early secondary school.

> Nothing in biology makes sense except in the light of evolution. (Dobzhanski, 1973)

INTRODUCTION

Educators are in a rare position in which, as of September 2015, an entirely novel topic has been introduced to the curriculum for primary schools – "evolution and inheritance". This inevitably has effects on the teaching requirements both preceding and following these academic years (i.e. affects before Year 6 and after Year 6 as the pupils' understanding needs to be tailored before and advanced afterwards compared to before the topic was introduced). Understanding evolution has been described as the keystone to understanding biological sciences. However, this topic is also known to hold tricky concepts and improper teaching can generate misconceptions and negative attitudes towards learning. Currently, not only are there few resources available for teachers to use in these introductory years, but also attitudes and concerns held by teachers, students and indeed parents are largely unknown regarding the teaching of evolution. This chapter examines how the process of evolution occurs and general thinking about evolution by students and teachers. The chapter will also delve into why understanding evolution does not mean a choice between religion or evolution and insight into how evolution can be taught in an effective and stimulating way. The activities presented in this chapter have been tested with teachers as well as students and their response to learning evolution in this way is positively highlighted in survey data and general feedback.

WHAT IS EVOLUTION?

The late Stephen Jay Gould, a highly influential evolutionary biologist, argues that the process of evolution is the most important and the most misunderstood of all biological concepts. Evolution was happening millions of years ago when dinosaurs dominated the earth, it was happening in the 1800s when Darwin was travelling the world on *HMS Beagle* and it is still happening today – and will continue to do so. Evolution had and is having an impact on every living species . . . right now and, yes, that *is* including humans! Evolution is not about just fossils, but fossils are useful in understanding evolution by following lineages. Evolution is about genes, mutations, populations and reproduction.

Evolution is change in the heritable traits of populations over generations. There are numerous examples to draw on to explain the process of evolution, however, the Galapagos finches (or Darwin's finches) are by far the most renowned and easily understood.

The finches are named after Darwin as he theorised that the 13 distinct species of finch were all descendants of one common ancestor. Each finch species eats a different type of food and has unique characteristics or traits that have arisen through evolution. The ground finch found on the island, Daphne Major, is an ideal species to study evolution as the finches have few predators or competition. Therefore, the main factor influencing the survival of the finches is the availability of food, which varies in relation to the weather. The finches have short beaks and eat mostly seeds. The individuals of the ground finch population naturally vary in size and shape, as does any population of individuals. This species of finch has been studied for decades on how environmental change is having an impact on the survival of the individuals within the population.

The first weather event monitored was a drought that lasted for 551 days without rain. The typically dominant food supply of small seeds was dwindling. The ground finches with larger beaks were able to take advantage of alternative food sources as they were able to open the harder, larger seeds. Smaller beaked birds were less able to do this and more likely to die of starvation. Larger beaked birds were more likely to survive and reproduce.

One year later, researchers returned to see the effect of the drought on the next generation of finches. They found that beak size in offspring was more than 3% larger than that of their grandparents. This is an example of evolution by natural selection. A change in the frequency of heritable traits in a population over generations. This example of evolution by natural selection has been adapted into a lesson plan at the end of this chapter.

WHY IS EVOLUTION IN THE CURRICULUM?

There are many important reasons as to why biological evolution is compulsory in the national curriculum. Evolution is said to be the underpinning and unifying theory of biological sciences. It forms the basis of research spanning over 150 years and ongoing research today and evolution is universally accepted among professional biology researchers.

British Humanist Association (BHA) education campaigner, Richie Thompson, commented:

> Scientists and educators have long told us that evolution is such a central idea to biology that it should be taught from a primary level instead of at GCSE. It is vital

that every young person has a good understanding of how life came to be and we are pleased that today's changes mean that from now on, young people will have more opportunities to learn about such an important topic and from an earlier age at that. We're pleased to see the fulfilment today of our decade-long campaign.

Science educators and policy emphasise learning the process of science, particularly the understanding and practice of scientific inquiry. This process involves developing testable hypotheses or questions that can be answered by scientific investigation. In current research, the answers to these questions continue to show the usefulness and validity of evolutionary theory for forming answerable questions in biology. Evolution is also one of the more current or relevant topics taught in school. Not only is it researched today, but it is also heavily involved in globally significant issues. Evolutionary research opens new vistas in healthcare, agriculture, technology and other contemporary topics. Understanding evolutionary processes is also essential in understanding the occurrence of antibiotic resistant bacteria. This is a problem that is becoming more and more relevant as antibiotics are becoming more redundant as a method to treat bacterial infections.

WHAT DO TEACHERS THINK ABOUT EVOLUTION AND SCIENCE AND RELIGION?

Teachers are more frequently being considered in policy as the instigators of change. As policy moves into the realm of practical implementation, its success relies on the professionals implementing it. This, in turn, is affected by their skills, experiences and attitudes towards the aforementioned policy and the transition from policy to practice. This means that the engagement with the policy is affected by external factors such as cultural and social structures that may impede teaching as well as the teacher content knowledge and strategies in place. This is particularly relevant to teaching evolution given current thinking around the topic as well as the absence of a "tried and tested" library of resources teachers can confidently rely on.

In addition to issues surrounding subject content and appropriate resources, there may also be angst among teachers concerning teaching evolution due to the potential conflict between science and religion. This aspect is by no means trivial in science education. Research, which has investigated how young people see relationships between science and religion, has shown that a majority perceive them to be opposites of one another (Billingsley et al. 2013; Hanley 2008; Bauser & Poole 2002). A perception of science and religion being necessarily mutually exclusive may instigate negative attitudes towards learning science and later considering a career in science (Reiss 2008). Indeed, research has shown that some students with a religious faith hold negative attitudes towards science, based on the fact that they perceive their religious beliefs to be in conflict with science as they consider it an alternative worldview (Hanley 2008). These concerns already surround science in general; considering the teaching of evolution, it is logical to assume the same outcomes or even that the issue is exacerbated by the nature of the topic, particularly given its portrayal in the media as an argument for or against religion or evolution.

A survey of over 150 teachers was conducted to find out their attitudes and needs around teaching evolution in primary school, as well as gauging their current ability to teach evolution. Results showed teachers hold three strong preferential support areas for teaching evolution: primary specific activities, subject content knowledge and information on the science and religion paradigm surrounding evolution. Delving into their ability to teach the new module, results show teachers do not have a sufficient understanding of the evolution subject content. Furthermore, teachers are aware of this deficit in their own understanding. This is reflected in not only their expressed concerns, but also proved by teachers' general inability to spot misconceptions put to them with a list of statements. Contrary to what we originally expected, teachers have prioritised external organisations coming into school to teach the curriculum over a free visit to museums, free resources, a FAQ site and other options. This leads to interesting interactions with their current thinking towards teaching approach, implications of teaching evolution and how to confidently navigate a potentially contentious subject between science and religion. With this resource, we aim to bring back the initiative to teachers to teach these topics, and use other strategies to enhance students' learning, rather than replace the teachers' own teaching.

The teacher's role is to enable students to learn about scientific concepts and to distinguish scientific from non-scientific concepts. Evolution is an entirely scientific concept. This, however, is not synonymous with "evolution is an entirely atheistic concept". As such, it is important that both the teacher and the students fully understand this.

A statement from the teacher survey was "Most children with a religious faith will not accept evolution". This statement's most common response by teachers was "Neither agree nor disagree". Teachers are not only uninformed on the thinking of mainstream religions, but they also do not know whether there will be a differentiated response to learning evolution based on their children's apparent faith. Moreover, teachers are not just uninformed on the positions of the mainstream religions on evolution, many also have the preconception that the theory of evolution is in conflict with a belief in creation (39.2%).

In fact, the majority of mainstream religions are in agreement with evolution and do not see this process as in conflict with their religious beliefs. For example bishops of the Church of England are in agreement with the theory of evolution. Pope Francis of the Catholic Church stated that: "Evolution of nature is not inconsistent with the notion of creation because evolution presupposes the creation of beings which evolve."

Although the vast majority of teachers were looking forward to teaching evolution (78.8%) and 85.8% believed evolution is an important idea for children in primary school to learn about, teachers are still concerned about teaching the new unit (31.4%).

Additionally, 68.2% of primary school teachers surveyed believe that it will be important to take into account children's religious beliefs when teaching evolution. Already, teachers are showing signs of teaching this aspect of the science curriculum in a different way to how they may normally teach a science unit. This is likely to stem from a combination of lack of teaching experience, awareness of a perceived conflict between evolution and religion and potentially their own understanding of the relationship. Teaching experience is something that cannot be gained from reading; however, this textbook will provide the necessary skills to prepare teachers to teach this topic confidently as well as some of the tools and resources to enhance students' learning.

Of teachers surveyed, 18.1% agree or strongly agree that parents should be informed that a lesson on evolution will take place and may remove their child. Almost one-fifth of primary school teachers surveyed believe that parents should be allowed to remove their child from a science lesson on evolution. This absolutely should not be the case. A science lesson or topic in the National Curriculum is mandatory and, given the information provided in this chapter, teachers should believe with confidence that they can teach this topic without anxiety and with quality resources to do so effectively. Most teachers may inform parents in their weekly newsletter, but this is by no means as a way to provide them with an option to remove their child from the lessons. It is interesting to think about how many other science lessons a teacher will provide the option to remove students from – likely none.

In an open question on what teachers would like help with in a session on teaching evolution, they identify three main areas of support:

■ access to primary focused resources
■ training in evolution subject content knowledge
■ information on the relationship between science and religion.

The last two areas are vital with respect to teaching science in a way that supports the idea that science and religion are compatible with most religions or at least that science is not a scientistic domain. Ineffective teaching of science or understanding of positions of religions leads to misconceptions in science and religion and negative attitudes towards learning science.

It is important to recognise that the issue of children not moving into a career in science is a multifaceted problem. Our research suggests that even at an early age, children are already forming perceptions that there is some conflict between science and religion. The problem does not lie solely with the students, however; teachers are also in a similar position. Furthermore, data suggest that these stances are influencing the way they are teaching science in school, which may in turn affect students' thinking around science and religion. Not only are children in need of guidance as to relationships between science and religion, but educators are seemingly also in need of this support. These problems stem from both a perceived view of science and religion, but also from misunderstanding or misconceptions of the process of evolution.

MISCONCEPTIONS OR MISUNDERSTANDING IN LEARNING EVOLUTION

Students can generate misconceptions in learning through a multitude of pathways, and misconceptions are rife in this topic. They can be formed from informal ideas inferred from everyday experiences, underdeveloped ideas from the classroom or flawed concepts formed by teachers and textbooks.

In biology, however, misconceptions can be caused from stimuli from areas outside the personal experiences of the learners (Sanders 1993). It is suggested that for certain scientific concepts that are concerned with abstract concepts or ideas concerning scientific phenomena not immediately apparent, children are not likely to have direct contact or experience of these mechanisms in daily life. Therefore, they are unlikely to have developed their own conceptions or explanations. This means any misconceptions they may have regarding these topics can be caused by ineffective learning or ineffective teaching in the classroom. This can arise from improper use of language in teaching evolution. Evolution is not teleological and, as such, use of terms implying thought or a goal to evolution must be avoided. Evolution is a natural process. Rather than a decision to evolve, evolution occurs as a result of a change in the frequency of heritable traits in a population.

Misconceptions around the learning of complex or abstract scientific phenomena may also result from a lack of understanding due to improper comprehension of prerequisite knowledge necessary for the construction of the new concept. Teachers have a responsibility to avoid this type of misconception arising by ensuring their students have mastered these prior units before they take on the more complex lessons. (Garnett *et al.* 1995). This means teachers should follow a recommended progression from topics needed to learn evolution before tackling the process of evolution. An example of a misunderstanding as a result of this is children saying "I've never seen an animal change into a different type of animal!" Additionally, adults say: "If mammals evolved from frogs, why are there no fronkeys?" These are the kinds of misunderstanding of the process of evolution occurring over generations of a population tiny changes over a long period of time. Therefore you do not *see* one animal changing into another or *see* intermediate "half an animal half another animal".

Misconceptions may also arise as a result of poor understanding of science subject content knowledge of the teacher. This can generate incomplete or flawed views from the student as a direct result of inaccurate teaching or improper use of textbooks (Sanders 1993). This type can be particularly prevalent with students who adopt a learning experience with unconditional trust or acceptance of the detail from the teacher – such as in primary schools. This can be exacerbated by misuse of scientific terminology. Although the teacher may have a sound understanding of the scientific concepts they are teaching, a careless or loose use of certain terms may instigate improper learning by their students. Misuse of terminology as a source of misconceptions has been documented in the literature (Amir & Tamir 1993). This can also arise during the teaching of evolutionary lineages. A very common misconception is that humans evolved from monkeys. Humans and monkeys *do* share a common ancestor, but the lineage separates or branches at this point, rather than a direct descent from monkeys to humans. Rather than using the well-known graphic that, unfortunately, generates this misconception, the use of an evolutionary tree would be a much more effective way of teaching. During interviews with Year 6 children with no prior teaching of evolution, it became clear that they were able to understand that living things are in some way linked through evolution, but were distinct species that share ancestors. (Show poor graphic and tree alongside or just evolutionary tree.)

TEACHING STRATEGIES AND RESOURCES

Education is in a perpetual state of change. This is not a localised issue; educators worldwide have to constantly devise new methods of teaching on topics both tried and tested as well as new. Currently, there is a gap between policy and practice in teaching. Particularly in the UK, a new curriculum has been introduced with a new format of pedagogy. Teachers and educators are in a position in which they not only have to alter teaching practice for previously taught units, but they also have to devise new methods for the teaching of novel units introduced to the curriculum. Below is a small guide to teaching the topic of evolution, including building the students' prerequisite knowledge of topics before attempting to teach the process of evolution.

Evolution is one of the topics teachers can really have some fun with and be creative. There are countless examples of evolution to use and interesting or unusual living things they can use images of or even bring into the classroom to show how organisms are adapted to their environment. However, the actual concept of evolution is a tricky one and requires a surprisingly large amount of prerequisite information.

The first idea to get across is the huge timescale that is typically required for noticeable changes to a population as a result of evolution. (The bird beak example is a great one for being able to see changes over generations of birds but within the lifetime of people.) The first signs of life were billions of years ago and the evolution of current living things from these ancestors has occurred over millions of generations. Teachers can get their students to be "newsreaders" and design their own report on the evolutionary history of life. They can report on the first signs of life in the ocean, to the first fish, animals colonising the land, first dinosaurs and so on. The key is to get the students to recognise the time-scale between these marked points in time – they are enormous! Recent interviews with Year 6 children have shown that the concept of a million years is something they struggle with. To put the time frames into some kind of context, if the history of life on earth fitted into a 12-month calendar, humans have only been around for the last few minutes of the final day.

As alluded to at the start of this chapter, fossils are useful tools for understanding how living things have changed over time from their ancestors. Hands-on activities we have designed have been used by teachers and have received great feedback. One such example is the fossils jelly, which has been used to teach children across the years in primary schools (not just Year 6). The children pour in different colours of jelly to signify different layers in the rocks and place different sweets within these layers. Children are encouraged to figure out that the top layers are usually the most recent (or youngest layers) and therefore will have the most recent living things in them. Similarly the living things in the bottom layer will be from a time further back in history. (Please see www.LASARcentre.com for printable handouts for teachers.)

Once the children understand the timescales evolution occurs over, you can intro-duce the idea of evolutionary adaptations. This topic is great for showing organisms adapted to their environments. The more extreme the environment, the easier it is to get this con-cept across. All students, when asked in interviews, know what a cactus is and where to find them in the wild. This makes them an ideal example to build this understanding by then encouraging them to think about how the cacti are adapted to their surroundings. A vital aspect of science education is to develop students' understanding of working scientifically. Asking questions such as *"what do you notice?"* and *"what features can you tell me about, which might help the animal fit into its environment?"* supports this. If children can generate explanations themselves this is exactly the kind of mind-set needed to be a scientist!

Finally, teachers can then approach the topic of evolution or how species evolve. Generally, this means talking about natural selection and this usually goes along with talking about Charles Darwin. As previously mentioned, this is a great opportunity to talk about the Galapagos finches and use the bird beak activity.

There are four key ideas teachers want to get across at this point to teach about evolution by natural selection:

■ **Time.** Evolution by natural selection is a process of traits becoming more prevalent in a population over time
■ **Variation.** Individuals within a population are different to one another
■ **Selection.** As a result of variation, some individuals are better at surviving and reproducing than others
■ **Inheritance.** Successful parents have offspring that are similar but not identical to their parents, increasing the frequency of these successful traits in the population.

CONCLUSION

This chapter has highlighted the importance of learning about evolution with respect to contemporary issues, learning in science and developing essential scientific skills. The chapter has also outlined a systematic way of teaching about the process of evolution including the prerequisite content necessary to be able to understand these tricky concepts. Although perceived in the media as potentially quite a contentious issue, this chapter has shown that a lot of faiths are in agreement with the theory of evolution. Although this is the case, teachers still hold reservations about teaching the topic and may even adopt different strategies for this topic compared to other science topics as a result. The aim of the chapter is to encourage teachers to teach evolution with confidence, including avoiding misconceptions, encouraging scientific enquiry and teaching in a way that does not generate misconceptions or deter students with a religious faith from learning about science.

[Please note that free resources and details about CPD for teachers are available at www.primaryevolution.com.]

REFERENCES

Amir, R. and Tamir, P. (1993) The light and dark reactions of photosynthesis – terminology as a source of misconceptions. In J. D. Novak (ed.), *Proceedings of the Third International Seminar on Misconceptions and Educational Strategies in Science and Mathematics* (New York: Cornell University).

Bauser, J. and Poole, M. (2002). Science education and religious education: possible links? *School Science Review*, 85(311), 117–124.

Billingsley, B., Taber, K. S., Riga, F. and Newdick, H. (2013). Secondary school students' epistemic insight into the relationships between science and religion—a preliminary enquiry. *Research in Science Education*, 43(4), 1715–1732.

Garnett, P. J., Garnett, P. J. and Hackling, M. W. (1995) Students' alternative conceptions in chemistry: a review of research and implications for teaching and learning. *Studies in Science Education*, 25, 69–95.

Gould, S. J. (1996) Three facets of evolution. In *How Things Are: A Science Tool-Kit for the Mind*, eds. J. Brockman and K. Matson, 81–87 (New York: Harper Perennial).

Hanley, P. (2008). Controversy in school?: origin of life and the science/religion overlap. Paper presented at the *British Educational Research Association Annual Conference*, Heriot-Watt University, Edinburgh, September (Edinburgh: Heriot-Watt University).

Reiss, M. J. (2008). Should science educators deal with the science/religion issue? *Studies in Science Education*, 44(2), 157–186.

Sanders, M. (1993) Erroneous ideas about respiration: the teacher factor. *Journal of Research in Science Teaching*, 30, 919–934.

Soyibo, K. (1995) A review of some sources of students' misconceptions in biology. *Singapore Journal of Education*, 15, 1–11.

Tamir, P. (1991) Professional and personal knowledge of teachers and teacher educators. *Teaching and Teacher Education*, 7, 263–268.

AIMS OF THE CHAPTER

- Introduce the idea of miracles and why they are potentially a controversial subject in the area of science and religion.
- To present the views held by students, their concerns and potential barriers to being open to science and/or religion as a result of the debate.
- To introduce the views of some scholars on the subject from a religious and non-religious background and also to introduce some scientists who believe in miracles and their explanations for their occurrence.
- To present some practical ideas that provide some challenges to assumptions about the incompatibility of science and religion in this area.

INTRODUCTION

Miracles are an important element of many religious traditions where they have a more defined nature than that encountered in much colloquial usage of the term. Within religious belief, miracles have a role in revealing the identity of key religious figures and their authority given from the god or greater being of that tradition. Perhaps more importantly, they are frequently seen as a sign of divine concern for and intervention in the world. As such they form an important part of the theology and daily teaching of these religions. For example, in Jewish tradition the escape from slavery of the Jewish people involved the miraculous parting of the Red Sea to enable the people to evade the pharaoh's army. This demonstrated the authority of Moses and the love of god for his chosen people. In Islam, the existence of the Quran itself is regarded as miraculous, placing its message as beyond that of human authority and the desire of Allah to communicate with his faithful and the whole world. In Christianity, the power and authority of Christ is revealed in numerous miracles, most notable in his resurrection from the dead. Many other traditions contain similar historical miracles and many also believe in their ongoing occurrence as signs of divine power and concern.

In this chapter, we will examine what is understood by the term "miracle" and what differentiates them, if anything, from daily events that have a beneficial or seemingly providential outcome. We will then consider what the potential conflicts with science might be, both in practical and philosophical terms. As part of this, we will consider how this may impact on the engagement of students with science education, including an examination of what students say when asked about the relationship between the scientific worldview and the idea of miracles. This will be set in the context of the same dialogue as seen through the ideas of a number of theologians and philosophers, particularly those who are encountered in the secondary curriculum for subjects such as religious education. The views of miracles held by a number of religious scientists are considered to see how experienced thinkers in the area have dealt with the concerns raised by young people and others. Finally, we present some resources and possible activities that could be incorporated into lessons to enable constructive dialogue between religion and science on the concept of miracles.

WHAT IS A MIRACLE?

At first glance, defining what a miracle is may seem quite straightforward and most people can give examples from various religious traditions. Clearly, they are something out of the ordinary. But at the same time it is not uncommon to hear people make assertions along the lines of "every day is a miracle" or "each person is a miracle". It would seem that what is being said here is that each day or each person is special or unique in some way and that this *seems* miraculous. It is certainly the case that uniqueness or special-ness is an element of what constitutes a miracle but if such conditions apply in each and every case then we start to move away from what we understand as miracles in a strict sense.

The RE curriculum in England specifies the study of miracles at GCSE and A-Level and a typical definition provided by examination boards of a miracle is "something impossible, something contrary to the laws of nature, something only God does" (AQA, 2014). This form of definition is one that has existed for several centuries and closely resembles that given by the philosopher David Hume in 1748 as *"a violation of the laws of nature"*. Clearly, if this definition is taken, then belief in miracles poses problems for those who see the laws of nature, on which scientific laws are built, as inviolable. It is here that we find one of the potential sources of conflict between science and religion in the school curriculum. This also presents a point at which students may find they are forced to choose between studying these subjects and to make choices in personal belief. In this chapter, we will consider a broader set of ideas about the nature of miracles as understood by theologians, philosophers and scientists and consider how these may help to ease some of the tensions we have encountered when working with students in this arena.

WHAT IS THE PROBLEM?

So, if we have a working definition of a miracle as:

■ something that violates the laws of nature
■ something unique or unusual in its occurrence
■ something impossible
■ something only God does

what problems does this raise with regard to science and science education?

As already mentioned, if a miracle is something that violates the laws of nature and consequently our understanding of those as expressed in scientific laws then this can easily cause some disquiet among scientists and those who hold such laws to be unchangeable. This would mean that scientific laws and theories as we currently understand them are entirely conditional on the mind of a God who seems very capable of changing his/her mind at will. This also raises questions for those of faith and for theologians who must then consider that God is capricious, altering the way the world works to suit the needs of some but not for others. It also raises the question of whether God is omnipotent and all-knowing or in some way limited as the laws of nature created by God seem to be insufficient to meet the needs of all occasions and require occasional interference and temporary changes or violations.

These questions have been at the heart of the debates surrounding the relationship between science and miracles, leading some to dismiss miracles as simple fiction or lies and others to dismiss scientific explanations of the world as erroneous or invalid. Without a doubt, it has been an area of heated discussion and one that pre-dates some of the more high profile moments of conflict such as debates over human origins. The role of miracles in faith and the centrality of unchanging laws in scientific method have ensured that these questions continue to form a central part of the discussions on science and religion encountered, and engaged with, by students.

WHAT STUDENTS SAY

In a survey looking at perceptions and beliefs relating to religion and science, over 300 secondary school students answered a range of questions looking at miracles.

When asked whether they believed in miracles that break the laws of nature, 38% of young people answered that they did, with 30% stating that they did not and the bulk of the remainder indicating that they were undecided. This would seem to suggest that, for a substantial majority, the issue of miracles as defined in the terms outlined above remains at least an open question with many accepting the possibility of miracles that break the laws of nature. Many of those expressing belief in miracles explained this in the context of a belief in God and indicated a belief in divine power to intervene *"because the* [sic] *God has power to do this"* being one comment reflecting this. The notion of evidence relating to miracles was also a common theme in belief: *"Yes, I have seen a few occur as miracles happen every day."* It was also presented as not being essential to belief: *"I believe but have never seen it happen."*

This suggests that, for many young people, evidence is important and also that their view of miracles is not limited to the technical definition provided here but does include the notion of miracles in the everyday.

Those indicating that they did not believe in miracles frequently held positions that referred to the issue of evidence, largely along the lines that they had not been convinced:

"I don't understand how they could exist."

"I don't necessarily believe in specifically miracles however there are some events which I don't know how to justify other than saying it is a miracle."

"Not all 'miracles' are performed by God, I believe that miracles are purely coincidental."

When asked whether they believed in God, 52% of the young people said they did, with 19% saying they did not and the remainder being undecided. Similar arguments to those seen for acceptance of miracles were put forward for belief or disbelief in God. The desire for proof was again raised by both groups and also those indicating that they were undecided on the matter:

"Where is the evidence God exists. He hasn't helped anyone I know yet . . ." (non-believer)

"I don't see any valid proof" (non-believer)

"There is not enough proof to prove or disprove whether there was a greater being" (undecided)

"There is no solid proof for this (even though I'm a Hindu)" (undecided)

Most of those who indicated a belief in God linked this with a particular tradition or their family origins:

"I am Christian."

"I am Hindu."

"I believe that God is called Allah."

"People have different opinions, and the way I've been brought up I've believed there to be a god as I am Sikh."

This linkage with tradition is unsurprising in one sense as acquired religion is a widely acknowledged feature among believers. It is worth noting, however, that there was an absence of more general or subjective notions of a deity or higher power and that the religious tradition of the respondent was important support for their position on this question. As such, students tended to have a clearly defined concept of God from a particular tradition and not a generalised notion of a deity.

Of those who said they believed in God, 63% also said that they believed in miracles. Thus, while an important part of many religious traditions, belief in miracles can by no means be seen as an essential component of belief or membership of a religious group among this cohort. Similarly, only 87% of those who expressed a belief in miracles as something that breaks the laws of nature also stated that they believed in God. This indicates that those who believed in miracles as actions that break the laws of nature do not necessarily presume that this is being done by some form of deity or greater being. This would suggest that there must be some form of "natural", as opposed to "supernatural", miracles which would seem to correspond to improbable events. Such "miracles" indicate a link with several of the explanations for miracles provided by scientists in their attempt to reconcile inviolable notions of natural law and suggest that, for some at least, it is not the violation of natural laws that is in question but the intervention of a supreme being that appears to be a barrier. The explanations provided by some scientists are considered below.

When asked whether they agreed with the statement "According to science, laws of nature determine everything that happens", 47% agreed and only 15% disagreed. Comments from students indicated a range of reasons for agreeing with the statement:

"I agree because science teaches their followers many theories that prove this."

"I think nature and situations interacting with each other make a change"

"and God could be the one who created those rules."

These suggest a diversity of reasons in agreeing with the statement, including positions that suggest that those who hold the "scientific" position as set out in this statement are incorrect in limiting their understanding purely to reductive or mechanistic understandings. Those stating belief in miracles showed a similar level of agreement to the general population of respondents with 46% agreeing. Of those agreeing with the statements about laws of nature, 51% stated a belief in miracles. This would seem to suggest that for about half of those who believe in miracles they see their position as in conflict with science.

Students were also asked whether they agreed with the statement "The scientific view is that it is impossible for miracles to happen". Overall, 54% agreed with this statement, 13% disagreed and the remainder indicated uncertainty. Of those who said that they believed in miracles a slightly higher proportion, 57%, agreed with the statement. While this difference does not appear significant, it does indicate that a large proportion of those who believe in miracles do tend to see that belief as placing them in conflict with a scientific worldview. Comments from young people indicated a range of positions among those who agreed. Some saw a fundamental incompatibility: "Science believes in the laws of nature, miracles are the opposite therefore it is incompatible for them both to be correct."

Others seemed to suggest a scientific equivalent of a "God of the gaps": "In science, with every abnormal thing, science always guesses the answer."

Those who disagreed with the statement did not then suggest agreement between a scientific view and the possibility of miracles but tended, rather, towards a position that indicated the limits of science and laws of nature as we understand them:

"Outside the dimensions of space and time, in a multiverse outside our own, there are no laws of physics."

The outcome of this study, then, is that many young people hold a belief in God and a belief in miracles, yet see this belief as in conflict with the way science sees the world and presents explanations of how things work. A key component of this conflict seems to rest in the role of evidence in providing reason for belief in miracles and, indeed, belief in God. The absence of evidence in line with that gathered by scientific method is seen as reason to reject belief in miracles or to see one's own belief as in conflict with science.

Miracles present students with a clear problem where they see conflicts between their view of science and their view of religion. On the whole, they have little experience of the relationship between science and religion beyond a model that suggests conflict. As such, they feel forced to choose. The following section presents the views of some notable scientists who maintain a belief in miracles and have attempted to explain their scientific and religious views. We will then go on to consider how introducing some of these figures and their views can help to open up students to broader considerations of the relationships that exist between science and religion.

SOME RELIGIOUS SCIENTISTS

The views and theories of miracles put forward here by some religious scientists each attempt to reconcile scientific and religious worldviews and argue against the conflict model that most students encounter as their only option. We have used the stories of these scientists and the explanations they provide to challenge assumptions of conflict and so offer the opportunity to think about and talk about the issues presented in a different way. The way in which each one is presented allows for their background and ideas to be communicated to students and also provides some discussion of the ideas and some possible criticism from scientific and religious standpoints. We have used this format in workshops with secondary students and they have proved effective in challenging assumptions and provoking new ways of thinking about miracles and science. An exercise that has proved useful is to summarise each position and allow discussion before asking students to think about which of the possible explanations they find most convincing.

Isaac Newton (1642–1727) is one of the most famous figures in the history of science and someone whom students will inevitably encounter in their studies. His laws of physics and, in particular, his study of gravity make him central to the science curriculum and culture generally. Newton famously had little difficulty in reconciling his faith and the physical laws he described and equally famously received robust criticism for this position. In his description of planetary motion, Newton recognised that from time to time his explanation was insufficient and so felt quite comfortable with the notion of God making adjustments to the course of planets and intervening in other ways. As such, Newton saw God making interventions in the world when he wished to as perfectly in line with a scientific description of the world. Miracles therefore are just one example of this.

The main criticism of Newton's position came from his contemporary, the philosopher and mathematician Gottfried Leibniz (1646–1716) who mocked the idea that God might make occasional adjustments to the way the world works: *"God Almighty wants to wind up his watch from time to time: otherwise it would cease to move. He had not, it seems, sufficient foresight to make it a perpetual motion."* To be fair, these two had a history of arguing between them that carried on for years after their deaths, not least about who first came up with calculus, but Leibniz does make an important point that raises an issue for many with regard to miracles and laws of nature. Why would a God who is all-powerful and all-knowing create laws that then need to be changed?

Harrison (1995) argues that, for Newton, and in a more developed way for his followers such as William Whiston, the absence of a sense of conflict between science and miracles was rooted in a view of natural laws that differs fundamentally from that presented by those such as Hume and Leibniz, who see rigid inviolable laws that have been fully described by scientific study. For Newton, natural laws are an expression of the divine creator's will and foresight and so all miraculous events, including also answers to petitionary prayer, are in essence pre-programmed into the laws which we observe. The fact that they appear anomalous is the product of our lack of understanding of the fullness of those laws (Harrison, 1995).

This position finds more recent expression in the thought of scientists such as Colin Humphreys, who presents a model of miracles as equivalent to musical accidentals embedded in the composition of natural laws. Humphreys is professor of materials science at Cambridge University but has also devoted his time to considering various Biblical events, including miracles. One analogy he presents is that miracles are like musical accidentals, embedded in the score by the composer from the beginning but unexpected in the key of composition. When listening to a piece of music with such accidentals, we are surprised by them, they appear to be anomalous, but they were always there and always meant to be there; it was simply our lack of knowledge of the composition and our assumptions that make them seem odd.

Newton's position and, similarly, Humphreys' do not require a violation of natural law but, rather, a new understanding of what is considered a law and the range of particular variations that can be encapsulated within a broader understanding of the physical universe. This does not mean that miracles are not interventions or signs by God but that they were embedded in the fabric of creation from the beginning. One difficulty that remains, however, is that God still appears capricious: why choose to intervene only in certain cases when from our perspective there are many worthy situations in which a miracle might seem appropriate?

Former professor of mathematical physics at Cambridge University and Anglican priest John Polkinghorne also sees the problem of a capricious god as central to the theological dilemma of miracles. He supports the definition of miracles presented by Swinburne (1968, p. 1) as:

> [A]n event of an extraordinary kind, brought about by a god, and of religious significance [and adds that god] . . . is no celestial conjurer, doing an occasional turn, but his actions must always be characterized by the deepest possible consistency and rationality. Therefore they must be endowed with meaning and be free from caprice. (Polkinghorne, 1989, p. 53)

In a similar way to Newton and Whiston, he presents a model of miracles as events that do not break laws of nature but simply involve a deeper understanding of the functioning of existing laws. His key example is that of boiling water and the apparent change of state and breaking of laws that might occur on observing it for the first time (Polkinghorne 1989, p. 60). Imagine you live in a world in which you have only ever been able to heat water to 70°C. If one day you walked into a room and saw water boiling but never managed to repeat this then you might consider it a miracle. Philosopher of science, Nancy Cartwright, in considering the boundaries of science, without specific reference to miracles, also presents a similar picture of what she terms a "dappled world", in which scientific theories and laws describe only parts of a patchwork and that assumptions about universal applicability are often overly presumptive.

An alternative perspective on the relationship between miracles and the laws of nature is exemplified by Humphreys (1995) again, who argues that perception of the miraculous is a matter of timing. In this model, the events of the miracle fall within the bounds of natural, and indeed normal if unusual, events with the extraordinary element being that of timings for the individuals involved and the significance of this in revelation of the will of god. An example of this might be the crossing of the Israelites over the river Jordan in which the river was blocked allowing them to cross. Humphreys has investigated this and believes that there is evidence of landslides causing just such blockages of the river. The miracle in this case is being in the right place at the right time.

A similar notion of miracles being due to natural events and providential timing is provided by the meteorologist Carl Drews, who modelled a circumstance that given sufficient wind strength acting on a bend in a river then waters could be parted. Drews argues that there are just such places in the northern reaches of the Nile Delta where the Israelites fleeing the Egyptians during the Exodus might be expected to cross. Drews suggests that while improbable as an event, it is *possible* and that the Israelites may have been led to the right place at the right time.

Timing, in a slightly different sense, is also central to the nineteenth-century writer and theologian Henry Drummond's notion of miracles and the action of an immanent god, in which he argues that the miracle is not the event but its product and can thus be a slow process rather than an event (Drummond, 1894). As such, the miracle of creation, or more specifically for Drummond the miracle of evolution, is not the event of creation but the product that is a being capable of love. Such a view completely eliminates any need for the miraculous to break laws of nature and relies entirely on subjective evaluation of the value of the outcome. In some ways, this corresponds with the position of the theologian Friedrich Schleiermacher (1799), who dismissed the notion of miracles as *"merely the religious name for an event"*. For both Drummond and Schleiermacher, subjective interpretation is far more significant than the nature of the event itself, both in terms of whether natural laws are broken or timing.

Of course, one of the drawbacks of these interpretations of miracles as natural events, or matters of timing, is that they appear to limit the power of God to working with the laws of nature. This raises the question of whether god is all-powerful or all-knowing and so may provide challenges to young people with a particular faith. Schleiermacher's position in particular reduces such events to simply natural occurrences that we project significance on to, whether intended by god or not. For those who hold a faith based in miraculous events, such as the resurrection of Jesus, this could prove extremely challenging.

The following section will now consider how these explanations provided by scientists and theologians can be used to explore miracles more deeply in a classroom setting and also suggests some activities to help demonstrate some of the core principles considered here.

A CLASSROOM SESSION ON MIRACLES

The learning outcomes of this session are:

- To be able to explain why some questions are more amenable than others to the methods of scientific enquiry.
- To appreciate that science and religion are not necessarily incompatible.
- To know that science and religion are mostly concerned with different types of question even when they are talking about the same topic.
- To appreciate that different types of question often call for different types of method and produce different types of answer.
- To understand that belief in miracles does not necessitate a rejection of science and vice versa.

One opening approach can be to think about the nature of science itself and the way we gather information. The three following activities can open up questions about the way science works and how we perceive phenomena.

Mystery shoebox

Show the students a shoebox that has a mystery item inside (two plastic forks works well or any small object such as cotton reels, pencils or small toys etc.). Shake the box – see if they can guess the object from the sound. Give the box to a student but tell them they may not open the box (if you have enough boxes you could distribute several for small groups to work with) and pose the question:

> How can you gather evidence to help you come up with a theory about what's inside? Does it roll? Does it slide? What material might it be? How many objects?

Point out if they may not open the lid, they will never know if they were really right. Much of science is like this: we construct theories about things that are too far away or too small for us to investigate directly – and we're ready to update the theory if new evidence comes along. (At this point you could also show a couple of news stories about black holes, relativity or particle physics as ways to highlight that physicists model the universe mathematically and this can produce some surprising ideas which they test by gathering evidence.)

This activity will help to establish that scientific evidence is gathered from many sources that are often indirect. These help to build up a picture but at any given moment our scientific understanding is subject to development and change as we gather further information.

Gravity-defying drum

In this demonstration, you can demonstrate that unexpected things can happen even within the laws of physics as we understand them. In this case, the law of gravity appears to be broken but, in fact, it is gravity working normally that creates the unexpected outcome.

Prepare a large empty drum of some sort, a paint can or empty catering drum of coffee/chocolate are quite good. Fix a heavy weight inside, don't make the weight too heavy or the drum might skid a little when you carry out the task. It may take a little trial and error to get the right weight.

Make a slope out of a short plank or by tilting a table. Give the drum some grip by making sure the surface isn't too smooth (if you can fix sandpaper or carpet to the slope this works well). Position the can so the weight allows it to roll downhill. Repeat this. (You could distract the students a little by getting them to time how long it takes to roll down so when the third attempt happens they are expecting a simple third repeat.)

On the third attempt position the hidden weight slightly to the uphill side. If you put the can onto the slope with the weight (hidden inside) positioned properly, when you let go the can rolls a little uphill. Snatch it up before it rolls down again. (See Figure 10.1.)

This is an unexpected outcome. You can repeat if you like to show that the phenomenon of the can rolling uphill is observable and repeatable.

Explain that, in this case, we can observe, repeat and investigate and finally explain but at first it was a real surprise! In fact, if you didn't know otherwise, it might appear to be a miracle.

The magic finger

This demonstration makes many of the same points that the gravity-defying drum does so you probably don't need to do both.

Fill a shallow tray with water to a depth of 1cm or so. Place some small triangles (or any shape really – it's just so they look like boats) of paper in a cluster in the water

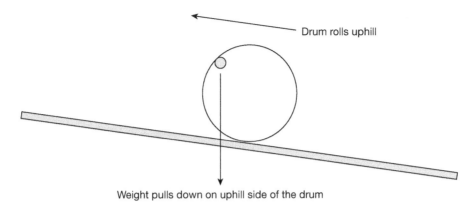

Figure 10.1

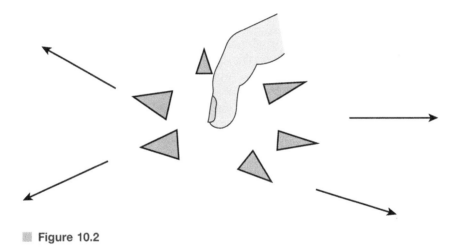

Figure 10.2

so they are floating together. If you place the index finger of you left hand gently into the water among the "boats" there is no real movement. But, when you do the same with your right hand the boats all move rapidly across the water! (See Figure 10.2.)

The difference is that, unknown to the students observing, you have secretly dipped your right index finger in some washing-up liquid and the break in surface tension caused by this causes the paper to move. It's important to emphasise that this isn't a conjuring trick but real science in action.

Now, this can only be done once without changing the water so is unexpected and non-repeatable: another possible "miracle" if you don't know what is happening.

Introducing miracles and thinking about them

Using the descriptions above you can now introduce the idea of miracles and how they are defined.

You could ask whether everyday things such as finding a parking space or the beauty of nature are miraculous and then move towards a definition as outlined in the curriculum and by thinkers such as Hume.

Once the students have a working definition of miracles ask them to discuss whether they think a scientist can believe in miracles. Our experience has been that most feel that scientists cannot accept miracles as defined in the RE curriculum.

An introduction to some scientists who believe in miracles such as Newton, Humphreys, Polkinghorne and Drews can provide a challenge to the assumptions held and create a little dissonance for students. If you have used some of the demonstration activities above you can draw parallels between the unexpected events and limited knowledge that some explanations are built on.

At the end, the same question about whether scientists can believe in miracles can then be revisited, perhaps alongside a question about how convincing students feel each explanation is.

CONCLUSION

In this chapter, we have considered the nature of miracles and the relationship between science and miracles. In presenting the views of several thinkers who hold that belief in miracles is compatible with a scientific worldview, and in many cases a scientific career, we have also attempted to challenge the assumption encountered in some students that the two are incompatible. The intention is not necessarily to create a belief in miracles, or their possibility, but instead to introduce the notion that they may be compatible with science or, at least, not necessarily in conflict. Whether students are convinced by the arguments put forward by the scientists here is up to them but the hope is that they are able to engage in a conversation that has no other obvious place to take place in school or even in their everyday life.

REFERENCES

AQA (2014). http://www.aqa.org.uk/subjects/religious-studies/gcse/religious-studiesb-4055/subject-content/unit-4.

Brooke, J.H. 1991. *Science and Religion*. Cambridge: Cambridge University Press.

Drummond, H. 1894. *The Ascent of Man*. Radford, VA: Wilder.

Fuller, M. 1995. *Atoms and Icons*. London: Mowbray.

Harrison, P. 1995. "Newtonian Science, Miracles and the Laws of Nature". *Journal of the History of Ideas*. Vol. 56 (4): 531–553.

Hume, D. 2008 (1748). *An Enquiry Concerning Human Understanding*. Oxford: Oxford University Press.

Humphreys, C. "The Star of Bethlehem". *Science and Christian Belief*. Vol. 5 (October 1995): 83–101.

Polkinghorne, J. 1989. *Science and Providence*. London: SPCK.

Poole, M. 1997. *A Guide to Science and Belief* (2nd ed.). Oxford: Lion Publishing.

Schleiermacher, F. 1799. *On Religion: Speeches to Its Cultured Despisers*. London: Paternoster (1893).

Swinburne, R.G. 1968. "Miracles". *The Philosophical Quarterly*. Vol. 18 (73): 320–328.

Ward, K. 2002. "Believing in Miracles". *Zygon*. Vol. 37 (3): 741–750.

Westfall, R. 1970. *Science and Religion in Seventeenth Century England*. New Haven: Archon.

GOD AND NATURAL DISASTERS

Bethany Sollereder

The television interrupts our daily pattern with breaking news. An earthquake has devastated part of the world. Pictures pour in of people sorting through collapsed houses, looking for their loved ones. Or a tsunami has swept away an entire coastline. Grainy videos of crowds running in vain away from an unrelenting flood play themselves out over and over again. We watch the desperate work of relief organisations to provide basic necessities to thousands of displaced people so that the casualties from the natural disaster do not climb still higher.

We are familiar with the statistics of loss in earthquakes: the 2004 Indonesia Boxing Day earthquake, 9.1 magnitude, claimed 230–240,000 lives; on 12 January 2010 in Haiti a 7.0 magnitude earthquake caused some 140,000 deaths; 11 March 2011 an undersea mega-thrust with a 9.0 magnitude covered 217 square miles of Japan with flood waters, taking 15,893 lives and causing a major meltdown of the Fukushima nuclear power plant.

Earthquakes are so big and unpredictable that they have unrivalled casualties among natural disasters, but other disasters can also have sizeable local effects. On 13 November 1985, the Nevado del Ruiz volcano in Colombia erupted. Landslides and mudslides caused by the force of the eruption engulfed a nearby town, killing over 20,000 people. In 79 CE, Mount Vesuvius erupted and covered the nearby towns of Herculaneum and Pompeii with ash and burning gases – 1500 deaths have been confirmed by uncovering body casts among the well-preserved remains. Estimates for how many lives the eruption actually took run over 10,000.

In light of such tragic natural disasters, by no means uncommon, how can theists believe in a God who is both powerful and good? The problem of suffering in light of a God characterised by the "omni"s—omnipotence, omniscience, and omnibenevolence—remains one of the greatest challenges in theology.

I am regularly asked to design and deliver talks and workshops for students, fellow academics, and for public audiences. I write, speak, and worship as a practising Christian theologian, and organisers who make the invitations anticipate that I can help frame how someone can believe in a good and loving God while being aware that reality includes disasters of this type. Teachers are likely to want to, and are encouraged to, expand the material and ideas offered here to include the perspectives of other faiths.[1] With that said, I hope the ideas and activities outlined here will be a useful and informative starting point.

In my workshop designed for secondary students, I begin by outlining the problem, as described above. Then we explore various Christian theological responses to the question of natural disasters. We take time examining, critiquing and analysing the implications of several different approaches. Some positions are well known and widely held, others represent some of the newest thought among academic theologians. All the positions are presented as possibilities, and none of them is given as "the Christian answer".[2] I explore seven positions, labelled as:

1 The sin approach
2 The Satanic influence approach
3 The kenotic approach
4 The development approach (or "nomic regularity")
5 The physical package deal
6 The co-suffering approach
7 Redemptive responses

In each, I try to show how the perspective is either supported or critiqued by the input of modern science. The aim is to show that theology does not have just one settled answer to difficult questions, but that there are various conversations going on, all of which engage with science in varying ways.

I give students a handout with quotations from authors representing the first five positions. I ask students to read the first quotation and provide a title for the position, or to give a 2–5 word summary of the author's approach. On the board, I gather student opinions, choose an appropriate title and ensure that the basic idea of the position is clearly understood. Then I give the students 2–4 minutes to discuss in pairs the theological strengths, weaknesses, and scientific merits (when applicable) of the newly entitled position. While they talk, I move from group to group gathering what is being said so that I can build a class recap from their discussions and logically order how I receive comments.

I cannot recap these discussions fully, but will outline each position below with suggestions or common positions taken by the students.

THEOLOGICAL APPROACHES TO THE QUESTION OF NATURAL DISASTERS

The sin approach

QUOTATION

"For it appears that all the evils of the present life, which experience proves to be innumerable, have proceeded from the same fountain. The inclemency of the air, frost, thunders, unseasonable rains, drought, hail, and whatever is disorderly in the world, are the fruits of sin." John Calvin[3]

SUMMARY

When humans first sinned (with reference to Adam and Eve in the Garden of Eden – Genesis 2–3) the non-human world was corrupted, or cursed, resulting in all the natural causes for suffering and death. God never intended suffering to happen, it is a result of human sin.

STRENGTHS

It preserves God's goodness, and puts the entire blame for all suffering on human choice. Had those humans chosen differently, a world without suffering could have been a possibility.

WEAKNESSES

It seems highly unfair. Natural disasters kill indiscriminately and disproportionately to the sin of those affected.[4] And it is highly unfair that humans born later should "inherit" the result of sins long preceding their own birth.

SCIENTIFIC MERIT

Very poor. First, behaviourally modern humans have only been around for 50,000 years, while earthquakes have been causing harm to life for all of the 3.8 billion years that life has existed. Calvin is not to blame for not incorporating these things: neither plate tectonics nor the old age of the earth were known in his time. But today, it is important to take the best science into account in theological work. The chronological problem here is insurmountable.

The Satanic influence approach

QUOTATION

"To save theism from the charge of contradiction, all the theist has to do is to argue that natural evil is possibly due to the activity of Satan." William Abraham[5]

"It seems reasonable to suppose that the defection and rebellion in the angelic realm will drastically disorder the material world . . . Within this view, death, disease, division, and predation are seen as symptoms of this distortion, consequences of the angelic Fall rather than part of the good order of creation." Michael Lloyd[6]

SUMMARY

If suffering and natural disasters were around before evil humans could be the cause, a different agent could be the source instead. Some scholars point to Satanic evil, or the fall of the angels, as a reasonable agent to account for natural evil.[7]

STRENGTH

It solves the chronological problem present in the first position and it protects God's blamelessness in relation to non-human animal pain and suffering.

WEAKNESSES

In the Old Testament, God regularly claims both that the world is good (Genesis 1) and that the uncontrollable elements of creation are particular points of pride (Psalm 104, Job

38–41). If they were the result of Satanic interference with an otherwise perfectly peaceful creation, it is a wonder that it is not stated more clearly.

SCIENTIFIC MERIT

Problematic. Darwin's famous insight was that the diversity, beauty, and skill of the natural world are inseparably linked to the pain, suffering and competition found in the natural world: "Thus, from the war of nature, from famine and death, the most exalted object which we are capable of conceiving, namely, the production of the higher animals, directly follows."[8] If Satan is the cause of Darwin's "war of nature", then Satan is also responsible for the developments of the beauty, skill and diversity produced by that conflict.

The conditions of life that humans and other animals need are created by the very same natural disasters that cause harm. Tectonic plate movement, for example, does cause earthquakes, but it also creates stable earth temperatures, the magnetic field that protects life from damaging solar rays, the renewal of nutrients in the soil, the existence of liquid surface water and many other benefits that make life possible.[9] It would be odd if Satanic agents that intended to corrupt or destroy life by causing earthquakes actually gave the means of life's continuation.

The kenotic approach

QUOTATION

"God cannot unilaterally prevent genuine evil. Because God's nature is first and foremost love, divine love is always and inherently uncontrolling. By 'uncontrolling,' I mean that God never controls creatures, situations, or worlds." Thomas Jay Oord[10]

SUMMARY

The "kenotic" approach is drawn from the Greek word *kenō* in the passage Philippians 2: 6–7 (NRSV), which says that Jesus, "who, though he was in the form of God, did not regard equality with God as something to be exploited, but emptied himself (*ekenosen*), taking the form of a slave, being born in human likeness." The basic approach is that although God has all power, God does not use power to control people or events, but takes the form of a servant and gives freedom to others.

By giving creation its "otherness", God also gives the world and all that is in it the ability to cause real harm. For Thomas Jay Oord, the nature of God's love is so completely uncontrolling that God cannot take away a creature's ability to do harm or experience harm without contradicting God's own love.

STRENGTH

It explains why God does not prevent the harm caused by natural disasters or by other agents, such as predators. God, in creating, has given freedom to the world to be itself.

WEAKNESSES

A strong kenotic approach, as Oord takes, stands in contrast to the majority of the Christian tradition's understanding of God's sovereignty and power. While these kenotic views have proliferated since the profound human suffering witnessed during World War II, and is prominent in the writings of Jürgen Moltmann, Paul Fiddes, Clark Pinnock, Charles Hartshorne and many others, it does not explain why God cannot create new conditions (or perform miracles) to reduce or prevent harm.

SCIENTIFIC MERIT

This metaphysical position confirms the uniformity seen in the natural world. If God has given up the ability to control events, then we would expect material to move predictably, even if sometimes ruthlessly, according to natural laws.

Development (or "nomic regularity" or "law-like regularity")

QUOTATION

"Why can't God suspend the regularities of nature whenever God had reason to do so? Consider a universe in which God could and did suspend at will the operation of (to begin with) physical regularities, a world (say) in which the murderer's bullet turned into a flower when it left his gun and floated gently to the ground . . . It is hard to see how the evolution of rational agency, not to speak of moral agency, would be possible in such a world." Philip Clayton and Steven Knapp[11]

SUMMARY

Everyone relies on the regularity of the world in order to learn, to build skills and to work out relationships with people and objects around them. If God interrupted that regularity to prevent people from being harmed, the end result would be a world in which no relationships could have integrity and no skills could be built. I sometimes use the following examples with students:

> Imagine a world where, when my brother and I fought as children, God always intervened to prevent harm. Every time I went to throw a punch, God created a feather pillow between my fist and my brother's arm. Or, every time he went to say something rude to me, God stopped the sound waves before they hit my ears. Would I have any real relationship with my brother? Similarly, if every time I slipped when running, God turned the road into marshmallow to soften my fall, would I ever really learn to run? I would begin to think that the miracle was the way the world really was.

Clayton and Knapp suggest that if God continually intervened, people and other living creatures could never build a true picture of the world, hold real relationships or build the basic skills for life.

STRENGTH

This approach is equally true for non-human animals. A mountain goat would never build its tremendous skill and strength if God prevented its being harmed by rocks and gravity.

WEAKNESSES

Taking this approach to an extreme prevents any allowance for miracles.

SCIENTIFIC MERIT

Again, this metaphysical position assumes the regularity of the world. It is also true that without an assumption of nomic regularity, no one could do science either.

The physical package deal

QUOTATION

"Which would you rather have, a bursting planet or an earthquake here and there?" Father Joseph Lynch[12]

   "The world is a package deal. We cannot experience the joys of existence without experiencing the aches of pain." Niels Gregersen[13]

SUMMARY

There are no physical alternatives. The occasional earthquake is the price for an earth's surface that is liveable on. The suffering that people experience is due to the same complex neural system that also allows them to feel profound joy and love. When worms, by contrast, are hit by natural disasters, they do not suffer. But worms cannot feel joy either.

STRENGTH

It is a strong argument: God is responsible for creating a world with conditions where life can, and often does, flourish. The only known conditions for life on our planet involve reliance on earthquakes and other natural disasters that cause suffering.

WEAKNESSES

While science can show that life on *this* earth requires plate tectonics for life to flourish, it cannot prove that there are no other conditions under which life might develop and flourish.

SCIENTIFIC MERIT

This approach appropriates all that we know about the causes and effects of earthquakes and other natural disasters.

   At this point, I take a break from looking at perspectives that try to explain why God allows natural disasters (or other natural harms) to occur, and ask instead about how

God might respond to the suffering of those caught up in these natural occurrences. Although I have included quotations below, I do not usually use them. I simply allow the students to mull over ideas in a brainstorming session and respond. Students usually come up with the idea that God might inspire people to give aid to those who are suffering, or to get involved in some other way. God might also be active in bringing healing to those who are physically or psychologically damaged. I then typically propose two last types of divine response to end the class.

The co-suffering approach

QUOTATION

"I can only suppose that God's suffering presence is just that, presence, of the most profoundly attentive and loving sort, a solidarity that at some deep level takes away the aloneness of the suffering creature's experience." Christopher Southgate[14]

SUMMARY

Some theologians have proposed that, alongside other responses, God suffers with creatures in pain. God accompanies every creature through every pain.

WEAKNESSES

There is a long-standing debate in the Christian tradition that would argue that it is impossible for God to suffer. Suffering would mean the world affects God, whereas traditional views of God's impassibility hold that God is unchanging in perfection. Another critique is that it does not help if God does suffer. If my arm is broken, someone who set my arm in a cast, rather than someone who allowed their own arm to be broken too, would be a better help.

STRENGTH

While this approach does not lessen the suffering of creatures, it does replace a certain view of God that I call the "Lord Farquaad God". In the movie *Shrek*, Lord Farquaad wants to rescue the Princess Fiona but is unwilling to go himself. Instead, he gathers a group of knights and commissions them with the task. In his speech, he includes the line: "Some of you *may die*. But it's a sacrifice *I* am willing to make." Divine co-suffering does not alleviate creaturely suffering, but it means that God does not nominate other creatures for suffering from which God is exempt.

Redemptive responses

QUOTATION

"Just as we hope that other human beings, given their propensities and needs, find appropriate fulfillment in life beyond death, we must hope that kindred creatures, given their propensities and needs, find fulfillment in life after death too ... What a pelican chick might know as fulfillment of needs would have its own kind of harmony and intensity, one quite different from what we humans might know. If there is a pelican heaven, it is a *pelican* heaven." Jay McDaniel[15]

SUMMARY

Thinkers from across the theological spectrum are increasingly proposing that life after death is not just for humans.[16] While some have held this view in the past (notably, John Wesley the founder of Methodism), it has never been a majority view. Now, it is becoming extremely prevalent. Heaven (or, better, the new creation) will incorporate the lives of non-human animals, particularly those who suffered, and allow them a chance to flourish.

WEAKNESSES

This can be evaluated as "too little, too late," or as improbable since a good and loving God was not able to give the suffering creatures a chance to flourish in this life. It raises the question: "Why didn't God just make heaven first?"

STRENGTHS

The ability of God to creatively redeem suffering stands at the heart of the Christian faith. Christians believe that God took one of the cruellest occurrences in human history—the crucifixion of the blameless Jesus—and used it, with the resurrection, as the grounds for the salvation of the world. Because of this, millions now wear an instrument of death, the cross, as a sign of hope. For God to redeem the suffering of all sentient creatures would align well with the primary message of Christianity.

If there is any time left, I recap the major positions, and reemphasise that the goal is not to come to a certain conclusion or a single answer, but to explore how different perspectives highlight different questions about who God is, and how God might be present in circumstances of suffering.

NOTES

1   My own expertise is insufficient to comment on how other faith traditions approach suffering.
2   The most innovative and recent works in theodicy (that branch of theology that deals with suffering) do not offer simple solutions, but hold that viable approaches must be compound. Various lines of argument should be held together, and even so, it is not commonly thought that these approaches give a final answer. Christopher Southgate, *The Groaning of Creation: God, Evolution, and the Problem of Evil* (Louisville, KY: Westminster John Knox Press, 2008), 15–16; Michael Murray, *Nature Red in Tooth and Claw: Theism and the Problem of Animal Suffering* (Oxford: Oxford University Press, 2008), 193–199.
3   John Calvin, *Commentaries upon the First Book of Moses called Genesis (1554)*. In *Calvin's Bible Commentaries: Genesis, Part I*, translated by J. King (Forgotten Books, 1847/2007), 113.
4   Newborn babies die quite as often as adults, for example. The issue of disproportionate "punishment" was a particular issue in the devastating 1755 Lisbon earthquake, which has become a classic case study in theodicy. Those in church on Saturday morning for the All Saints' feast day had the great stone churches crumble on top of them. Worshippers who escaped the churches were threatened by fire and ran to the harbor for shelter, at which point three tsunami waves crashed on them. People visiting brothels on the edge of town on the feast day survived much better.

5   Abraham, William J. *An Introduction to the Philosophy of Religion* (London: Prentice-Hall, 1985), 68.

6   "Are Animals Fallen?" in *Animals on the Agenda*, Linzey & Yamamoto, eds. (London: SCM, 1998), 159.

7   C. S. Lewis, author of *The Chronicles of Narnia* also said this: "It seems to me, therefore, a reasonable supposition, that some mighty created power had already been at work for ill on the material universe, or the solar system, or, at least, the planet Earth, before ever man came on the scene." *The Problem of Pain* (New York: HarperCollins, 1940/1996), 138.

8   Charles Darwin, *The Origin of Species* (London: John Murray, 1859), 490.

9   See Peter Ward and Donald Brownlee, *Rare Earth: Why Complex Life is Uncommon in the Universe* (New York: Copernicus, 2004).

10 Thomas Jay Oord, *The Uncontrolling Love of God* (2015), 167; "Divine Action as Uncontrolling Love", available online at http://biologos.org/blogs/jim-stump-faith-and-science-seeking-understanding/divine-action-as-uncontrolling-love#sthash.F8SoklGq.dpuf.

11 Philip Clayton and Steven Knapp, *The Predicament of Belief: Science, Philosophy and Faith* (Oxford: Oxford University Press, 2011), 47.

12 John Joseph Lynch, SJ, "In Defense of Earthquakes," quoted in Eric R. Swanson, *Geo-Texas: A Guide to the Earth Sciences* (College Station, TX: Texas A&M University Press, 1995), 74

13 Niels Gregersen, "The Cross of Christ in an Evolutionary World", *Dialog* 40: 3 (Fall 2001): 192–207, 201.

14 Christopher Southgate, *The Groaning of Creation* (Louisville, KY: Westminster John Knox, 2008), 53.

15 Jay McDaniel, *Of God and Pelicans: A Theology of Reverence for Life* (Louisville, KY: Westminster John Knox, 1989), 45.

16 See also work by David Clough, Christopher Southgate, Nicola Hoggard Creegan, Tom Wright, Elizabeth Johnson, Paul Griffiths and Trent Dougherty.

SCIENCE AT THE MOVIES

REMEDIATING THE MISCONCEPTIONS AND DEVELOPING ETHICAL REASONING

Siew Fong Yap

AIMS OF THE CHAPTER

- ▓ To introduce an innovative and engaging approach of teaching science that addresses common misconceptions in scientific concepts using the popular medium of films or movies.
- ▓ To promote ethical thinking and reasoning through the use of socio-scientific issues raised through the medium of films or movies.
- ▓ To outline a lesson utilising this approach and present some students' responses on the socio-scientific issue of "climate change" based on a teaching module which incorporated viewing of the film *The Day After Tomorrow*.
- ▓ To present some implications from this study that establish the plausible connections between the teaching of science and faith values in the classrooms.

INTRODUCTION

We all love the movies! Well, perhaps not all of us, but if you give most young people the choice between a science lesson or watching a movie, the smart money will be on the latter. The great thing is that they are not mutually exclusive. It is certainly true that you can't teach everything through this medium but there are some great opportunities to make some important learning points and stimulate vibrant discussion on difficult or controversial topics such as those considered throughout this book.

The following chapter sets out an approach for the use of films in looking at socio-scientific issues with the example used here being climate change. Climate change is an important, perhaps the most important, environmental issue of our time and is rightly an important part of the science curriculum in Australia and many countries around the world. It is not, however, simply a matter of the science as climate change has become a highly charged global political issue; perhaps most notably in the United States but also in many developed economies. Denial of climate change is inevitably linked with economic and social priorities but it is also frequently linked with the issue of the relationships between science and religion. Christian evangelicals have been linked with climate change denial but they are by no means alone. It is possible that part of this is due to the close link between certain religious groups and political parties that have policies that deny or seek to minimise the significance of climate change but there are also some deeper theological issues. For those who take creation accounts in scriptures literally and presume a young Earth of about 6000 years of age, there is a fundamental challenge brought by the climate science that presumes an ancient Earth and compares the current climate to that of tens of thousands of years ago. Additionally, for traditions that resist any notion of population control as part of their faith then there is an instinctive resistance to much evidence of environmental change.

Climate change, then, provides an excellent model for the use of movies in science education and the issue of science and religion in bringing together complex and important science and socio-political matters and some key issues in science and religion that relate to other areas such as evolution, ethics and divine action.

From an educational perspective, researchers, policy makers and practitioners all over the world wish to understand how education innovations propel emerging ideas and systems from good to great to first rate and how their trajectories will provide insights for reforms in the education system, schooling innovation and classroom practices. It is a learning environment that promotes the development of creativity, innovativeness and capability for self-directed lifelong learning in students that will have a distinct focus on constructivist learning, rather than one of teacher-centred learning. Being innovative is about looking beyond what we do well now, identifying the sterling ideas of tomorrow and putting them into effective practice.

In what follows, we seek to explore and implement an engaging approach towards integrating science, societal values and religion through the use of socio-scientific issues using films and/or movies in the middle school and upper secondary science classrooms. Such a pedagogy resonates with a social constructivist approach towards learning, involving higher order thinking skills such as the remediation of misconceptions and the development of argumentation and ethical reasoning in a positive and collaborative learning environment. In a more immediate way, it helps to draw students of all abilities into complex subject matter and helps to introduce what are often foreign ideas, such as science and religion, in the context of mainstream science lessons.

USE OF SOCIO-SCIENTIFIC ISSUES (SSI) AS A VIABLE EDUCATIONAL FRAMEWORK

In the past decade, socio-scientific issues (SSI) have emerged as an educational construct influenced by ideologies embedded in the science–technology–society (STS) tradition but informed by theory and scholarship from philosophical, developmental and sociological traditions that characterised them as a category on its own.

SSI provides "entry points" into science curricula that are of pedagogical importance to the larger science education community of researchers and practitioners. SSI focuses on the nature of science issues, cultural issues, discourse issues and case-based issues as a way to help develop scientific literacy in a broader sense. Such *broad* entry points in the

SSI curriculum allow for the cultivation of scientific literacy by promoting informal reasoning in which students are encouraged to analyse, evaluate, discuss and argue varied perspectives on complex issues that are ill structured. The *open-ended* nature of the themes raised in SSI provides a fertile medium for developing higher order thinking skills and ethical reasoning.

THE MEDIUM OF FILMS (OR MOVIES)

Film has the ability to create concrete images of the natural world on the screen and thus in the audience's mind. Such images may include what a comet looks like, how birds evolve, how the Earth's core rotates, how genetic modification of a T-rex works and so on. Take for example what is called "sensuous elaboration" in communicating the dangers of plagues and environmental change in the films *Contagion*, *The Day After Tomorrow* and *San Andreas*. These perils are no longer seen as abstract but are made more concrete in the mind through the visualisation provided through the cinema which helps generate public awareness of their impact on large populations and the environment. The cinema's sensuous elaborations of disaster highlight the need to acquire scientific knowledge and new technologies in order to prevent these disasters.

Thus, films can be employed as a visual medium captivating the imagination of our young minds and hearts and these could be tapped into as starting points for generating viable discussions as well as highlight misconceptions or alternate conceptions that could be further modified and corrected.

FAITH VALUES AND RELIGION IN SSI

Scientific literacy, in the broad "functional" sense in which we understand it, necessarily includes the evaluation of moral and ethical factors in making judgements about both the validity and viability of scientific data and information relevant to the quality of public and environmental debates. Thus, scientific literacy entails the ability to make informed decisions, analyse, synthesise and evaluate varied sources of data and information, use moral reasoning to attend sensibly to ethical issues and understand the complexity of connections inherent in SSI.

It is also important to recognise that any approach that privileges scientific reasoning over other approaches on matters related to SSI but neglects to consider and attend to factors such as motivations, personal values and social milieu will likely fail. Thus, inclusion of personal values and social milieu necessitates the careful consideration of the diverse religious backgrounds of students and the worldviews that influence and shape their underlying belief systems.

On faith/values framework in relation to ethical reasoning, research has shown from students' responses on socio-scientific issues that intuitive reasoning can be influenced by religious convictions/religious knowledge (Yap, 2012). To an appreciable extent, students' faith did affect or influence their moral reasoning capacity. Faith can provide a basis for reasoning. In some cases, faith could also take precedence over other forms of reasoning in opting for a more simplistic acceptance rather than a logical rationalistic step-by-step approach in reconciling differences in facts and reality. In summary, research studies indicate there are several problem-solving strategies in making moral judgements. It suggested that allegiance to belief systems and ideologies can sometimes override the influence of one's own sense of fairness in making decisions of moral rightness. This is an important factor to consider in mapping out curricula on moral education and socio-scientific education.

REMEDIATING THE MISCONCEPTIONS

Research has shown that students commonly hold alternative ideas that are inconsistent with the science to be learned and these often get in the way of learning important scientific concepts. It is important to understand learners' alternative conceptions in a topic before teaching them and then to explicitly challenge them.

A range of studies suggests that learners' ideas about scientific topics are actually quite diverse in nature, as might be expected when considered as knowledge "under development" (Taber, 2014). Ideally, learners would be presented with activities, demonstrations and opportunities for dialogue that would allow them to recognise the superiority of scientific concepts and models presented in the classroom to their own alternative conceptions.

Research to understand the nature and characteristics of students' conceptions continues because understanding the precise nature and status of different types of reported conception is important in understanding how conceptual change may be best brought about. Various instructional methods have also been used in science education for overcoming intuitive interference including teaching by analogy, conflict teaching, calling attention to relevant variables, raising students' awareness of the role of intuition in their thinking processes and conducting practical activities.

CLIMATE CHANGE AND GLOBAL WARMING

Globally, many countries have experienced extreme weather events at increasing frequency over the past few decades. Australia, the context of the study considered here, has been impacted by severe weather events (bush fires and flooding) and unprecedentedly high temperatures in recent years. Also, in a recent study of Western Australian high school students' understanding about the socio-scientific issue of climate change (Dawson, 2015), a sample of 438 Year 10 (14–15-year-old) students exhibited a mixed understanding of the greenhouse effect and climate change with about one in three students able to give a correct or partially correct definition of the greenhouse effect and climate change. More than half of the students expressed one or more of 10 alternative conceptions.

The following is an outline of the process in which a teaching module on Earth science was given to one of the participating schools. Two classes of Year 10 students were taught a term (8 weeks of 6 periods [duration of 40 minutes] on Earth science, followed by a week on "socio-scientific reasoning", which utilises Toulmin's argumentation and the use of ethical frameworks (Yap & Dawson, 2014) in the form of case studies and classroom discussions. Students participated by providing written responses in the form of questionnaire and select groups of students were interviewed.

In the Year 10 Australian Science Curriculum, the Earth science module covers global systems, including the carbon cycle, the greenhouse effects, climate change and the various interactions involving the biosphere, lithosphere, hydrosphere and the atmosphere. Under the *Science as a Human Endeavour* strand, students learn to use scientific knowledge to evaluate whether they should accept claims, explanations or predictions.

Climate change is defined as "a change in the average pattern of weather over a long period of time. Greenhouse gases play an important role in determining climate and causing climate change" (Australian Academy of Science, 2010). The greenhouse effect is a natural phenomenon in which "light from the sun heats the Earth's surface which then releases this heat into the air. Greenhouse gases in the air, such as carbon dioxide, absorb this heat". This radiation is emitted in all directions including the Earth's surface. An increase in greenhouse gases increases the temperature of the Earth.

This is the rationale presented to the students: climate change is increasingly viewed as a subject that has brought about much debate in the media and members of the public have different, often opposing views regarding the science, consequence and causes. Given that climate change impinges on ethical, political and social dimensions, it is recognised as a socio-scientific issue that requires global co-operation and collaboration to be addressed effectively. *The Day after Tomorrow* is one of the movies chosen to address this socio-scientific issue of "climate change" as it highlights the tension between science and politics.

The following is an example of a teaching resource (Yap, 2016) that was used to engage students in a science class discussion on climate change (pp. 26–28).

STUDENTS' RESPONSES ON THEIR UNDERSTANDING OF CLIMATE CHANGE AND ITS CAUSES

Student A: "I think climate change is something to do with the greenhouse effect and the temperature rising and something to do with ice melting. We hear about Alaska ice melting and erosion causing villagers to relocate."

Student B: "The greenhouse effect is destroying the ozone layer, so more heat enters the atmosphere and reaches the Earth. That is why our waters are warming up so much. Quite a lot of the corals in the Great Barrier Reef are bleached!"

Student C: "Climate change is when the ozone layer traps more solar heat than is needed because gases build up in the atmosphere. This trapped layer of heat gradually increases the average temperature in different parts of the world which can melt ice caps, and make hot places even hotter. The scientist in the movie talks about the change in ocean current – why didn't they act sooner?"

Student D: "I think that climate change is when the temperature of the climate changes quickly – becoming hotter and hotter over a short period of time, causing environmental problems. The movie shows all these are happening quite rapidly and over such a big chunk of the continent and all over the major cities. It is quite frightening to see it happen all so fast!"

Student E: "[The greenhouse effect] is when heat coming to the Earth cannot escape because we have this thickened atmosphere due to pollution. Air pollution is really bad – it really affects those of us with asthma!"

ALTERNATE CONCEPTIONS OR MISCONCEPTIONS IDENTIFIED – SUMMARY OF ANALYSIS 1

1   There was a prevalent misconception that greenhouse effect was caused mainly by ozone.

2   Student responses were categorised into two types. The first was that the greenhouse effect and/or greenhouse gases are destroying the ozone layer, thus allowing more

SCIENCE AT THE MOVIES – REMEDIATING THE MISCONCEPTIONS

MOVIE – *THE DAY AFTER TOMORROW* (2004)

■ **Figure 12.1** Image contributed by Mya Tint Te Htaik (Year 12 student)

Synopsis. Climatologist Jack Hall (Dennis Quaid) is largely ignored by the United Nations officials when presenting his environmental concerns. In this movie, his research proves true with the development of an enormous "superstorm" setting off catastrophic natural disasters throughout the world. In his fervent attempt to get to his son, Sam (Jake Gyllenhaal), who is trapped in New York with his friends, Jack and his crew travel by foot from Philadelphia, braving the elements to get to Sam before it is too late.

Australian Curriculum (Year 10 Earth science)

Science inquiry skills

Communicate scientific ideas and information for a particular purpose, including constructing evidence-based arguments and using appropriate scientific language, conventions and representations.

Science understanding

Global systems, including the carbon cycle, rely on interactions involving the biosphere, lithosphere, hydrosphere and atmosphere.

Science as a human endeavour

USE AND INFLUENCE OF SCIENCE

People can use scientific knowledge to evaluate whether they should accept claims, explanations or predictions. Advances in science and emerging sciences and technologies can significantly affect people's lives.

Pre-movie questions

1   What do you understand by climate change?
2   What do you understand by global warming?
3   Is climate change the same as global warming? Are they the same or different? Why?
4   How did you come to know the answers to these questions?

Alternatively, students may complete a multi-choice question quiz provided at the end of this activity.

Lesson on climate change and global warming

Note. Concepts of climate and weather difference, confusion between ozone depletion and global warming, influence of movie on risk perceptions and public understanding of global climate change.

Post-movie discussion questions

1   What are some effects of global warming that are portrayed in the movie?
2   From what you have learned in class, what seems to be in conflict with the story in the movie?

3   What is one major misconception portrayed in the movie? List them all if you can identify more.

4   What causes global warming?

5   What are the Australians' attitude(s) to climate change? Can you suggest why?

[The following question is a new addition to the activity provided in the E-book.]

6   The following are speeches made by some prominent politicians and religious figures. Discuss the content presented and answer the following questions:

7   In terms of environmental stewardship, what responsibility/obligation/debt does a present generation have to a future generation?

8   What is the appropriate response for the *individual* in developed and developing nations to global warming and the Kyoto Protocol?

9   What is the appropriate response for *society as a whole* in developed and developing nations to global warming and the Kyoto Protocol?

"From Australia we come with confidence and optimism", he said. "We are not daunted by our challenge of climate change. Innovation and invention could solve climate change." (Malcolm Turnbull, Australia Prime Minister at the Paris UN Climate Change Conference 2015; http://www.smh.com.au/environment/un-climate-conference/tale-of-two-leaders—trudeau-and-turnbull—at-the-paris-un-climate-conference-2015–20151130-glbyu4.html (accessed 20 April 2016))

"Climate change is one of the most serious threats facing our world. And it is not just a threat to the environment. It is also a threat to our national security, to global security, to poverty eradication and to economic prosperity. Now my country, the United Kingdom, is playing its part . . . In fact, it was Margaret Thatcher who was one of the first world leaders to demand action on climate change, right here at the United Nations 25 years ago. Now since then, the UK has cut greenhouse gas emissions by one quarter. We have created the world's first Climate Change Act. And, as Prime Minister, I pledged that the government I lead would be the greenest government ever. And I believe we've kept that promise . . . As political leaders we have a duty to think long-term. When offered clear scientific advice, we should listen to it. When faced with risks, we should insure against them. And when presented with an opportunity to safeguard the long-term future of our planet and our people, we should seize it." (David Cameron at the UN Climate Change Summit 2014; https://www.gov.uk/government/speeches/un-climate-summit-2014-david-camerons-remarks (accessed 20 April 2016))

"Humans have a moral obligation to protect the environment and that doing so is a key part of the challenge of lifting the world's least fortunate from poverty. The poor stand to suffer from extreme weather events that are already regularly wreaking havoc across the planet. We need a conversation which includes everyone, since the environmental challenge we are undergoing, and its human roots, concern and affect us all. Regrettably, many efforts to seek concrete solutions to the environmental crisis have proved ineffective, not only because of powerful opposition but also because of a more general lack of interest."

(Pope Francis on the First Encyclical, 23 December 2015; http://www.usatoday.com/story/news/world/2015/06/18/pope-francis-catholic-church-climate-encyclical/28910615/ (accessed 7 March 2016))

"Why should we be concerned about the environment? It isn't just because of the dangers we face from pollution, climate change, or other environmental problems – although these are serious. For Christians, the issue is much deeper: we know that God created the world, and it belongs to Him, not us. Because of this, we are only stewards or trustees of God's creation, and we aren't to abuse or neglect it. The Bible says, 'The earth is the Lord's, and everything in it, the world, and all who live in it' (Psalm 24: 1). When we fail to see the world as God's creation, we will end up abusing it. Selfishness and greed take over, and we end up not caring about the environment or the problems we're creating for future generations." (Billy Graham, Should Christians work to protect their environment? 22 April 2015; http://billygraham.org/story/billy-grahams-my-answer-global-warming-and-the-environment/ (accessed 7 March 2016))

heat or radiation to enter the atmosphere or to reach the earth. This brings about global warming and climate change. The second type related to general confusion caused by combining features of both phenomena. Climate change is when the ozone layer traps more solar radiation than necessary because of the build-up of gases in the atmosphere. The trapped radiation gradually increases the average temperatures across different parts of the world. The greenhouse effect is a natural process caused by the ozone layer around the earth. The gases in the ozone layer are like greenhouse gases; they insulate and protect the world with solar heat radiating from the sun.

3   The second alternate conception or misconception is that carbon dioxide alone caused the enhanced greenhouse effect.

4   The third common misconception is that greenhouse gases were harmful and are "poisonous" so they cause air pollution. Climate change is a difference in temperature caused by an increased greenhouse effect because of the pollution from burning fossil fuels and releasing poisonous gases into the atmosphere.

STUDENTS' RESPONSES ON HUMANS' RESPONSE TO CLIMATE CHANGE

Student A: "When we see the effects of climate change in so many places, we need to ask why Christians are not united in acting responsibly in cutting down these environmental problems. We all believe God creates this beautiful planet and he sure wants us to take good care of this."

Student B: "If the debate tells us that climate change is caused by men, we should do something about this. I am not sure if we are really loving one another if we are destroying bit by bit the very place we are living in, even if it has started in places quite far from us. Philippians 2: 4: 'Each of you should look not only to your own interest but also to the interests of others.' "

Student C: "We all have knowledge of science – even so – this is wisdom given by God – whether it comes from the scientist or the weather prediction patterns, we should choose to listen and act before it is too late."

Student D: "It all happened so fast in the movie. I am not sure this is really what happens in real life. If this is spread out over a long period of time, nature would work to even this out. I think movies have a way of being overly dramatic. Sometimes, science can be proven wrong too."

Student E: "It is not fair that some people have to suffer because others are not considerate. The atmosphere is what God gives us to support life here on earth. We are not honouring our creator God when we do not take good care of it."

PERSONAL BELIEFS AND VALUES EXPRESSED/ CLARIFIED – SUMMARY OF ANALYSIS 2

1   Students' responses reflected informal reasoning patterns; namely intuitive, rational- istic and emotive reasoning. Intuitive reasoning described considerations based on immediate reactions to the context of a scenario. Rationalistic reasoning described reason-based considerations. Emotional reasoning described care-based considera- tions. One or more of these patterns may be used to justify the students' viewpoint.

2   Moral reasoning based on one's values and belief systems can become explicit when this is made explicit in the form of a scripture quoted (as with Student B) or an imperative expressed in the form of what ought to be done (as with Students A, C and E). It is prudent for individuals, churches, communities, and governments to act now to curb actions that are causing degradation of the environment and ultimate global destruction.

3   The question of choice and individual right is raised by Student C. The use of ethical frameworks has brought to students' awareness the need to consider how choices are made. Students had a lengthy discussion on Galatians 5: 13: "For you were called to freedom, brethren; only do not turn your freedom into an opportunity for the flesh, but through love serve one another." There are choices to be made and there are different outcomes to be experienced depending on what we choose. God makes that clear. We are all free in Christ to decide if we care. It is not a guilt thing or an obligation thing. Our knowledge should lead us to care and action to alleviate this human-induced global warming effect.

4   The quest for the power of knowledge and the limitation of scientific theory are called into question (as in Student E) when our imperfect knowledge, our motive and partiality will influence our interpretation of events and shape the decision we make, and the final outcome.

PRACTICAL IMPLICATIONS AND SUGGESTIONS

The following are some implications from this study that establish the plausible connections between the teaching of science and faith values in the classrooms:

1   Films (movies) can be a powerful and engaging medium with which to highlight alternate conceptions or misconceptions of science and remediate these using inquiry- based teaching strategies.

2   Through the visualisation process captured on film, teachers can steer students' discussion so that the coherence of the scientific concept is compared with misconception(s), making this comparison more apparent and explicit.

3   The rethinking processes, generated by watching a movie followed by a post-movie discussion, provide students with another opportunity to ponder, evaluate, assess and reassess the validity of their scientific conceptions and in doing so, address any cognitive conflict retrospectively.

4   In addressing the alternative conceptions of science through dialogic and discourse-oriented forms of teaching within collaborative settings, teachers are teaching students the tools of scientific thinking themselves. Integral to these higher order thinking skills are argumentation, ethical thinking and informal reasoning (intuitive, rationalistic, emotional and moral) approaches that are increasingly important in the teaching and learning of science in recent years.

5   It may also be argued that rationalistic reasoning is not necessarily the superior form to other forms of reasoning such as intuitive or emotive because how we think is governed not only by our cognitive development but our emotional capacity to grasp and empathise, and relate to our previous experiences that are culturally conditioned and communally shaped since our childhood. Intuitive reasoning and emotive reasoning inevitably shape decisions which are primarily personal (although may affect immediate family circles) and integrally moral in nature.

6   In implementing effective science and faith values education, it is important to provide opportunities for reframing and shaping moral reasoning processes. The place for rationalistic and/or intuitive approaches in moral reasoning in a collaborative, open-ended setting (interacting with a popular medium) will have implications for educational endeavours in creating suitable science classroom environments for developing ethical reasoning and shaping a more holistic faith-value-integrated learning of life issues.

CONCLUSION

The instructional approach in this chapter acknowledges the need to align science curriculum design with cognitive and affective goals. It not only demonstrates a shift from a content-driven science approach to one inherently associated with its conceptual content. It also affirms that values, ethics, practices and perspectives of science are integral parts of science education. While values and beliefs have a cognitive dimension, values and attitudes are developed within an affective domain.

The use of movies as a medium of reasoning, evaluation and analysis serves as a tool for students' critical engagement with important issues existing in the societal domain. This instructional approach also highlights the relationship between the values inherent in society and the values embedded in science. It underlines the philosophy (UNESCO, 1991) suggested that the process of science curriculum development should focus on an effective value-oriented science curriculum that is strongly relevant and refreshingly engaging while emphasising the interdependency of science and technology, and their benefits to society. It also enhances accessibility of complex concepts and enables engagement on differing levels appropriate to the abilities of the student.

The approach advocated here is quite simple. Films, either in their entirety or presented as extracts, can initiate discussion through which the teacher can determine current levels of understanding of the scientific concepts and preconceptions. Often, this can be done reasonably informally through observation and conversation. You may wish to develop a brief quiz to look at these aspects to allow some form of baseline to be established, allowing focussed teaching that addresses genuine misconceptions without dwelling too long on those that may be presumed by the teachers beforehand. A follow-up session can revisit these issues, and perhaps even sections of the movie, and provide focussed input and further discussion. Of particular importance in this second phase are the cultural and religious assumptions that can lead to misconceptions. Here, identified alternative presentations from scholars or religious teachers that are congruent with the scientific understanding required can be introduced. There are many examples of this elsewhere in this book. These can challenge positions and provide the opportunity for students to think differently without feeling the need to dismiss either their faith background or the scientific material presented.

Currently, there is a paucity of teaching and learning activities for teaching socio-scientific issues with reference to addressing misconceptions in science as well as ethical reasoning in science education. To address this need, the following two resources have been specially written for secondary school students (14–17 years old) in Western Australia:

Dawson, V. & Carson, K. (2014). *Climate change and the greenhouse effect*. Perth: University of Western Australia.
Yap, S.F. (2016). (E-book). *Science at the movies – remediating the misconceptions*. Perth: SF Publications.

It is hoped that, in some way, this chapter will contribute towards the development trajectory of science teachers' teaching of socio-scientific issues and, in turn, enhance student-centred learning, improve scientific literacy, cultivate ethical reasoning, foster values education as well as strategically develop responsible, active citizenship among young people.

REFERENCES

Australian Academy of Science. (2010). *The science of climate change. Questions and answers.* Canberra: Author.
Dawson, V. (2015). Western Australian high school students' understanding about the socio-scientific issue of climate change, *International Journal of Science Education* 37(7), 1024–1043.
Dawson, V. & Carson, K. (2014). *Climate change and the greenhouse effect*. Perth: University of Western Australia. Retrieved from http://spice.wa.edu.au/ resource/gse.
Eastwood, J.L., Schlegel, W.M. & Cook, K.L. (2011). Effects of an inter-disciplinary program on students' reasoning with socio-scientific issues and perceptions of their learning experiences. In T.D. Sadler (Ed.). *Socio-scientific issues in the classroom*. Dordrecht: Kluwer Academic Press.
Heywood, D. (2015). A crisis of meaning: promoting new directions in science education, *Cultural Studies of Science Education* 10, 505–514.
Hodson, D. (2010). Science education as a call to action, *Canadian Journal of Science Mathematics and Technology Education* 10(3), 197–206.
Kolsto, S.D. (2001). Scientific literacy for citizenship: tools for dealing with the science dimension of controversial socio-scientific issues, *Science Education* 85, 291–310.

Latour, B. (2005). *Reassembling the social: an introduction to actor–network theory.* Oxford: Oxford University Press.

Levinson, R. (2014). Practice and theory of socio-scientific issues: an authentic model?, *Studies in Science Education* 49(1), 99–116.

McClelland, R.T. (2010). Moral education: too little, too late?, *Christian Scholar's Review* 39(4), 439–456.

Murphy, C. (2015). Reconceptualising the learning and teaching of scientific concepts. In *The Future of Learning Science: What's in it for the learner?* Zurich: Springer International Publishing.

National Research Council (2012). Eds. S.R. Singer, N.R. Nielsen & H.A. Schweingruber *Committee on the status, contributions and future directions of discipline-based education research, board on science education, division of behaviour and social sciences and education.* Washington, DC: National Academic Press.

Reinfried, S. & Tempelmann, S. (2014). The impact of secondary school students' preconceptions on the evolution of their mental models of the greenhouse effect and global warming, *International Journal of Science Education* 36(2), 304–333.

Sadler, T.D. (2011). Situating socio-scientific issues in classrooms as a means of achieving goals of science education. In T.D. Sadler (Ed.). *Socio-scientific issues in science classrooms: teaching, learning and research.* Dordrecht: Springer.

Sampson, V., Simon, S., Amos, R. & Evagorou, M. (2011). Metalogue: engaging students in scientific and socio-scientific argumentation. In T.D. Sadler (Ed.). *Socio-scientific issues in the classroom.* Dordrecht: Kluwer Academic Press.

Santos, W.L.P. (2009). Scientific literacy: a Frierean perspective as a radical view of humanistic science education, *Science Education* 93, 361–382.

Storksdieck, M. (2016). Critical information literacy as core-skill for lifelong STEM learning in the 21st century: reflections on the desirability and feasibility for widespread science media education, *Cultural Studies of Science Education* 11, 167–182.

Taber, K.S. (2014). *Student thinking and learning in science: perspective on the nature and development of learners' ideas.* New York: Routledge.

UNESCO. (1991). *Values and ethics and the Science and Technology Curriculum: a Sourcebook.* Bangkok: UNESCO-PROAP.

Yap, S.F. (2012). Developing, implementing and evaluating the use of ethical frameworks in teaching bioethics in a year 10 biotechnology program. [Unpublished PhD thesis]

Yap, S.F. (2013). *Classroom teaching strategies in bioethics education: promoting ethical thinking and reasoning in the middle school years.* Perth: SF Publications.

Yap, S.F. (2016). (E-book). *Science at the movies – remediating the misconceptions.* Perth: SF Publications.

Yap, S.F. & Dawson, V. (2014). The use of ethical frameworks for implementing science as a human endeavour in year 10 biology, *Teaching Science Journal* 60(4), 17–33.

CHAPTER 13

BEYOND EXPERIMENTATION

TEACHING A BROADER MODEL OF WHAT SCIENTISTS DO

Richard Brock

AIMS OF THE CHAPTER

- To introduce a broader model of the work of scientists that goes beyond an understanding of scientific practice as only conducting experiments.
- To introduce a range of activities that may be used in the classroom to model the work of scientists.

STUDENTS' UNDERSTANDING OF THE RELATIONSHIP BETWEEN SCIENCE AND RELIGION

Students tend to assume that the science and religious education classrooms are contrasting spaces, where different kinds of knowledge claim are made and differing levels of authority exist (Billingsley, Brock, Taber & Riga, 2016). Many students believe that science and religion conflict (Taber, Billingsley, Riga & Newdick, 2011) but this perception of difference is built on assumptions about the nature of science as both an academic discipline and a school subject. A large body of research has highlighted that students' interpretations of the nature of science differ from those suggested by philosophers of science (Deng, Chen, Tsai & Chai, 2011). However, defining the nature of science and demarcating it from other disciplines is a challenging task and a subject of ongoing debate (Pigliucci, 2013). The unresolved status of the nature of science presents a challenge for teachers who wish to define what science is and what it is not for the students in their classroom. Teachers and students will have preconceptions about what "doing science" means and what kinds of activity are appropriate for the science classroom. This chapter examines some of those assumptions and presents a range of suggested activities that might encourage both students and teachers to adopt a broader model of the nature of scientific activity.

SCHOOL SCIENCE

Students often make the assumption that "doing science" must involve doing practical activities (Keeley, 2014, p. 1). Practical work is an important part of the science student's experience in school for a number of reasons. First, in doing practical work, students learn experimental techniques and skills related to data presentation and analysis. Second, the empirical data gathered may be used to support the validity of knowledge claims being taught. Third, students typically enjoy carrying out practical work and the activities can increase students' interest in and motivation to study science. Fourth, it can be argued students learn general skills from the tasks such as working in groups, following instructions carefully and learning to problem solve, among others. However, scientific inquiry is not always experimental (Hodson, 1993) and a number of other routes to coming to know about the world are observed in the work scientists carry out. For example, knowledge may be generated through thought experiments or as the outcome of debate. The argument in this chapter is not intended to be a critique of the practical work that is already routinely carried out in the classroom. Instead, the aim is to highlight that carrying out experimental work is only part of the work of scientists. A number of activities are suggested that might help students develop a broader understanding of what "doing science" means.

School science differs from scientists' science (Izquierdo-Aymerich & Adúriz-Bravo, 2003) as the activities have different goals and methods. It wouldn't make sense to assume that the goal of the science classroom was to uncover or to test novel scientific knowledge. Hodson (1988) suggested a distinction between learning science (the propositional content of the discipline), learning about science (learning about the nature of the discipline) and doing science (gaining expertise in using the methods of science). The practical activities carried out in school science are, in some cases, explicitly or implicitly presented as models of the practice of scientists. However, it may be that the activities carried out in a typical classroom do not present a broad representation of how scientists develop knowledge. Therefore, this chapter sets out to propose some activities that represent some of the work scientists engage in beyond the laboratory that contributes to the generation of knowledge.

WHAT DO SCIENTISTS DO?

When students are asked to draw a scientist, a common representation involves a person in a white coat in a laboratory surrounded by practical equipment (Chambers, 1983). However, the reality of the kind of work scientists do is more complicated than this view presents. Although carrying out experiments is an important part of scientific work, scientists engage in other activities that assist in knowledge generation. One group of scientists, theoretical scientists, do scientific work by proposing novel theoretical models and hypotheses. Although ideas generated theoretically tend to require repeated empirical testing before they become part of accepted scientific knowledge, the work theoretical scientists do in generating propositions is no less doing science than the experimental verification work done by their colleagues. The tasks of data analysis and the design of novel experiments are also part of the activities of scientists. Another facet of scientists' work beyond the laboratory comprises the activities of collaborating, critiquing and arguing that lead to the construction of consensual ideas. Scientists develop ideas by engaging with the criticisms of peers and developing persuasive arguments. In the classroom, this aspect of scientific work is often marginalised as the context of school science is largely focused on developing students' understanding of a consensual body of scientific concepts. The next sections discuss these ideas in greater detail and outline some activities that may be used in the classroom to introduce students to some less well-known ways of doing science.

Non-experimental ways to do science in school

THINKING ABOUT WHAT DOING SCIENCE MEANS

As has been suggested earlier in this chapter, students may perceive the activity of science as largely related to what scientists do in the laboratory. In order to broaden students' perceptions of the types of activity that scientists engage in, the card-sorting activity below has been adapted from an activity developed by Keith Taber (2007, p. 38). The activity presents students with a set of cards labelled with an activity that some scientists might do:

- Collecting data with practical equipment
- Building practical equipment
- Mending broken practical equipment
- Giving presentations
- Arguing with colleagues
- Critiquing colleagues' papers
- Giving presentations at a conference
- Sitting and thinking
- Teaching students
- Watching television
- Reading fiction
- Going for walk
- Playing sport

Students, working in groups, would be asked to sort these activities along a continuum, which runs from doing science to not doing science. Once they have completed this task, they should develop a set of criteria for which activities count as doing science and which do not. These criteria can then be shared between groups and discussed.

THOUGHT EXPERIMENTS AS A WAY OF DOING SCIENCE

A thought experiment is a mental simulation of a scenario constructed to investigate a particular idea or phenomenon. A well-known example is the scenario proposed by Galileo:

- Imagine two objects of different mass in free fall. Do they fall at different rates? Now imagine that a light rod joins the two objects. How is their motion altered?

It has been argued that thought experiments are under-represented in descriptions of the history of science and Winchester (1990) notes that thought experiments are rarely set as activities in textbooks. Although a number of thought experiments are found in the work of physicists, they are less common in biologists' and chemists' writing. However, it is possible to imagine a number of examples that could stimulate learning in the classroom, for example:

- Imagine if a griffin, a creature with the body of lion and the head and wings of an eagle, were discovered. How would a taxonomist decide what class of organism it was?

▨   What would the world be like if Van der Waals forces stopped acting?

▨   If the woolly mammoth were re-introduced into an ecosystem in small numbers, what consequences might result?

▨   Is it possible for a completely unreactive substance to exist?

Introducing these kinds of thought experiment has a number of potential benefits in the classroom. First, they emphasise that scientific work does not have to be experimental. This observation could prompt a discussion of how knowledge claims are justified in science. For example, a debate could spring from the question: in the interval between Einstein's proposition of special relativity from thought experiments and its experimental verification, was the theory scientific knowledge? Second, thought experiments can be a useful stimulus for practising the skills of academic debate and also for raising ideas about the manner in which scientific consensus is reached. Third, thought experiments can be a prompt for demonstrating and teaching cognitive skills such as visualisation and mental modelling.

Thought experiments might work well as starters or plenaries as they are provocative and stimulate interest but also require creative thought that goes beyond the taught material. A typical approach to using thought experiments might be to set the problem and require students to think about the case individually for a few minutes. It may be useful to introduce students to a couple of techniques to support their thinking such as imagining a single variable in the situation were set to an extreme value (for example, if one of the masses in Galileo's thought experiment were much larger than the other) or finding an analogous case with which they are familiar (for example, likening the impact of mammoths to that of elephants). After an opportunity to think individually, allow the students to share their perceptions of what will occur with their peers and emphasise the significance of attempting to justify their perceptions. It may be engaging in some cases if you, as the teacher, indicate that you don't know the "right" answer to the case but model your own thinking in attempting to reach the best possible answer.

DOING SCIENCE IN THE CONTEXT OF DISCOVERY – MOMENTS OF INSIGHT AS A WAY OF DOING SCIENCE

A distinction is sometimes drawn between the context of discovery and the context of justification (Reichenbach, 1938), that is, there is a difference between the processes used to conceive a theory or model and those used to subsequently validate and support it. In the science classroom, there is a focus on replicating the context of justification through the use of practical work to justify theoretical claims. It is much more challenging to allow students to experience the processes that occur in the context of discovery. In the context of discovery, a scientist may have experienced a moment of insight, that is, the sudden conscious awareness of the links between concepts, that arrives with little conscious control (Brock, 2015). Moments of scientific insight can be highly motivating for scientists and there are reports that indicate students may also experience moments of sudden developments in conceptual understanding in the classroom. The nature of school science may lead students to believe that science is a subject that requires only the formulaic application of methods to problems. This would seem to be an impoverished model, which is likely to negatively affect students' interest and motivation to study the subject. Allowing students to experience moments of sudden clarity may both be motivating and represent the importance of creative thought in scientific practice.

It is untenable to imagine that students can be expected to experience conceptual revolutions every time they encounter a new concept on the curriculum. For example, it is not realistic to expect students to develop Newton's laws in a moment of inspiration. However, it may benefit students if they become aware of, and even occasionally experience something like, the processes that scientists experience in the context of discovery. One approach is to introduce students to reports of scientists' moments of insight. These may present a more human and engaging model of science rather than one in which scientists follow formulaic rules to discover new ideas. The examples in the list below might act as useful models for students (more examples can be found in Irvine, 2015):

- Kekulé's insight into the structure of benzene following a dream.
- Feynman's description of his sudden understanding of the superfluidity of helium.
- Einstein's advance in thinking about relativity while talking to his friend, Michele Besso.
- Loewi's experiments on nerve conduction that developed from undecipherable notes written down after a dream.
- Tesla's insight into the design of a direct current generator achieved while walking, reciting a stanza from a play.

While it is useful to highlight to students that there are historical cases of scientists' ideas advancing without doing empirical science, students might also be supported to experience the context of discovery for themselves. This is a challenging undertaking and moments of insight cannot be guaranteed to occur in all students. However, it might be motivating to occasionally set students the type of problem that might lead to a moment of insight (Brock, 2015). For example, books such as *Thinking Physics* (Epstein, 2009) and *The Flying Circus of Physics* (Walker, 2011) list puzzling physics questions that may cause students to experience moments of insight. These kinds of question typically involve skills such as the development of mental simulations or the reformulation of the problem into a simpler case. A couple of sample, potentially insight-provoking questions are listed below:

- An ice cube floats in a glass of water filled to the brim. Will the glass overflow as the ice cube melts?
- A helium balloon floats in a car travelling at constant velocity. If the car brakes, which way will the balloon move?

Setting these kinds of problem could lead to a discussion about whether the knowledge developed in a moment of insight would count as scientific knowledge and therefore if theoretical scientists can be considered to be doing science.

DATA ANALYSIS AS A WAY OF DOING SCIENCE

The history of science contains a number of examples of scientists whose work involved the analysis of data, rather than its collection. For example, Johanes Kepler was employed to analyse the astronomical data collected by Tycho Brahe (Ferguson, 2002) and Watson and Crick's discovery of the structure of DNA used data extracted from an X-ray diffraction pattern collected in practical work carried out by Rosalind Franklin (McElheny, 2004). Data analysis activities may be preferred where a particular experimental activity is not practical due to cost, time or safety constraints. For example, it is unlikely to be commonly practicable for students to collect their own data on the absorption spectra of galaxies in order to calculate red shifts and using a pre-existing data set is likely to be preferable. Data analysis activities can be a useful way of introducing the subjective nature of the interpretation of some kinds of data set. For example, consider the constructed data below concerning the relationship between students' performance on a test and the duration of sleep they experienced the night before the assessment (Table 13.1).

Students working in groups could be asked to describe the conclusion they would draw from the data and then discuss their decision with other groups. This activity could lead to a discussion of the nature of uncertainties in data and an examination of the criteria that might lead to a consensus conclusion for the experiment. An alternative to using constructed data is to subject freely available data sets to secondary analysis. A number of sources of such data are available:

■   The United States National Oceanic and Atmospheric Administration has a number of classroom ready data sets related to climate change and aquatic ecosystems: http://www.noaa.gov/resource-collections/data-resources-for-educators.
■   The TinkerPlots website lists a number of data activities including an analysis of 100 m sprint times and an exercise on the distribution of fish lengths: http://www.tinkerplots.com/activities/data-analysis-and-modeling-activities.
■   The NASA website lists a number of lesson plans that encourage students to use NASA data sets: http://mynasadata.larc.nasa.gov/lesson-plans/multi-day-lesson-plans/.
■   The Natural History Museum makes available a large amount of data, which could be used to develop lesson plans: http://data.nhm.ac.uk.

One approach to data analysis that reflects the work of scientists is to allow students to develop models that generate predictions. For example, data sets related to global average temperature change can be found on the United Kingdom's Meteorological Office website (http://www.metoffice.gov.uk/hadobs/hadcrut4/data/current/download.html). Students can import this data into a graph-drawing package, such as Microsoft Excel, and plot the change in temperature over time. Excel allows the students to attempt to fit different types of line of best fit to the data and so produce different predictions for the temperature in five, ten

■ Table 13.1

Test score (%)	Hours of sleep experienced the night before the test
98	9
75	9
72	8
65	7
45	9.5
12	8

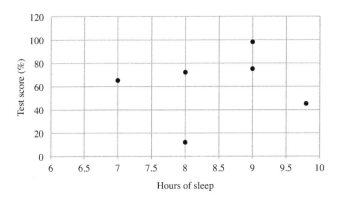

Figure 13.1

or a hundred years. A slightly different approach might be to give the students a data set for temperature change in the past and set them the challenge of producing the best prediction of the current average global temperature. Students can then be encouraged to compare their models and reflect on the challenge of developing mathematical models to fit empirical data.

DESIGNING EXPERIMENTS AS A WAY OF DOING SCIENCE

Before experimental work can be carried out, a significant task for scientists is to develop experimental methods that can test hypotheses or explore novel phenomena. For example, Newton predicted that the Earth's density is five times greater than that of Jupiter and suggested that this claim could be supported by data derived from measuring the deviation of a plumb line close to a mountain or by measuring the attractive force between two spheres (Lauginie, 2007). Newton doubted whether these methods were feasible and several iterations of approach by Bouguer, Maskelyne, Hutton, Michell and Cavendish were required to refine the techniques and to develop increasingly precise measurements (Lauginie, 2007). The history of the measurement of the Universal Gravitational Constant might act as a useful example for the manner in which experimental design is a creative and iterative process in the work of scientists.

One approach to demonstrating the ingenuity of experimental designers is to set students the challenge of designing approaches that replicate well-known experiments. For example, depending on the age, ability and prior knowledge of students, some of the tasks in the list below might present an interesting challenge.

Design an experiment to:

▨ Show that a ring is made of pure gold (cf. Archimedes' displacement method).
▨ Show that oxygen combines with materials on combustion (cf. Lavoisier's synthesis of water over mercury).
▨ Measure the charge on an electron (cf. Millikan's oil drop experiment).
▨ Show diseases are spread by microorganisms (cf. Pasteur's broth experiments).
▨ Measure the circumference of the Earth (cf. Eratosthenes' calculation).

Once students have devised their own approaches, they can be compared and contrasted with the historical versions of these experiments. Alternatively, students could design experiments to answer open questions that relate to their own experiences, for example:

▓ Is there a link between the consumption of caffeinated drinks and test performance?
▓ How does the consumption of different sports drinks impact athletic performance?
▓ Which hair gels are most effective in maintaining a hairstyle?
▓ Does holding a car's remote key fob next to your head increase its range?

Addressing such questions would require students to address the issue of how variables such as "test performance" or "most effective" could be defined. Once students have designed experimental approaches, they might present their ideas to the class and their peers could discuss the effectiveness of the different approaches across a number of facets:

▓ Will the method answer the question?
▓ Is it a valid approach, that is, are there other factors that could affect the outcome?
▓ Is it practical to carry out the approach this way?

This type of approach might not only encourage students to reflect critically on experimental approaches, but also help students to begin to develop an appreciation of the skill of experimental design as a way of doing science.

CREATING A META-ANALYSIS AS A WAY OF DOING SCIENCE

Students will doubtless be aware of the contradictory scientific claims that appear in the media, for example:

▓ "Study: Eggs are nearly as bad for your arteries as cigarettes" (Fung, 2012)
▓ "Eggs are no longer considered a health hazard – in fact, they are incredibly good for you" (Dillner, 2015)

Articles such as these may be used to provoke a discussion of the consensual nature of scientific knowledge claims. To further this debate, students could be given a set of cards printed with a range of topics such as: the mass of an electron, the chemical reaction for photosynthesis, the best diet for a healthy life, the harmfulness of cigarettes, the harmfulness of bacon etc. The students can then be asked to form a continuum based on the level of agreement they believe exists about these statements in the scientific community. This activity could lead onto a discussion of the nature of processes that lead to the development of consensus in science, for example discussions at conferences and the process of peer review.

This discussion may be followed by an introduction to the process of systematic review or meta-analysis, that is, the process of collecting all existing data on a particular question and, by reflecting transparently on the kind of methods and analyses used, coming to a conclusion on the issue (Goldacre, 2012). Constructing systematic reviews is a challenging process and involves careful scientific work. This process can be modelled in the classroom in the following approach. Choose a question on which a number of contradictory studies exist, for example:

Table 13.2

Authors of study	
Conclusion related to question	
How strong is the description of the effect?	
Is the sample appropriate?	
How well are extraneous variables controlled?	
Comments on the method used (e.g. criticisms of technique and potential sources of bias)	

- Are vegetarian diets healthier than ones that include meat?
- Are mobile phone masts dangerous?
- Is taurine, which is found in energy drinks, harmful?

You may wish to pre-select and edit a number of studies to ensure that they contain information that is at an appropriate level for your students. For example, you might summarise the abstract of a paper to give a few details on the method and conclusions reached. Alternatively, you may choose to let students find their own studies on the Internet and make their own choices about criteria for inclusion or exclusion. It will be helpful to create some kind of structure for students to collate the information from the studies to focus their attention onto key features, such as that found in Table 13.2.

After constructing a summary of the findings of a number of studies, the students should be encouraged to draw a conclusion related to the initial question, possibly describing the level of certainty of their claim. Then students might compare their findings with others and reflect on why their conclusions agreed or differed. This kind of activity may allow students to develop an understanding of the complexity of reaching definitive answers to some kinds of scientific question and therefore the important scientific work of data synthesis.

DEBATING AND REACHING A CRITICAL CONSENSUS AS A WAY OF DOING SCIENCE

Part of the work of scientists is to present a persuasive case for their work such that it is accepted by other members of the scientific community. However, it has been observed that some science classrooms may lack opportunities for students to develop the skills of proposing and defending scientific arguments (Jiménez-Aleixandre, Bugallo-Rodríguez & Duschl, 2000). One approach to understanding how scientific argument proceeds is to examine the nature of historical scientific debates, such as those between proponents of the positions listed below:

- Rutherford's and Thompson's model of the atom
- The steady state and big bang theories

■ The miasma and germ theories of the spread of disease
■ Vibration theory and lock and key theory of smell

For example, the mechanism of the detection of smell is an unresolved question and therefore presents an authentically open problem for students to consider. Students might be divided into two groups to research the opposing positions and then attempt to persuade their peers, before a vote is taken to see which side was the most persuasive. In the three other cases listed above, a generally accepted consensus position exists and the cases may be usefully studied as historical examples. Students might produce an essay or a poster describing the claims made by proponents of the two views and describe how the dominant side came to general acceptance.

A different approach for modelling the discursive nature of the scientific process is to simulate a scientific conference in the classroom. For example, groups of students could carry out the same practical or be given existing data collected from an experiment. Using pre-prepared data has the advantage of allowing you to construct contradictions between different data sets that can become discussion points at the conference. In order to facilitate the discussion of methodological issues, a description of the methods that would have been used to collect the data should be included. The groups of students would be asked to develop their own interpretation of their data set and present their conclusions to their peers, either in the form of a poster or as an oral presentation. As a final activity the students could be encouraged to discuss which interpretation of the data they felt was the strongest and to reflect on what factors they felt contributed to a strong argument. They might be encouraged to consider how social processes influenced the development of a consensus. Students may need support to develop a nuanced approach to understanding interpretations of data, and that there is not always a single correct interpretation of certain kinds of data.

CONCLUSION

Students may develop a model of scientific activity that does not reflect the work of scientists. This is unsurprising as students are likely to extrapolate their perceptions of the activities of scientists from their classroom experiences and hence may develop a partial model of what it means to engage in scientific work. Not only do some school science practicals differ from the kind of experiments scientists carry out, but at least part of scientists' work does not involve practical work and even experimental scientists engage in significant work beyond the laboratory. The ideas suggested in this chapter are intended as possible additions to lessons to give students a broader image of what it means to be a scientist. Carrying out the activities proposed might act as a starting point for discussions about the nature of scientific practices and the processes by which science generates knowledge claims. It is hoped that by challenging students' perceptions of the work of scientists they may begin to develop a more nuanced model of the nature of science. Such an understanding might help students to gain insight into the kinds of knowledge claim made in science and how they are supported by evidence from practical work and other sources, such as thought experiments. Students who have a greater insight into the diversity of practices that develop knowledge claims in science will be better placed to understand the relationship between science and other disciplines, such as religious studies. Students are reported as perceiving the science classroom as a space in which objective or factual claims are reported (Billingsley et al., 2016); the activities suggested above may present a useful means by which to broaden students' interpretations of what it means to do science.

REFERENCES

Billingsley, B., Brock, R., Taber, K. S. & Riga, F. (2016). How students view the boundaries between their science and religious education concerning the origins of life and the universe. *Science Education, 100*(3), 459–482.

Brock, R. (2015). Intuition and insight: two concepts that illuminate the tacit in science education. *Studies in Science Education, 51*(2), 127–167.

Chambers, D. (1983). Stereotypic images of the scientist: the draw-a-scientist test. *Science Education, 67*(2), 255–265.

Deng, F., Chen, D. T., Tsai, C. C. & Chai, C. S. (2011). Students' views of the nature of science: a critical review of research. *Science Education, 95*(6), 961–999.

Dillner, L. (2015, March 29). Should I eat more eggs? *Guardian*. Retrieved from: https://www. theguardian.com/lifeandstyle/2015/mar/29/should-i-eat-more-eggs.

Epstein, L. C. (2009). *Thinking Physics* (3rd ed.). San Francisco, CA: Insight Press.

Ferguson, K. (2002). *The Nobleman and His Housedog: Tycho Brahe and Johannes Kepler – The Strange Partnership That Revolutionised Science*. London: Headline Review.

Fung, B. (2012, August 14). Study: eggs are nearly as bad for your arteries as cigarettes. *The Atlantic*. Retrieved from: http://www.theatlantic.com/health/ archive/2012/08/study-eggs-are-nearly-as-bad-for-your-arteries-as-cigarettes/261091/.

Goldacre, B. (2012). *Bad Pharma*. London: Fourth Estate.

Hodson, D. (1988). Experiments in science and science teaching. *Educational Philosophy and Theory, 20*(2), 53–66.

Hodson, D. (1993). Re-thinking old ways: towards a more critical approach to practical work in school science. *Studies in Science Education, 22*(1), 85–142.

Irvine, W. B. (2015). *Aha!: The Moments of Insight that Shape our World*. Oxford: Oxford University Press.

Izquierdo-Aymerich, M., & Adúriz-Bravo, A. (2003). Epistemological foundations of school science. *Science & Education, 12*(1), 27–43.

Jiménez-Aleixandre, M. P., Bugallo-Rodríguez, A. & Duschl, R. A. (2000). "Doing the lesson" or "doing science": argument in high school genetics. *Science Education, 84*(6), 757–792.

Keeley, P. (2014). *What Are They Thinking?* Arlington, VA: National Science Teachers Association Press.

Lauginie, P. (2007). Weighing the earth, weighing the worlds. From Cavendish to modern undergraduate demonstrations. In P. Heering & D. Osewold (Eds.), *Constructing Scientific Understanding Through Contextual Teaching* (pp. 119–148). Berlin: Frank & Timme.

McElheny, V. K. (2004). *Watson and DNA: Making a Scientific Revolution*. New York: Basic Books.

Pigliucci, M. (2013). The demarcation problem. A (belated) response to Laudan. In M. Pigliucci & M. Boudry (Eds.), *Philosophy of Pseudoscience* (pp. 9–28). Chicago, IL: University of Chicago Press.

Reichenbach, H. (1938). *Experience and Prediction. An Analysis of the Foundations and the Structure of Knowledge*. Chicago, IL: University of Chicago Press.

Taber, K. S. (2007). *Enriching School Science for the Gifted Learner*. London: Gatsby Science Enhancement Programme.

Taber, K. S., Billingsley, B., Riga, F. & Newdick, H. (2011). To what extent do pupils perceive science to be inconsistent with religious faith? An exploratory survey of 13–14 year-old English pupils. *Science Education International, 22*(2), 99–118.

Walker, J. (2011). *The Flying Circus of Physics*. Hoboken, NJ: John Wiley & Sons, Inc.

Winchester, I. (1990). Thought experiments and conceptual revision. *Studies in Philosophy and Education, 10*(1), 73–80.

14 GENES, DETERMINISM AND HUMAN IMPROVEMENT

John Bryant[1]

AIMS OF THE CHAPTER

- To present that there are interactions between "nature and nurture" in genes.
- To argue that there is evidence that religious experiences can lead to behavioural changes.

INTRODUCTION – GENES, CHROMOSOMES AND GENOMES

Before launching into the deep water of genetics, genetic determinism and genetic selection we need to be clear about some definitions, as follows.

DNA is the chemical substance that makes up our genes; it exists as linear "strings" of chemical building blocks called bases. There are only four types of base but the huge length of DNA molecules means that a *code* can be built into the linear arrangement of the bases. A *gene* is a specific tract within the linear array of bases and in a given gene, the code, i.e. the sequence of bases, provides a specific "recipe" (not a blueprint) that instructs the organism to make something. DNA molecules are organised as *chromosomes* and thus each chromosome is a linear array of genes, albeit tightly coiled to fit into the cell's *nucleus*. Each chromosome is therefore like a recipe book and our total chromosome set is like a small library of recipe books. We can also say that our chromosome set comprises all of our genes, i.e. our *genome*. Our genomes therefore contain all the recipes needed to build and run a human, at least at the physical level. Changes in the DNA code are called *mutations*[2] and some of these mutations cause biological malfunctions, including certain diseases. We need to distinguish between *recessive* mutations and *dominant* mutations. If a person possesses one copy of a recessive mutation, the mutation generally has no effect. It takes two copies (remembering that we have two sets of chromosomes, one maternal, one paternal) for the effect of the mutation to become apparent. By contrast, a single copy of a dominant mutation will have an effect.

We hear a lot about genes, often in relation to diseases and other pathological states but sometimes also in relation to features such as athletic prowess. We also hear a lot about genomes, the totality of genes that an individual possesses. Thus the UK's *100,000 Genomes Project* involves sequencing[3] the genomes of 70,000 people suffering from rare heritable diseases plus the genomes of 30,000 cancer patients and their cancerous cells. It is hoped that this will lead to the discovery of the specific genetic changes that cause disease (and we should note here that for many inherited diseases, we know this already, as will become apparent) and also to identifying those cancers which are caused by genetic changes within the cells of the patient. All this is very good and will certainly lead to better, more focussed treatments – indeed, for some conditions it has already done so. However, there is the danger that medicine will become "over-geneticised". Perhaps too much focus will be placed on genes or too much will be attributed to them, especially when we consider that factors such as social conditions and diet still play a large role in affecting a person's health. It is not an exaggeration to say that the postcode of a person's residence may be at least as informative about their health as are their genes. But, by the same token, that does not mean that we should ignore genetics: we need a balance.

NATURE AND NURTURE – EXAMPLES AND IDEAS

"We need a balance"; the words that ended the previous section are very relevant for the nature–nurture debate. The first point we should make is that genes regulate our physical make-up – the structure and metabolism of our cells, the organisation of our cells into tissues and organs, the minute-by-minute working of those tissues and organs and so on. We also understand that the minute-by-minute working of our body is responsive to a range of signals, both internal and external/environmental and that some of those responses involve regulating the activity of genes. For example, ingestion of food, especially carbo-hydrate-rich food, causes the pancreas to make and secrete insulin in order to regulate the amount of sugar in the blood. However, long-term over-eating, especially of sugary foods, damps down the insulin response which is why many obese people suffer from type-2 diabetes. On a more positive note, regular exercise leads to increases in activity of genes involved in muscle fibre development and muscle energy metabolism.

A very tragic example of nature–nurture interaction was the discovery made in respect of the children who had been kept in Romanian orphanages during the rule of Nicolae Ceauşescu in the 1980s. Although their basic needs had been met, these children were almost totally deprived of emotional warmth and ongoing human contact. Scans revealed that brain development had been badly affected, with actual holes in their brain structure. Further, many of these children were past the point at which these lesions could be completely reversed.[4] Similar, but much less dramatic effects have been reported elsewhere (including the UK) in which children who experience some degree of emotional deprivation show slight but significant changes in brain structure. There are also inevitably effects on behaviour.

At the population level, the average height of humans in most areas of the world has increased significantly since the beginning of the 20th century. However, this has not occurred because of widespread changes in our genes. It has been ascribed to two main factors, namely the decrease in the frequency of severe infectious diseases in childhood and the general improvement in nutrition. These factors thus act on some or all of the genes that affect our stature without affecting the structure of the genes themselves. By contrast, some changes at population level do involve changes in genes. It is very likely that the majority of those who read this chapter are lactose tolerant, i.e. they are able to digest lactose, the sugar that occurs in milk. This is because of a mutation which causes us to retain the ability to metabolise lactose after weaning. The prevalence of that mutation has increased very markedly in human populations that have kept animals and used their milk (and milk products) in their diet. Indeed, the mutation is now so prevalent that lactose intolerance in our society is quite rare. Nevertheless, we can still find human tribes that have not traditionally kept cattle or consumed milk/milk products and among whom lactose *intolerance* remains the norm after weaning. It is a classic example of natural selection at work.

I have presented these examples to show that even with genes that contribute to the structure, function and minute-by-minute activity of our bodily systems, there are interactions between "nature and nurture" and further that some of those interactions may be complex. The situation becomes even more complicated when we consider features such as personality, behaviour and intelligence. We should certainly expect genes to influence these features. They are all dependent on the brain and on its structure and working mechanisms. If the brain suffers traumatic damage, personality changes may ensue. On a less dramatic level, patterns of behaviour may change if brain biochemistry is disturbed, for example by alcohol. Further, genes obviously regulate the mechanisms by which neuronal connections ("brain wiring") are made but they cannot control which changes in wiring occur as we learn new things and have different experiences through life.

But how much do genes actually contribute? The first thing to note is that it is difficult to quantify these features and even with rigorous psychometric analysis it may be difficult to obtain data with a high level of reproducibility. Nevertheless, based on studies with identical and non-identical twins and using examples of "normal" upbringing together and upbringing in separate homes and families, we can come up with figures on the heritability of these features of human personhood. Different studies come up with different figures but the clear overall picture is that these features show a high degree of heritability of around 40–50%, but probably a little higher for personality.[5] This ties in with something we already knew (albeit at an anecdotal level): identical twins may, in some ways, be uncannily similar but they are not identical people. Thus genes are not the sole determining factors, as some genetic "essentialists" or determinists have claimed. This 40–50%+ level of heritability resides in contributions from a large number of genes. Further, with a small number of specific exceptions, we have not been able to discover what most of those genes actually do. Nevertheless, this "genetic element" is important when we consider what we can do with genes (as we discuss later).

The 40–50%+ heritability of behaviour, personality and intelligence leaves a lot of room for "nurture" but in this context what do we mean by this term? It can certainly embody experience and learning, both academic and social; in the latter context, there is a lot of evidence that what people (and especially women) learn, often subconsciously from their parents (especially mothers), has a major effect on their own parenting styles. This gives just one example of the many that could have been mentioned. However, there is a larger question to think about. Is it possible that spiritual influences may also affect behaviour and personality? There is certainly a lot of evidence that religious experiences can lead to clear behavioural changes and sometimes changes in personality traits too. As a Christian, I ascribe this to the activity of God. Further, even those who are sceptical about the possibility of a spiritual level of existence may still admit that whatever a particular religious experience actually entails, it nevertheless can influence behaviour.

GENES AND HUMAN IMPROVEMENT

The previous section is important in that it tells us that genes are not everything. We do not "simply dance" to the tune of DNA, as Richard Dawkins has written.[6] Nevertheless, since the late 19th century, there have been attempts to improve the human species by what effectively amounted to selective breeding, e.g. by sterilisation of those considered to have undesirable traits relating to behaviour, personality and intelligence or, in its milder form, discouraging such people from breeding while encouraging those considered more desirable to have more children. This is called *eugenics* (from the Greek *eu* – good, *genos* – birth) and was first proposed at the end of 19th century by Francis Galton, a cousin of Charles Darwin. Mention of eugenics leads us to think about the Nazi regime in Germany, which was certainly its most brutal practitioner. However, eugenic laws, usually involving forced sterilisations of women, existed in many European countries (but not the UK), in Canada and the USA in the first half of the 20th century. In Sweden, for example, the last sterilisation on eugenic grounds took place in the mid-1970s. In the USA, 60–70,000 women were sterilised on eugenic grounds between the 1920s and mid-1950s. Even more shocking is the fact that abortions and sterilisations were still being forced on Native American women as recently as 1978.

However, one programme in the USA has been described as "eugenics with a smiling face". In American Jewish communities (many of which are descended from the Ashkenazi Jews of Eastern Europe), Tay-Sachs disease (a severe neuro-degenerative condition causing death in early childhood) is common. It is recessive (see Introduction to this chapter); a child born to a couple both of whom have the Tay-Sachs mutation has a one-in-four chance of inheriting two copies of the gene and thus having the disease. Prior to the availability of genetic tests on embryos (see below), couples of whom both carried one copy of the mutation were discouraged from having children of their own (or even discouraged from marrying each other in some traditional communities). This has reduced very significantly the incidence of the disease among Americans Jews of Ashkenazi descent.[7]

GENES, EMBRYOS AND IDEAS OF PERFECTION

As mentioned in the first section of the chapter, some mutations are harmful and lead to the development of disease. Indeed, we know of several thousand disease conditions for which a genetic mutation is solely or largely responsible. A common example in the UK is cystic fibrosis: about one in 25 people among the white population of Britain has one mutated copy of the gene but does not have the disease because it is a recessive condition. People in this category are therefore *carriers* of the mutation. If two carriers have babies together, each baby has a one-in-four chance of inheriting two copies of the mutated gene and therefore having cystic fibrosis (as with Tay-Sachs disease, discussed above). For dominant mutations such as the one that causes Huntington's disease, the situation is different. Someone possessing the mutation is bound to develop the disease (Huntington's is a disease that usually develops in a person's 40s). Further, if a person with the mutation has babies with someone who does not, each baby has a 50:50 likelihood of inheriting the mutation.

For a large and increasing number of genetic diseases, the specific mutation has been identified and can be detected in a person's DNA. Alongside that, nearly 40 years of IVF have led to greatly increased skill in handling embryos. When we combine the two technologies together we have the possibility of testing human embryos, created by IVF, for the presence of particular genetic mutations. In the UK, this technique was first used in 1989 and in recent years has become available within the NHS. So how does it work? Imagine a couple who wish to have a baby but both of whom are from families in which cystic fibrosis has led to the deaths of several people in previous generations and who have a sibling with the disease. They are able, in the first instance, to have their own DNA checked to see if they are carriers of the mutation. Let us suppose that indeed they both *are* carriers. The one-in-four chance mentioned above applies to each baby that they might have. What is to be done? They can have babies via IVF with the added step of testing each embryo before it is implanted into the womb. This is called *pre-implantation genetic diagnosis* or PGD.[8] Only embryos without the cystic fibrosis mutation[9] will be used to start a pregnancy.[10]

So, what has happened here? First, the couple themselves will have babies who do not have cystic fibrosis. In the sense of being healthier, these babies are in some way *better* humans, humans who do not have a specific serious genetic condition. The corollary of this is that the birth of babies with that condition has been prevented; embryos with the mutant gene were not used to start a pregnancy and will eventually be disposed of.[11] Second, the couple have established a lineage that is free from cystic fibrosis (except in the rare event of the mutation re-appearing spontaneously in subsequent generations). It is, in the health sense, a lineage of better humans. But all this raises a question: *is it eugenics?*

In the UK, licences for testing particular genes in PGD are granted by the Human Fertility and Embryology Authority; currently the list of genes runs to several hundred,[12] many of which certainly cause very serious diseases and on those grounds their presence on the list is justified. But this raises another issue under the umbrella of the eugenics question posed above: how serious does a genetic condition have to be for it to be included in the HFEA list? I will use one example to illustrate the problem. Achondroplasia is a condition that causes skeletal abnormalities and, in particular, short stature. The mutation is dominant so that if someone with achondroplasia has babies with someone who does not have it, each baby has a 50:50 chance of inheriting the condition (as described earlier for Huntington's disease). The gene is on the HFEA's list but this raises much disquiet. People with achondroplasia experience some limitations because of their short stature but other than that can lead full lives and enjoy success in their careers. For example, Tom Shakespeare, a well-known advocate for disability rights and who has achondroplasia, is a professor in the Medical School at the University of East Anglia in Norwich. He expresses the view (and is not alone in doing so) that if we use PGD to discriminate against conditions such as achondroplasia then we are narrowing the idea of what we regard as normal or acceptable[13] and that in such cases, use of PGD becomes an attempt to seek an idea of "perfection". This then leads back to our question: *is this eugenics?*

The question will become harder to answer as our knowledge of genetics increases. Sequencing techniques have become so much faster and genomic analysis so much more sophisticated that our knowledge is expanding at an astonishing rate. While this is certainly good in relation to understanding and treating genetic diseases, it will also raise more issues of the type we have just discussed.

I want to discuss one more case relating to medicine before widening the debate. The first child born to Jack and Lisa Nash in Denver, Colorado, suffered from Fanconi anaemia. This is a severe recessive genetic condition that leads to death in childhood or in the teenage years. Like Tay-Sachs disease, it is more common in people of Ashkenazi

Jewish heritage than in other groups (although rarer than Tay-Sachs). The Nashes did not know they were genetic carriers[14] of the Fanconi mutation until Molly was born. Molly could be cured by a stem cell donation from a Fanconi-free, immune-compatible donor. After much searching, the Nashes only option was to undergo IVF with PGD. The latter was not only for avoiding Fanconi but also for selecting a compatible stem cell donor. We note then, that some Fanconi-free ("healthy") embryos were rejected. After several attempts, baby Adam was born and stem cells from the umbilical cord were infused into Molly, who was by then eight years old and very sick. This was successful and Molly's life was saved; she is now (in 2017) 23 years old. At no point was Adam required to donate stem cells from his bone marrow, although we surmise that it might have happened had the first transplant not been successful.

Despite this success, considerable disquiet was expressed about this case.[15] Not only were there issues relating to discarding embryos but some people said that Adam had been conceived only to save his sister – he was a commodity. I personally do not accept that view but neither do I accept the view that he is a "better" human because he saved his sister; he had no choice in the matter.[16] One final point needs to be made in relation to the eugenics theme. Molly's bone marrow works properly because the stem cells came from Adam and have his genes. However, Molly's own genome still has two copies of the Fanconi mutation; she will pass one or other of these to any children she may have.

Because of our knowledge of the human genome there are now many genes for which we could test via IVF-PGD, including a large number that regulate traits that are not directly related to disease conditions. I started to write this while the Olympic Games were happening in Rio; indeed the temptation to leave my desk to watch the action on TV was sometimes very strong! We have a great tendency to put our successful sportsmen and sportswomen on a pedestal. Indeed, they are often called "heroes" as if they were better humans. But let us look at just one sport-based example concerning what might be achieved by embryo selection. In our muscles, most of us have about a 50:50 mix of fast- and slow-twitch fibres. This is a feature under genetic control and some variants of the relevant gene lead to an over-abundance of fast-twitch fibres – a very good trait for sprinting and explosive events – while another variant gives an over-abundance of slow-twitch fibres – a very good trait for endurance events such as long-distance running.[17] I like to joke that Mo Farah and I (as a former county-level long-distance runner) have at least one thing in common, namely the "slow-twitch" gene. And further, this is a genetic trait that could be tested for in IVF-PGD, selecting for embryos that have at least a potential to be good athletes.[18] Would we want to?

Using sport as an example opens the door to a much wider discussion. Should we be allowed to select embryos in respect of appearance (not entirely straightforward but becoming possible for some traits)? Suppose we eventually pin down some of those genes that each make a small contribution to intelligence, behaviour and personality, would it be ethical to select embryos so as to have children who may have slight advantage over others? At present, selecting for aspects of these features is just a theoretical possibility (with a handful of exceptions),[19] but may well not remain so. In an article written ten years ago, the journalist and commentator Madeleine Bunting imagined a situation in the year 2031 in which use of genetic and pharmacological interventions was readily available to those who could afford them.[20] Big questions are raised throughout the article. If we used our knowledge in this way, would we be practising eugenics or creating better humans? What sort of society would we be creating? What would it mean for our humanity? Would it be an ethical use of scientific and medical knowledge? And I will add a question especially for those of us with a religious faith: from where do we get our ethical guidance?

CONCLUDING REMARKS

In this chapter, I have tried to show how advances in genetics have given parents choices in respect of genes that affect their children's health. Even if we limit our discussions to just this one medical area, there are those, mainly from among the Roman Catholic and conservative evangelical faith communities, who oppose these developments. However, most of us give a cautious welcome to these techniques provided they are used wisely and ethically. But then there are the possibilities of using the techniques for a much wider range of traits, as discussed immediately above. We need to make up our mind on this issue. There are certainly some, including the moral philosophers John Harris and Julian Savulescu who would welcome such developments and indeed believe that we should embrace them.[21] However, many (I include myself here) do not support the widening of embryo selection to non-medical areas.

Finally, I am aware that I have not mentioned *direct* intervention in an embryo's genes, in the forms of genetic modification and genome editing. Genetic intervention by these methods is certainly possible but needs a chapter of its own to do it justice.[22] However I invite our readers to keep an eye out for developments in the application of these techniques, and especially genome editing, with human embryos.

NOTES

1. Emeritus Professor of Cell and Molecular Biology, University of Exeter; Bioethics Advisor, Higher Education Academy; Past-President, Society for Experimental Biology; Former Chair, Christians in Science

2. Note the word *mutation* is not in itself sinister, even though it is often used in a sinister way. It is simply derived from the Latin word for change

3. Sequencing means determining the order of the DNA bases in DNA molecules

4. There is a good summary here: Bardin J. (2012) *Social deprivation hurts child brain development, study finds.* http://articles.latimes.com/2012/jul/24/science/la-sci-orphan-brains-20120724

5. Strictly, heritability in this context means the extent to which variance in a particular feature in a population can be ascribed to genes. However, in practice it probably makes very little difference if we simply say that genetic effects contribute 40–50% to development of personality.

   See Nuffield Council on Bioethics (2002) *Genetics and Human Behaviour: the Ethical Context,* Nuffield Council, London; Willmott C. (2016) *Biological Determinism, Free Will and Moral Responsibility.* Springer, Cham, Switzerland

6. Dawkins R. (1995) *River Out of Eden*, Weidenfeld & Nicolson, London

7. A fuller version of this can be found in Bryant J. (2013) *Beyond Human?* Lion, Oxford

8. This is possible, first, because only one cell is needed for a DNA test and, second, because mammalian embryos can tolerate removal (and therefore loss) of one cell at the eight-cell stage

9. Each embryo also has a one-in-four chance of having *no* mutant copies of the gene

10. Note that exactly the same technique can now be used in relation to Tay-Sachs disease, discussed earlier

11. Behind all this is the debate about the moral status of the early embryo; space does not allow discussion here but may be found in Bryant J. (2013) *Beyond Human?* Lion, Oxford

and in Bryant J. (2015) Medicine in the moral maze. *Reform*, May 2015. http://www.reform-magazine.co.uk/2015/ 04/medicine-in-the-moral-maze/

12 http://guide.hfea.gov.uk/pgd/

13 For example Kerr A., Shakespeare T. (2002) *Genetic Politics: From Eugenics to Genome.* New Clarion Press, Cheltenham

14 See the start of this section if you want to refresh your understanding of the term "carrier"

15 Indeed, some of the reactions in the USA among sections of the Roman Catholic and conservative evangelical faith communities were very fierce. On a gentler note, this case was one of the events that gave Jodi Picoult ideas for her book *My Sister's Keeper* (Atria, New York 2003). Other "catalytic" events included the illness of her own son.

16 A much fuller account of this can be found in Bryant J. (2012) *Learning to Play God.* https:// thirdway.hymnsam.co.uk/editions/janfeb-2012/features/learning-to-play-god.aspx

17 Readers with a special interest in this will like Hansen A. (2016) *Elite Athletic Genetics.* Amazon Media EU S.à r.l, Luxembourg.

18 There is a fuller discussion in Bryant J. (2013) *Beyond Human?* Lion, Oxford

19 Discussed more fully in Willmott C. (2016) *Biological Determinism, Free Will and Moral Responsibility.* Springer, Cham, Switzerland and Alexander D (2017) *Genes, Determinism and God.* CUP, Cambridge and New York

20 Bunting M. (2006) *There is no stop button in the race for human re-engineering.* https://www.theguardian.com/comment/story/0,,1697702,00.html

21 For example, Savulesco J., Kahane G. (2009) The moral obligation to create children with the best chance of the best life. *Bioethics* 23, 274–290

22 But see Bryant J. (2016) *Thinking About . . . Genes and Embryos.* Christians in Science, Oxford. http://www.cis.org.uk/wp-content/uploads/2016/02/23802–16-Thinking-about-Genes-and-Embryos-AW-lr.pdf

HOW DO I OBTAIN RELIABLE KNOWLEDGE ABOUT THE WORLD?*

Ard Louis

AIMS OF THE CHAPTER

■ To show how a scientist's experiences can shed light on the big questions of life.
■ To argue that the alternative to the scientific method is not irrationality.
■ To illustrate that people have different worldviews – a set of values and assumptions on which people base their lives.

> It is not to science, therefore but to metaphysics, imaginative literature or religion that we must turn for answers to questions having to do with first and last things. (Sir Peter Medawar, *The Limits of Science*)[1]

That there is indeed a limit on science is made very likely by the existence of questions that science cannot answer and that no conceivable advancement of science would empower it to answer. These are the questions that children, in the classroom or at home, ask – the "ultimate questions" of Karl Popper. I have in mind such questions as: "How did everything begin?" "What are we all here for?" "What is the point of living?" The big question of life is sometimes framed in science vs. religion terms because people consider science to be a reliable way to obtain knowledge and may think that other ways (including religious ones) are, by contrast, unreliable. Questions regarding how to obtain knowledge about the world are terribly important to each of us; they help determine how we live our lives and evaluate the choices we make. They have also been the subject of sustained professional debate, particularly in philosophy and theology. For example, the (very relevant) question of God's existence has been debated by many of the greatest minds in history:

> The debate between atheism and religious belief has gone on for centuries, and just about every aspect of it has been explored to the point where even philosophers seem bored with it. The outcome is stalemate.[2]

This quotation comes from my Oxford colleague, Professor Alister McGrath. Although these subtleties are well known to philosophers and historians of science, public discourse on science and religion often operates as if blissfully unaware of them.[3] So, perhaps with some trepidation, I will revisit the question of the title and ask: Can my experience as a scientist shed any light on these big questions of life?[4] I'll start with a definition of science.

DEFINING SCIENCE IS NOT THAT EASY

The problem of where to draw the lines around science has vexed generations of philosophers. Like many unsolved philosophical questions, it has been given its own name, "the demarcation problem". Although one can determine with some degree of consensus what the extremes of the science/non-science continuum are, exactly where the boundary lies can be fuzzy. This doesn't mean, however, that we can't recognise science when we see it,[5] but rather that a watertight definition is difficult. What is clear is that the old-fashioned idea (still taught in many schools) that scientific practice follows a well-defined linear process from first making an observation, then a hypothesis and then testing that hypothesis, is certainly far too simple.

Science as a tapestry of many threads

Rather than attempt a careful and precise definition of science or scientific practice, I will instead resort to a favourite metaphor of mine. It originates with one of my former teachers at Cornell University, the physicist David Mermin, who describes science as a "tapestry" woven together from many threads (experimental results, interpretations, explanations, etc. . . .).[6] It is only when one examines the tapestry as a whole that it will (or will not) make a convincing pattern. Creating scientific tapestries is a collective endeavour among the scientific community, building on mutual trust and the communal experience of what kinds of argument and evidence are likely to stand the test of time. In part because the skill of weaving reliable scientific tapestries relies on subtle judgements, a young scientist may work for years as an apprentice of older more experienced practitioners before branching out on her own. Many parallels could be drawn with the professional guilds of old. I am fond of this metaphor because it describes what I think I experience from the inside as a scientist. Moreover, it also emphasises the importance of coherence and consistency when I weave together arguments and data to make an "inference to a best explanation."[7]

The strong communal element inherent to scientific practice has sometimes been seized on by sociologists of science to argue that scientific knowledge is just one more type of human construct with no more claim on reality than any other form of knowledge. Scientists as a whole have reacted badly to this proposition.[8] Although they agree that all kinds of economic, historical and social factors can play a significant role in the formation of scientific theories, they would argue that, in the long run, the scientific process does lead to reliable knowledge about the world. The view of nature that most scientists I know take could be described as critical realism. They are realists because they believe that there is a world out there that is independent of our making. The adjective critical is added because they recognise that extracting knowledge about that world is not always straightforward. Thus the primary role of the collective nature of scientific process is to provide a network of error correcting mechanisms that prevent us from fooling ourselves. The continual testing against nature refines and filters out competing scientific theories, leading to advances in the strength and reliability of our scientific knowledge tapestries.

The unreasonable effectiveness of mathematics in the natural sciences

Although there are similarities between the ways scientists in distinct fields assemble their tapestry arguments, there can also be subtle differences. These are forced on us in part by the types of problem each field attempts to address. For example, as a theoretical physicist, I've been trained in a tradition of the "unreasonable effectiveness of mathematics", a phrase coined in a famous article by the Nobel Prize winner, Eugene Wigner:

> The miracle of the appropriateness of the language of mathematics for the formulation of the laws of physics is a wonderful gift, which we neither understand nor deserve. We should be grateful for it and hope that it will remain valid in future research and that it will extend, for better or for worse, to our pleasure, even though perhaps also to our bafflement, to wide branches of learning.[9]

An iconic example would be an astounding calculation by Paul Dirac, who showed in 1928[10] that it is necessary to postulate antimatter (the positron) when you derive a description of the electron that combines quantum mechanics (the theory of very small things) with Einstein's special relativity (the theory of very fast things) in a mathematically consistent way. I remember very clearly being confronted with this as an undergraduate in Utrecht, in the Netherlands. How can mathematics demand something so fantastical from nature? I was sure it couldn't be true and spent many hours trying to find a way to prove it. When I finally gave up and saw that there was no way around Dirac's result, it gave me goosebumps. I remember thinking that even if I never used my years of physics training again, it would have been worth it just to see something so spectacularly beautiful. Most things that we can calculate with the methods of theoretical physics may not be that spectacular, but they still have their own sort of beauty. An elegant mathematical description of the natural world, especially one that reveals something unexpected, never ceases to amaze me.

Physicists believe, based on a history of spectacular success, that mathematical consistency between threads is a key indicator of strong tapestries. These days, I spend much of my time interacting with biologists who view my confidence in the ability of theoretical models to extract knowledge about the physical world with great suspicion.[11] I, by way of contrast, am often instinctively sceptical of the huge error bars that can afflict their data.[12]

To an important degree, these cultural differences are necessary given the kinds of question we study. Physics is self-limiting because we simply don't deal with the level of complexity that biologists encounter every day. If an experiment is too messy, we tend to define it away by declaring "That isn't physics" and moving on. Similarly, molecular biologists can often afford to be pickier about their data than medical scientists or psychologists are.[13] But, in spite of these cultural differences, which can lead to heated and sometimes exasperating discussion, we do agree on a number of ground rules for what makes a tapestry strong. For example, what we either predict or measure should be repeatable. If I claim to see an effect in an experiment, someone else in a different lab should be able to reliably measure the same.[14] That simple requirement has all kinds of implication for the types of problem we are able to address.

THE LIMITS OF SCIENCE

As Peter Medawar makes very clear in the quote at the beginning of this chapter, there are many questions that simply are not open to purely scientific analysis. The most important decisions in life cannot be addressed solely by the scientific method, neither do people really live as if they could. In the words of Sir John Polkinghorne, former professor of mathematical physics at Cambridge, and an Anglican priest:

> We are entitled to require a consistency between what people write in their studies and the way in which they live their lives. I submit that no-one lives as if science were enough. Our account of the world must be rich enough – have a thick enough texture and a sufficiently generous rationality – to contain the total spectrum of human meeting with reality.

THE ALTERNATIVE TO THE SCIENTIFIC METHOD IS NOT IRRATIONALITY

But just because we don't live life by the scientific method doesn't mean that the only alternative is irrationality. For example, imagine that I want to get married. A truly irrational approach to finding a wife would be to just pick a random woman off the street. Instead, assuming I find a potentially willing partner, it is wise to get to know one another. We may ask for the opinion of wise friends. There are helpful counselling programmes and myriad compatibility tests to which we can submit ourselves. Such tests, in fact, often apply knowledge that scientific techniques have extracted from our collective experience and wisdom. But, at the end of the day, I can't demand scientific certainty before deciding to marry someone. Neither is it often advisable to perform repeatable experiments! In order to marry, I must make a step of faith because there are aspects of marriage that I can only see from the inside.[15]

Another example of a method of obtaining knowledge is the legal process, which, although it is a tightly organised system, is not strictly scientific. Similarly, a historian will use a combination of evidence (manuscripts etc.) and understanding about the thinking patterns of a particular era to make informed judgements about what happened in the past. Each of these represents a non-scientific, yet widely accepted, means of acquiring knowledge and evaluating information.

EVERYONE HAS A WORLDVIEW ON WHICH THEY BASE THEIR LIVES

The big questions of how to extract reliable information about the world and how to separate fact from mere opinion are clearly complex. Unfortunately, that doesn't mean that we can simply ignore them or remain agnostic about them. These questions are critical to the construction of our *worldview*, that is, the set of values and assumptions on which we base our lives. Our worldview may be carefully thought out or it may consist of a hodgepodge of unexamined ideas that we have picked up from family, friends, school or the media. However it emerges, every person has a worldview and it plays a critical role in how we live our lives.

NOTES

*   Much of this text has appeared in the author's *Biologos* article: http://biologos.org/blogs/archive/ miracles-and-science-part-1, which was a translation of A.A. Louis, "Wonderen en wetenschap: De lange schaduw van David Hume", *Omhoog kijken in Platland*, eds. Cees Dekker, René van Woudenberg and Gijsbert van den Brink, Ten Have (2007).

1   P.B. Medawar, *The Limits of Science* (Oxford University Press, Oxford, 1987).

2   Alister McGrath, *Dawkins' God: Genes, Memes and the Meaning of Life* (Blackwell, Oxford 2005), p. 92.

3   A good example would be Richard Dawkins, *The God Delusion* (Bantam, London 2006). Contrast the confident verities proclaimed in his book with this extract from the professional literature by the atheistic (naturalist) philosopher Quentin Smith, who commented that:

> If each naturalist who does not specialize in the philosophy of religion (i.e., over ninety-nine percent of naturalists) were locked in a room with theists who do specialize in the philosophy of religion, and if the ensuing debates were refereed by a naturalist who had a specialization in the philosophy of religion, the naturalist referee could at most hope the outcome would be that "no definite conclusion can be drawn regarding the rationality of faith", although I expect the most probable outcome is that the naturalist, wanting to be a fair and objective referee, would have to conclude that the theists definitely had the upper hand in every single argument or debate . . . Their justifications have been defeated by arguments developed by theistic philosophers and now naturalist philosophers, for the most part, live in darkness about the justification for naturalism. They may have a true belief in naturalism, but they have no knowledge that naturalism is true since they do not have an undefeated justification for their belief. If naturalism is true, then their belief in naturalism is accidentally true. (Q. Smith, Philo 4, 2, 2000)

The disconnect between Dawkins' analysis of science vs. religion questions and that of the professional literature may explain the remarkably caustic review of *The God Delusion* by the Marxist literary critic Terry Eagleton, entitled *Lunging, Flailing, Mispunching*, which starts with the sentence: Imagine someone holding forth on biology whose only knowledge of the subject is the *Book of British Birds* and you have a rough idea of what it feels like to read Richard Dawkins on theology.

4   In the interests of accessibility, I will try to avoid as much as possible philosophical terms such as "epistemology" or "ontology". I am aware that commonly used words such as "knowledge" do not have simple definitions. I hope that those with a more formal philosophical training will forgive my simplifications.

5   I am reminded of a famous quote by US Supreme Court judge Potter Stewart who, when asked to distinguish between art and pornography, noted that although it was hard to define: "I know it when I see it" (*Jacobellis v. Ohio*, 1964).

6   N. David Mermin, "The Golemization of Relativity", *Physics Today* 49, 11–13 (1996).

7   Peter Lipton, *Inference to the Best Explanation* (Routledge, London, 2004).

8   In the 1990s this tension between sociologists and the scientific community erupted into the so-called "science wars". See e.g. J.A. Labinger and H. Collins (eds.), *The One Culture? A Conversation about Science* (University of Chicago Press, Chicago, 2001), for a good overview.

9   E. Wigner, "The Unreasonable Effectiveness of Mathematics in the Natural Sciences", *Communications in Pure and Applied Mathematics*, 13, I (February 1960).

10   P.A.M. Dirac, *Proc. Roy. Soc. A*, 117, 610 (1928).

11   The differences in culture between more mathematically minded physical scientists and more empirically minded biological scientists are discussed by Evelyn Fox Keller, in a fascinating book: *Making Sense of Life: Explaining Biological Development with Models, Metaphors, and Machines*, Harvard University Press, Boston, MA (2002).

12   Such instinctive reactions are what make interdisciplinary research so difficult. Clearly, biology has been incredibly successful despite the differences with my scientific culture.

13   I also suggest that as the questions we ask become more ambitious (often the case for applied subjects like medicine) then tapestries, by necessity, become more fragile.

14   I realise that this is subtler for historical sciences such as geology and cosmology (we have, for example, only observed one universe). Nevertheless, even in these fields, parallel concepts apply.

15   There are interesting analogies here to making a religious commitment. Christians would argue that important aspects of the Christian life can only be understood and experienced from within a relationship with Christ. That is not to say that a step of faith is just a blind leap in the dark. It should be a decision that is informed by careful thinking and weighing of evidence. But it is more than just that.

CHAPTER 16

AWE AND WONDER IN SCIENCE

Simon Peatman

Patterns exist everywhere in the world around us – from the double helix structure of DNA molecules inside our cells, tens of thousands of which would fit across the width of a human hair, to immense spiral galaxies, so vast that even a ray of light, the fastest thing in the universe, takes 100,000 years to cross from one side to the other.

Scientists are fascinated by patterns. In fact, it could be argued that a scientist's job is to spot patterns and then understand why they occur. However, that does not mean that you have to be a scientist in order to appreciate them. Consider some of the patterns seen in nature, shown here in Figures 16.1, 16.2 and 16.3.

Many people would surely admire the beauty or elegance in these and the many other patterns we see around us. Of course, it is also possible to admire beauty in man-made art. The difference is that patterns seen in the world around us are not created by a human mind but emerge directly from nature itself – from the laws of physics or biology, for example.

These patterns were not made by design. Or were they?

For some scientists, the awe and wonder we may feel when seeing beauty in nature points us towards a Creator God who did design all things, so the patterns we see around us could be thought of as works of art after all, with God as the artist. For others, providing a rational, scientific explanation of natural phenomena does away with our need for God, removing these phenomena from the world of spirituality into the realm of the purely physical.

Figure 16.1

Figure 16.2

Figure 16.3

This chapter provides a framework for exploring these two lines of thinking, using as an example an experiment that can easily be performed as part of a lesson. A discussion follows, which, it is hoped, will introduce ideas and questions to aid pupils in weighing up these ideas for themselves and debating them in the classroom.

THE RANDOMLY OSCILLATING PENDULUM

A standard pendulum consists of a weight (the "bob") on the end of a piece of string, which is allowed to swing freely back and forth (Figure 16.4a). Try setting up a pendulum by clamping the top end of a piece of string on a retort stand and tying a weight to the bottom end. How long does it take the pendulum to make a full swing (there and back)? Does this depend on a) how far the pendulum is first pulled back before being released or b) the length of string used? Can you create a pendulum that could be used for a grandfather clock (that is, it takes one second to swing one way and another second to swing back again)?

This simple setup is well understood by physicists. Provided that the angle of the swing is kept relatively small, you should find that the time for each swing does not depend on how far the pendulum is pulled back to start with; and that the longer the piece of string, the longer the swing takes. With a bit of experimentation it should be possible to verify that the duration of a complete swing in seconds is approximately found by taking the square root of the length of the string (in metres) and then multiplying by two. Thus, a grandfather clock requires a pendulum about one metre long.[1]

Of course, the pendulum does not have to swing just backwards and forwards. It can swing in two dimensions, so it can travel round in a circle or ellipse. This is, of course, possible with the setup we already have, but let us move to the setup in Figure 16.4b. Here, we use a magnet as the pendulum bob and place another magnet on the desk beneath. Make sure that the magnets attract (so if the pendulum bob has its north pole facing downwards, the magnet on the desk has its south pole facing upwards, and vice versa), and that the string is long enough that the pendulum bob is close to the desk but without quite being able to touch the magnet. It should be possible to make the pendulum swing in a roughly circular path, orbiting round the magnet. Gradually, due to friction and air resistance, the pendulum will slow down and ultimately come to rest over the magnet.

(a)

(b)

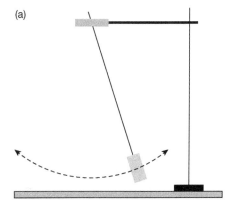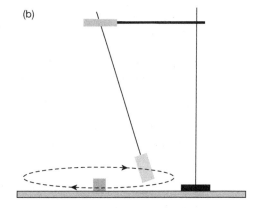

■ **Figure 16.4**

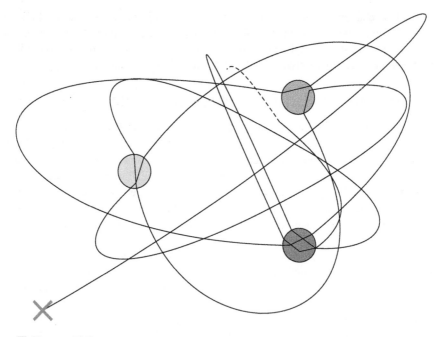

■ Figure 16.5

So far, there is nothing particularly surprising about the behaviour we have seen. However, the value in this experiment is that we can very simply change the setup and obtain a striking result. Instead of a single magnet on the desk, now use several magnets. Figure 16.5 shows a plan view, with the circles representing the magnets and the cross indicating a possible starting point for the pendulum's swing . Try with three magnets to begin with, then try increasing the number. It does not matter whether these magnets are placed in a neat arrangement or at random. It may take some trial and error to set this up, but you should find that the swing of the pendulum ceases to be simple and predictable. Rather, it becomes *chaotic*, as indicated by the example of the curve in Figure 16.5.

To describe the behaviour as chaotic (that is, it obeys *chaos theory*) is to say that there is a limit to how long one can reasonably predict the path of the swing. Try starting the pendulum's swing from one particular position, noting the path that the swing takes for the first few seconds, then restarting from the same position to try to recreate exactly the same swing. You will find it is extremely difficult! Only a short time into the swing the pendulum's path is already so unpredictable, and so sensitive to the precise starting position, that it is impossible to recreate an identical swing pattern consistently.

Recall that in the single-magnet setup the pendulum bob eventually came to rest over the magnet, as it gradually slowed down. With multiple magnets, again, it is usually the case that the bob will eventually come to rest over one of the magnets (depending on the precise arrangement of the magnets on the desk it is also possible that it will come to rest *between* the magnets). Suppose we plot a graph showing which magnet the bob ultimately comes to rest over, depending on where we allow it to begin its swing. For example, in Figure 16.6 three starting positions are shown (A, B and C). Suppose that from position A, the bob ends up over the dark grey magnet. We therefore label this location as dark grey. Similarly, from positions B and C the bob ends up over the light grey and black magnets respectively. Note that, even though these last positions are very close together, the system is so sensitive that the bob ends up over different magnets.

SCIENTIFIC DISCOVERIES AND RELIGIOUS EXPERIENCE

To complete the picture for all possible starting locations in Figure 16.6 would be a very arduous task, but we can do so using a computer simulation[2] as shown in Figure 16.7. Here the entire region uses different shades of grey according to which magnet the bob ends up hovering over (Figure 16.7a). This graph has a very surprising and interesting structure. Not only is the end magnet very sensitive to the starting position, indicated by the very fine structure in some regions of the graph, but we see very intricate geometrical patterns. No matter how far we zoom in on this shape (Figure 16.7b, which shows the region in the white box in Figure 16.7a.) we see increasingly intricate patterns occurring. In mathematics, such a shape is known as a *fractal*. Even to a trained physicist it would likely be a surprise and a delight to see such a complex result falling out of such a simple experiment. It requires no expert scientific knowledge to perform the experiment in a classroom and it is easy to see how the pendulum is pulled around and about, seemingly at random, by the array of attracting magnets beneath it. However, a mathematical description of the fractal shape would be far from simple.

Many scientists would even go so far as to use words such as "beautiful" or "elegant" to describe the patterns seen in Figure 16.7, just as with those we saw in Figures 16.1, 16.2 and 16.3. It is important to note at this point that a scientist is unlikely to use such subjective terminology when formally publishing their work, but in conversation with their

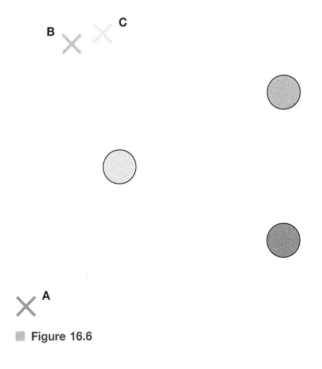

■ Figure 16.6

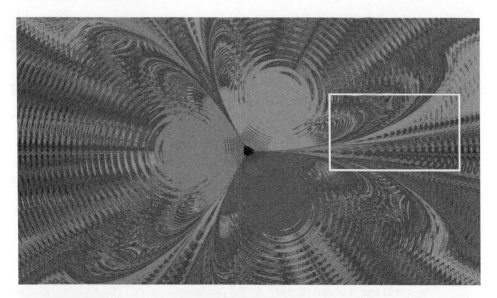

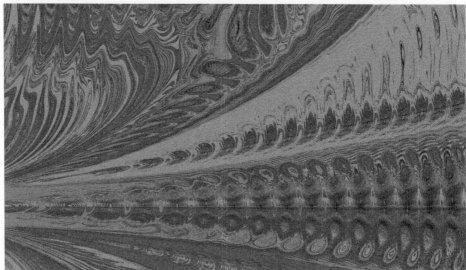

▨ Figures 16.7a and b

colleagues or their friends, or even when contemplating their work in their own mind, they may well ascribe concepts such as beauty or elegance to their scientific findings. They may also talk of having a sense of awe and wonder at nature when they make scientific discoveries.

Another group of people who often talk about the beauty and wonder they consider to be found in nature is religious people. Of course, some scientists are themselves religious, while others are not. But is there any connection between the way in which scientists and religious people talk about these matters?

First, consider how you felt when first learning that the fractal shape emerges from the magnetic pendulum experiment. Was it interesting, exciting, impressive or beautiful? Did it inspire a sense of awe and wonder? Or did it seem underwhelming, boring or mundane? It is quite natural that in a class of students there will be some who are fascinated by such an experiment and others who are unimpressed. After all, not everybody has a strong interest in science. But it is worth exploring these questions of how scientific discoveries make us feel.

Moreover, imagine you were the first scientist in the world to have made a particular discovery so that, for a short time at least, you know you are the only person ever to have known this one fact. How would that make you feel? Would that make the discovery even more exciting? Which, in fact, is the more exciting – the scientific fact itself or the process of discovering it?

Now consider the feelings of people who claim to have "religious experiences". This does not necessarily mean that they claim to have witnessed something miraculous or supernatural (although in some cases this is exactly what they mean). Instead, it could be witnessing something such as a beautiful view from a mountain top, which causes them to admire what they see as God's creation. Or it could be the experience of going through a time in their life when they feel especially close to God. How do you think religious people might talk about those experiences?

In answering these two sets of questions – how scientists, on the one hand, and religious people, on the other, talk about their respective experiences – did you tend to give similar answers in each case or very different ones? For example, did you find yourself using similar vocabulary in each case or similar concepts?

For some religious scientists, the two types of experience are certainly linked. Some would even say that their scientific work points them towards a faith in God and that their faith in God drives them to make scientific discoveries. Consider the following two quotations. The first is from Rebecca Goldstein, a philosopher and atheist. For her, the process of scientific discovery replaces any need we might have for religious notions. The second is from Jeff Hardin, a biologist who believes in God.[3] For him, everything we discover in science is God's handiwork:

> Maths, music, starry nights. These are secular ways of achieving transcendence, of feeling lifted into a grand perspective. It's a sense of being awed by existence . . . Religious people think of it as an essentially religious experience but it's not. It's an essentially human experience. (Rebecca Goldstein)

> Science for a Christian, in some very real sense, is an exercise in art appreciation . . . For me, being a Christian means that I need to take the contingent world as it is and understand it as well as I can, in the same way that someone who's studying a work of art must take it as it is and try to understand it for its own sake. (Jeff Hardin)

Discuss what you think Hardin and Goldstein are each trying to tell us in these quotations. Which – if either – do you agree with and why? Note that, although Hardin is a Christian, members of other religions may agree with his view on the relationship between science and God.

It is certainly the case that, while many scientists would agree with Hardin, there are also many who would agree with Goldstein. The view that science replaces our need for God tends to prevail amongst the general public, especially in the media, but it is important to know that scientists hold a range of opinions on these matters.

Let us finish with one view that is often attributed (perhaps apocryphally) to Werner Heisenberg, the 20th century quantum physicist. Again, some scientists will agree and others will not, but these words sum up the sometimes confusing world that is the interface of science and religion, and how the awe and wonder we see in one might be able to lead us to the other: "The first gulp from the glass of natural sciences will turn you into an atheist, but at the bottom of the glass God is waiting for you."

NOTES

1   The formula for the duration of the swing in seconds is $2\pi \times \sqrt{(l/g)}$, where π is the number pi (3.14159 . . .), l is the length of the string in metres and g is the strength of the Earth's gravitational field (approximately 9.81 m/s^2). Therefore, a period (swing there and back) of two seconds requires l = 0.99396 . . . or 99.4 cm.

2   Created using *Visions of Chaos*, http://softology.com.au/voc.htm.

3   https://scienceandbelief.org/2011/10/13/worship-at-work (viewed 08/10/2017).

CHAPTER 17

EVOLUTION AND RELIGION

MARY ANNING – EMBRACING FAITH AND SCIENCE

Keith Chappell

AIMS OF THE CHAPTER

- To evaluate Mary Anning's role in the development of different branches of science.
- To provide an example of a scientist with faith.
- To illustrate that Mary Anning presents a picture of science rooted in observation and deduction.

> She sells seashells on the seashore.
> The shells she sells are seashells, I'm sure.
> So if she sells seashells on the seashore,
> Then I'm sure she sells seashore shells.

Most of us are probably very familiar with this challenging tongue-twister, which was written in 1908 by Terry Sullivan. As with most nursery rhymes, tongue-twisters and popular tales, it relates to an historical figure, in this case, the famous nineteenth century fossil hunter, Mary Anning. An understanding of Mary Anning's role in the development of the sciences of geology, paleontology and evolutionary theory, and her significance for women in science, is now rightly a part of the primary science curriculum in the United Kingdom. This chapter looks at her life, work and faith and sets her important contribution to science in the context of her deeply held religious belief. In addition to providing an example of a scientist with faith, the story of Mary Anning also presents a picture of science rooted in observation and deduction rather than the notion, held by many children, that science is purely experimental and done in the laboratory.

LIFE OF MARY ANNING

Mary was born in Lyme Regis, a small seaside town in the south-west of England, on 21 May 1799. She lived there for the rest of her life, indeed, only leaving Lyme Regis on one occasion. The story of her family is one typical of many families of the time; she was one of ten children but only Mary and her brother Joseph grew to be adults. Most of her brothers and sisters died as babies. At the time diseases such as smallpox and measles meant that most children did not reach the age of five. Today these diseases are almost unknown in the developed world thanks to the development of vaccines. One of her older sisters died aged four after her clothes caught fire and when Mary was born she was given the name of this sister. Mary herself famously nearly didn't make it past 15 months old when lightning struck a tree at a fair killing the woman holding Mary and two other women with them. Mary survived and her father would tell that her health and personality were greatly enlivened following the experience. Others in the town would later attribute her curiosity and genius to this moment.

Mary's family were poor throughout her life. Her father, a carpenter, would help to supplement their income by selling shells and fossils to tourists visiting the town as part of the new fashion for seaside holidays. Due to wars on the continent, the English seaside had become very fashionable with the rich and royalty, which encouraged others to follow.

■ **Figure 17.1** An Ammonite Fossil

Mary was soon included in this part of the family business and would spend time hunting fossils with her father on the now famous "Jurassic Coast" on which Lyme Regis sits. Many important fossil finds have been found in this area and millions visit the area each year in search of fossils. Many millions of years ago that part of England was under the sea at the equator, producing a range of sedimentary rocks containing the fossils of sea creatures. Mary was, in many ways, a pioneer in understanding the diversity and significance of the fossils to be found in the area and more broadly. Mary and her father didn't know that what they were selling were fossilised animals and simply called them "curiosities"; it was only later that she came to understand that the "curiosities" were animals from long ago that had become hardened into stone. In fact, at the time, the fossils had many descriptive nicknames, which gave a good visual idea of what they were: names such as vertiberries, snakestones, ladies fingers, devils toenails; and many stories existed about where they had come from. Snakestones, for example, are what we now know as Ammonites (see Figure 17.1) but they were believed by some to be snakes that had been turned to stone by ancient saints.

When Mary's father died, when she was still only 11 years old, from complications after falling from a cliff while fossil hunting, the already poor family were left without his income and in debt. They became dependent on what they could gather and sell at the seashore. Mary, Joseph and their mother worked together for several years but when Joseph became apprenticed to be an upholsterer it fell to Mary to take on responsibility for most of the fossil collecting. From then on she could be found every day on the beach collecting fossils with her faithful companion, Tray, a small dog that would often guard fossils while Mary went to get extra equipment or help.

Mary proved to have a great talent for fossil collecting and as well as making some valuable income she also made some important scientific discoveries. Many of her finds were sold to collectors and museums and would sometimes command large prices (the equivalent of thousands of pounds in today's money). Fossils found by Mary were bought by many universities and can still be found today in the Natural History Museum in London and others around the world. Mary and Joseph together found the first fossil of an Ichthyosaur when she was only 12 years old. Joseph found the skull and Mary the rest of the skeleton and this fossil can still be seen in the Natural History Museum in London. The Ichthyosaur is over five metres long and when it was first found it was believed to be a fossil of a crocodile. It was this fossil that first attracted the attention of the scientific community to the work that Mary and her family were doing as some geologists realised it could not simply be a crocodile but a whole new species like nothing ever seen before. The name Ichthyosaur means "fish lizard" and as a result of work on this fossil and others found by Mary, scientists came to accept that there had been past times when some whole groups of animals had existed that have no close relatives alive today.

MARY'S EDUCATION AND CONTRIBUTION TO SCIENCE

As was the case with many children at the time, and especially for girls, Mary's education was quite limited. Her parents were members of a Congregationalist Christian church and there she did receive some basic education, learning to read and write. Churches were the main source of education for poor people of her day but many girls still received little or no education. The fossils her family sold caught the attention of an expert called Elizabeth Philpot who took Mary to see her own collection and introduced her to the latest thought about fossils, including the understanding that these were preserved creatures from many years ago. This thought was a challenge to many who still believed that the world was only a few thousand years old. Mary appears to have been a keen and able student and taught herself a great deal through reading whatever she could find on the subject. This meant that Mary not only collected fossils and sold them but came to understand what she was dealing with and the significance for science of many of her finds.

Mary would often look for fossils after storms that had caused landslides and revealed new layers of rock but these were dangerous and required great care. One day while walking along the beach she noticed a very unusual large rock. The rock didn't show anything on the outside but Mary's educated eye and her instincts told her that there was something unusual inside. It was too large to lift by herself so she asked some local quarry men to help her take it to her house. There she spent weeks gradually chipping away at the rock to reveal a remarkably large and unusual fossil that had never been found in its complete form – a Plesiosaur. This fossil can still be seen today in the Natural History Museum in London. She would go on to discover the first Pterosaur (a type of flying dinosaur) in Britain and many other rare or unique fossils.

As the years passed great men came from around the country to see her fossils and talk to Mary about her ideas. Many would go on to publish research papers in prestigious journals based on fossils Mary found and using her ideas but they did not name her or acknowledge her contribution. It was not considered necessary, or appropriate, to acknowledge the role of women in academic pursuits – especially one from a poor background. Women were not allowed to be members of the Geological Society of London where the palaeontologists of the day met. Indeed, women were not even allowed to visit. Treatment like this today would be considered scandalous but despite the offence this caused to her at the time Mary continued to look for fossils and develop a greater understanding of the animals they revealed because she was passionate about her subject. This doesn't mean she took it quietly. According to Christopher McGowan, in his 2002 book *The Dragon Seekers* about early fossil hunters, one of Mary's companions, Anna Pinney, reported a conversation:

> She says the world has used her ill . . . these men of learning have sucked her brains, and made a great deal of publishing works, of which she furnished the contents, while she derived none of the advantages. (p. 217)

As McGowan notes she did have a great deal of celebrity while still alive (McGowan, 2002, p. 217) and after her death in 1847 the Geological Society paid for a stained glass window to be installed in the parish church in Lyme Regis honouring Mary and her work. It was only a long time after her death that the full degree of her contribution was acknowledged by the scientific establishment but by 1925 books were being written about her celebrating her huge contribution to palaeontology (Forde, 1925). There is little doubt that her work had important influences on scientists for generations, including figures such as Charles Lyell, who consulted with her, as did many university professors, including the tutor of Charles Darwin. Mary has since been the subject of plays and novels about her life, such as *Remarkable Creatures* by Tracey Chevalier and *Curiosity* by Joan Thomas, which look at her role as a scientist and her treatment by the male scientific community. In 2010 the Royal Society declared Mary Anning as one of the top ten most influential British women in science.

RELIGION AND EVOLUTION

The Anning family were Christians and worshipped as part of a Congregationalist community where Mary received much of her early education. At around the age of 30 Mary converted to become a member of the Church of England following changes in the local Congregationalist church. A new pastor was unpopular with many of the members and this may have been a factor influencing Mary's decision. Also, many of her customers who bought fossils were clergy in the Church of England and it was seen to be more socially respectable to be an Anglican. She remained an active member of her local church for the rest of her life. She was well known for her religious faith and could often be seen praying.

As mentioned above, when Mary Anning first discovered Ichthyosaurs, many assumed the animal must be a crocodile or a creature that lived somewhere remote and hadn't been discovered alive. The concept of its no longer existing – i.e. extinction – was shocking to many Christians. Even if they accepted that the world was older than a few thousand years, it was difficult to accept the idea of extinction. The idea challenged the accepted belief that God did not make mistakes and would never create an animal only to have it die out. If animals and plants had been created by God why would he be so wasteful to make species that he would then eliminate? Why would he then turn them into fossils in rock form to be found later? This certainly provided some challenges for established ideas about the origins of life. Mary Anning didn't seem to have any problems and saw her life of faith and life as a scientist as part of the same thing.

All of these new ideas were controversial. Indeed, when Darwin came up with his ideas about evolution and the origin of species, he kept quiet about it for 20 years in part because he knew this challenge to religious beliefs would cause an outcry – as they still do to some. Mary Anning died 12 years before Darwin went public with his theories, but she was doubtless aware of these issues. She said little about them – she was struggling to make a living and had little time for debate. The closest she came to supporting a theory about how the past might link to the present was in a letter of 1844:

> I can only remark on it generally as truly believing from what little I have seen of the fossil world and Natural History I think the connection or analogy between the Creatures of the former and present world excepting as to size much greater than is generally supposed.

In other words, creatures from the past were related in some way to those of the present. Perhaps she would not have been surprised by Darwin.

CLASSROOM SESSION

Key aims of session

- Science and religion can fit together.
- Science explains how nature works. Religion answers different questions to those posed by science.
- Expose children to people in science who are also religious.
- Relate key aspects of the evolution and inheritance unit to optional curriculum points in religious studies.

National Curriculum links

KEY STAGE 2 (PRIMARY)

■ Recognise that living things have changed over time and that fossils provide information about living things that inhabited the Earth millions of years ago.

Learning objectives

■ Be aware that the scientific community is diverse and there are people in science who are also religious.

■ Understand that Mary Anning is an example of a woman who advanced our scientific understanding of what life was like millions of years ago. She was also religious and was commended for her advances in science by both scientists and the Church of England.

Differentiated outcomes

ALL: Mary Anning was a scientist and religious.

MOST: Will be able to explain how Mary Anning studied fossils, which show us what lived thousands and indeed millions of years ago and was a leading expert in her field. She was also a Christian.

SOME: Explain that you can be a scientist as well as being religious. Mary Anning found fossils and examined what kind of living things the fossils used to be. The geological society and the Church of England commemorated Mary Anning for her advances in science.

Lesson in context/prior learning

This unit examines an example of a scientist who lived in the past who looked at fossils, which provide information about what living things existed millions of years ago.

Pupils should already be aware of what a fossil is and how fossils are made from previous lessons in both Year 6 and in other years that look at fossils i.e. Year 3. Pupils will be asked to consider the idea that science and religion can go together – they are not necessarily in conflict. Mary Anning is an example of a leading scientist who was also religious.

The session looks at the life of Mary Anning. It also delves into how she searched for and found fossils as a child. As she collected these fossils and grew up and went to school, she built up her understanding of fossils. She used evidence from the fossils to figure out what things lived in the past.

The key idea for students is that you can go into science from any background.

Resources

■ PowerPoint presentation
■ Quiz answer sheets
■ Optional quiz prize!

Session plan

(What the children (and teacher!) need to know before they start this lesson.)

Element	Purpose	Timing	Summary
Learning orientation	Introduce the lesson and key purpose	Five minutes	Explain that we are going to learn about science and religion. How they can go together and we will be looking at an example of this in Mary Anning. See if any children have heard of her before. Mention she looked at fossils and get the children to think-pair-share either what a fossil is or ask children whether they think science and religion go together.
Introduction of contemporary religious scientists	Expose children to examples of scientists who are also religious	Five minutes	Select a diverse range of current scientists who are also religious. Emphasise that there are specialists in many different scientific disciplines who are also religious.
Mary Anning presentation	Provide an in-depth look at a scientist who was also religious	Fifteen minutes	Mention a quiz on the presentation! Mary Anning grew up in Lyme Regis, a great place to go fossil hunting. As she grew up her knowledge of fossils increased and she became a leader in her field of fossils. Throughout her lifetime she was religious. She regularly read the Bible and looked to God and scripture in times where she felt closer to God, e.g. after scares from landslides when fossil hunting. She was Anglican and was commemorated when she died by the Church of England and the Geological Society of London. She was the first woman to have a stained glass window made in her honour to acknowledge her advances in science.
Main activity	To recap in depth on the life of Mary Anning who embraced her passion for science and faith	Ten minutes	Following the presentation, the class will be in teams for the quiz on Mary Anning. Read out the questions to the group – all questions are covered on the slides or slide notes that are read out at the time of the presentation.
Main plenary	Children need to understand that science and religion are not necessarily in conflict with one another	Five minutes	The teacher will recap on the information they have covered. Discuss the many different religious scientists from a broad range of disciplines. Repeat that Mary Anning was a great example of a person who embraced her faith throughout her life. She also was a leading specialist in her field of science – fossils.

Plenary

Conclude to the class that there are many religious people who are also scientists. Science and religion do not necessarily go against each other. The scientific community consists of a diverse group of people. As well as the fact there are religious people in science, there are also examples in which both science and religion have rewarded people for their work. This reinforces a positive outlook on science and religion as the heads or leaders in science and religion come together to commemorate people for the work they have done.

REFERENCES

Forde, H.A. *The Heroine of Lyme Regis: The Story of Mary Anning the Celebrated Geologist* (1925).

McGowan, C. *The Dragon Seekers: How An Extraordinary Circle of Fossilists Discovered the Dinosaurs and Paved the Way for Darwin* (Cambridge, MA: Perseus, 2002).

CHAPTER 18

THINKING BEYOND THE CLASSROOM

Jane Borgeaud

All the materials provided in this book could be used within a single one hour lesson or series of lessons, fitting into the normal timetable and the typical format of lessons within your school. However, there are also other ways to extend or enrich the way in which you use the materials. This chapter seeks to provide some inspiration for how this could be achieved.

THEMED DAYS OR WEEKS

The 2013 OFSTED report "Religious education: realising the potential" (OFSTED, 2013) questioned the common practice of delivery, at the time of the report, of teaching RE topics through a six week block of 45 minute to 60 minute lessons. This practice has a tendency to prevent deep understanding and exploration of key issues, contributing to the often superficial learning that the report highlighted in many schools. This issue is not limited to RE and has increasingly led schools to adapt the structure of the timetable to take children off timetable for a themed day or week.

Many of the materials provided within this book lend themselves to inclusion within such an approach, within a theme that is not specific to religion and science. For example, the Mary Anning materials could be used in a week focussing on women in science, the Galileo or Newton materials could be included in a topic on space and so on. The inclusion of these materials normalises the idea that scientists can have a religious faith. It is easy to assume that this will be obvious to children, but an investigation into the views of Year 6 pupils on science and religion found that the children frequently indicated that they did not know of scientists with a religious faith (Billingsley and Borgeaud, 2015). Often, despite studying scientists such as Einstein and Newton, who did indeed have a religious faith, the children were often unaware of this or even assumed that they were not religious.

Equally, the choice to create a themed day or week specifically centred on science and religion would allow a deeper study of the diversity of views different people hold of the relationship between science and religion. The use of a range of different materials from this book within a single themed week would allow the children to gain a cumulative understanding of how religious scientists respond to different "big questions" commonly investigated by scholars interested in these areas. This would also seek to normalise the idea that it was safe for these two themes to be discussed together and that teachers were not averse to ideas from science and RE lessons being brought together. This would address another key finding from Billingsley and Borgeaud (2015) that children perceived that this was not an appropriate thing to do, either due to the need to stick to the topic of the named subject on the timetable or due to perceptions that the discussion of religion and science together was somehow inappropriate or even impolite.

Taking the whole school off timetable to study the same topics in age appropriate ways facilitates a sense of status for the topics and the opportunity to make use of whole school opportunities for learning such as an assembly to launch the week or a sharing assembly or finale event at the end of the week. Parents and carers could be invited to such events, raising the events' status and giving parents an insight into what has been studied to support them in continuing conversations at home. A book or newsletter could be produced with contributions from all the classes involved.

USE OF VISITING EXPERTS

The use of a visiting expert, such as an author, professional athlete, or person from a particular country or religion, to support the teaching of the curriculum is very beneficial in many ways. Children often enjoy the experience of hearing a voice different from that of their everyday teachers. The interaction with someone who is deeply immersed in the field or way of life in question can be extremely beneficial to the children as they can explore what it really means to live or work in that way. The area being studied comes to life in a way that is not possible without personal contact with a relevant individual. Furthermore, a person practising a particular faith or involved in a particular field of expertise can answer questions from children in a way that comes from intensely held personal beliefs or experience and personal connections between ideas.

Scientists and people with religious faith are often groups about whom children have particular stereotypical ideas. The opportunity to encounter a real scientist who follows a particular faith can have a significant impact in broadening children's views of these groups and this can have far greater impact than simply on the connections between science and religion (for example, the stereotype of scientists as male could be challenged implicitly by inviting in a female scientist to talk also about her religious faith).

It may be particularly useful to invite a scientist with a religious faith into the classroom towards the end of a topic that has made use of the materials within this book and to provide the children with an opportunity to interview them, asking questions that they have prepared in advance. This is likely to ensure that maximum impact is achieved, since the children have already focussed on the topic being studied and developed knowledge of the key concepts involved before being given the opportunity to investigate and enrich their understanding further by asking the questions that are most pertinent to them.

Year 6 pupils have been found to be very accepting of the notion of a person being entitled to pursue a career and religious faith of their own choosing. However, they lacked any real insight into what this would be like for an individual, tending to view this as problematic (Billingsley and Borgeaud, 2015). Therefore, it is likely to be particularly valuable for children to hear the detailed personal logic line of how a scientist with a religious faith makes sense of the interrelationship between their faith and science.

As well as the obvious choice of a religious person working in a scientific field, it can also be useful to invite in people who will be significant to the children in relation to a particular faith, such as a local imam or vicar in order to enable the children to understand that people who clearly have a strong commitment to their faith are not necessarily in opposition to science or particular scientific ideas, such as evolution. The discovery that the local vicar who visits school assemblies has a science degree might be as significant a moment for the children as discovering that the scientist from the local power station has a religious faith, for example.

In inviting in people known to the school by association, such as the parish priest, local imam or rabbi or a parent with a particular faith or career, it is important to ensure there is a shared understanding of the purpose of the exercise. It is important for the school to be confident that there is no misunderstanding of the goals of the session in order to avoid the damage that could be done by, for example, an inappropriate attempt to evangelise or a comment that was disrespectful to another group. Furthermore, it is important to emphasise that a personal response is what is required, if this is the case, rather than setting the expectation for a parent to speak for the entire range of people within their religious faith or to have in depth theological knowledge. The understanding that a "normal person" can have a religious faith that is compatible with science can be as powerful as a deeply theological discussion, for example. Furthermore, many of the people whom you may wish to invite in may have little or no experience of speaking to 30 primary school children and may appreciate a discussion of how the session will be managed.

Some local SACREs and local authorities have lists of people who are willing to come in and speak about their faith schools. Organisations such as Christians in Science (www.cis.org.uk) and REinspired (http://www.reinspired.org.uk/) may be able to put you in touch with appropriate local visitors.

It is important to note that there is no single view of the relationship between science and religion either among scholars studying this area or between people of the same religious faith. The aim of the activities in this book is not to replace the notion that science and religion are incompatible with the notion that everyone thinks that they are easily compatible. Therefore it is particularly powerful to bring children into contact with, for example, people from the same faith who have different views on this question or scientists with different ways of understanding the relationship between science and faith. Equally, there is value in enabling children to meet scientists who are themselves atheists but are respectful of the religious beliefs of their peers. Atheist scientists do not necessarily see an inherent split between science and religion and may have reasons for being atheist that are not primarily scientific in nature. This insight can enable children to further unpick the intricacies of views of science and religion as something other than a pair of intrinsically opposing standpoints.

GETTING OUT AND ABOUT

School trips, planned well, are experiences that children often remember throughout their lives. Incorporating a school trip into the study of a topic can be a fantastic way to cement its importance in the children's minds.

Depending on your school's location, there are many ways to enhance the topics within this book through a trip. For example, the topic of evolution could be brought to life by a trip to one of several science museums around the country to view fossils. This would enable children to gain first-hand experience of the validity of the fossil record and see the evidence that has informed scientific understanding. A visit to a wildlife park or zoo (or even bug hunting in the local park) would enable children to seek to be scientists and suggest reasons for adaptations, mirroring the way in which zoologists and evolutionary biologists think about adaptations.

If your school is within the local area of Lyme Regis, where Mary Anning hunted for fossils, or travels to that area for a residential trip, the power of visit to the beaches where she hunted for fossils or to St. Michael's Church where the window commemorating her life can still be found would be likely to greatly enrich the children's experience of the topic.

A visit to a planetarium, such as that at Winchester Science Centre or a visit from a travelling astrodome, such as that owned by Bracknell Discovery Centre or the mobile Polestar Planetarium in the north of England, is likely to inspire significant awe and wonder for children. This might naturally lead to the opportunity to discuss the ideas of religious scientists such as Galileo who viewed science as delivering greater understanding of the wonders of God's universe. Pupils are likely to have far greater understanding of what Galileo meant by wonders in an environment such as a planetarium that helps them to access an understanding of the vastness and beauty of space.

As well as specific events, such as those provided by the LASAR project at Canterbury University and a 2016 Primary Science Fair at Winchester Cathedral, which specifically seek to link science and religion, a beneficial avenue to explore would be the potential to incorporate a visit to a place of worship or science laboratories (for example, at a local university or secondary school). As well as the general benefits that such a visit obviously holds in enriching children's school experience, the simple implication that places of worship are not adverse to a discussion of science within their walls, or that a science laboratory is a place where religion can be talked about gives a powerful message about the capacity for the two disciplines to "work together like friends". Such a visit could be combined with the opportunity to talk to scientists and religious people about science or religion, in a similar way to bringing an expert into school.

OPPORTUNITIES FOR CROSS-CURRICULAR LEARNING

One of the criticisms made by the 2013 OFSTED report (OFSTED, 2013) was that RE is a subject that is less likely to be incorporated into cross-curricular topics than other subjects. The materials within this book already move this situation forward by linking religion to science, but the opportunities to widen the links between these materials and other curriculum areas can be much richer than simply RE and science.

The study of historical figures such as Galileo, Mary Anning and Newton can enrich the study of the periods in which they lived. In turn, an understanding of the significance of their discoveries is significantly enhanced by a wider understanding of what the world was like in their time.

The powerful story of Galileo discovering the telescope after watching children playing with lenses would provide a golden opportunity for children to work through design and technology to design their own telescopes, developing an understanding of the science behind how they work. In a similar way, children could use the story of the stained glass window created to commemorate Mary Anning as a spring board to design their own stained glass windows to commemorate the life of an important figure or their experiences at the school when they leave in Year 6 linking to the art curriculum.

This list of possible cross-curricular links is clearly not exhaustive and schools will find their own way of linking the materials in this book into their own schemes of work.

However, it is worth highlighting the positive benefits of any cross-curricular links that connect the study of RE with the wider curriculum, rather than leaving it as a separate, odd subject within an otherwise connected curriculum. This arguably better mirrors the way in which a faith position, or indeed agnosticism or atheism, are a constant part of the life of an individual that is alongside them whatever other endeavours they pursue.

ENGLISH, LITERACY AND TEXT TYPES

Although the connection between English curriculum and the materials in this book could well be included under the previous subheading of cross-curricular study, there are particular aspects of this particular connection that are worthy of further explanation.

Year 6 pupils have been shown to tend to be unaware of the possibility of religious people approaching religious texts as something other than literal, historical narrative (Billingsley and Borgeaud, 2015). OFSTED findings suggest that topics such as miracles, where this issue may be particularly pertinent, were taught in a way that did not allow this concern to be explored: "For example, Christian stories, particularly miracles, were often used to encourage pupils to reflect on their own experience without any opportunity to investigate the stories' significance within the religion itself" (OFSTED, 2013: 13).

Given that children are given substantial opportunity to explore different text types and ways of using language in the National Curriculum for English, both as authors and as readers, including literal and figurative language, this provides a golden opportunity for children to make connections with the English curriculum to deepen their understanding of the different ways in which religious language can be interpreted and explore the richness of language in religious texts and ceremonies. A particularly pertinent route into this topic could be through the materials on Galileo, since there was already, in his time, discussion among theologians about passages within the Bible that might not be best suited to literal, narrative interpretations.

This issue of the different ways in which people, including those within the same faith, interpret religious texts is an extremely pertinent one, since the extent to which historical texts are taken as literal narrative is critical in how consistent the interpretation of these texts is with scientific discoveries (in combination with an individual's understanding of the power and limits of science). The fact that the children will be familiar with different uses of language and interpretation of texts from English lessons provides a useful route into such discussions.

In addition, the materials within this book provide valuable contexts for children to engage in writing a variety of text types, including explanations, reports on interviews with scientists or the lives of particular characters. Equally, there are many opportunities for speaking and listening activities.

A word of caution is needed around using science and religion as a vehicle for debating or for writing arguments or persuasive texts. While the topic appears to provide many opportunities for this type of writing, using this subject as a context for this type of communication without ensuring that children are aware of the ways in which science and religion can be seen as compatible, can further entrench the view that science and religion are opposing viewpoints that are in conflict with one another and cannot, therefore, both be true.

REFERENCES

Billingsley, B. and Borgeaud, J. (2015) "Miracles and the Nature of Science: Primary School Pupils' Perspectives on Whether a Belief in Miracles is Consistent with a Scientific Worldview", AULRE Conference: Belief in Dialogue, St Mary's University, Twickenham, 1–3 September 2015.

OFSTED (2013) *Religious education: realising the potential*. Manchester: OFSTED Publications.

INDEX

Note: bold page numbers indicate tables; italic page numbers indicate figures; numbers preceded by n are chapter endnote numbers.